Contents

What do you think of this book? We want to hear

Microsoft is interested in hearing your feedback so we can conti
books and learning resources for you. To participate in a brief online survey, please visit:

www.microsoft.com/learning/booksurvey/

What do you think of this book? We want to hear from you!

Microsoft is interested in hearing your feedback so we can continually improve our
books and learning resources for you. To participate in a brief online survey, please visit:

www.microsoft.com/learning/booksurvey/

Introduction

The 70-480 exam is a detailed examination of your skills with using HTML5 and CSS3. This book will guide you through the necessary objectives that you are expected to know to pass this exam. It is expected that you have at least 2 years' experience working with these technologies. This book is structured such that it provides a reference to the key information required for each objective. This book does not teach every concept but provides an account of the details you are expected to know for each objective covered on the exam.

This book covers every exam objective, but it does not cover every exam question. Only the Microsoft exam team has access to the exam questions themselves and Microsoft regularly adds new questions to the exam, making it impossible to cover specific questions. You should consider this book a supplement to your relevant real-world experience and other study materials. If you encounter a topic in this book that you do not feel completely comfortable with, use the links you'll find in text to find more information and take the time to research and study the topic. Great information is available on MSDN, TechNet, and in blogs and forums.

Microsoft certifications

Microsoft certifications distinguish you by proving your command of a broad set of skills and experience with current Microsoft products and technologies. The exams and corresponding certifications are developed to validate your mastery of critical competencies as you design and develop, or implement and support, solutions with Microsoft products and technologies both on-premise and in the cloud. Certification brings a variety of benefits to the individual and to employers and organizations.

> **MORE INFO**   **ALL MICROSOFT CERTIFICATIONS**
>
> For information about Microsoft certifications, including a full list of available certifications, go to *http://www.microsoft.com/learning/en/us/certification/cert-default.aspx*.

Free ebooks from Microsoft Press

From technical overviews to in-depth information on special topics, the free ebooks from Microsoft Press cover a wide range of topics. These ebooks are available in PDF, EPUB, and Mobi for Kindle formats, ready for you to download at:

http://aka.ms/mspressfree

Check back often to see what is new!

Errata, updates, & book support

We've made every effort to ensure the accuracy of this book and its companion content. You can access updates to this book—in the form of a list of submitted errata and their related corrections—at:

http://aka.ms/ER480R2

If you discover an error that is not already listed, please submit it to us at the same page.

If you need additional support, email Microsoft Press Book Support at mspinput@microsoft.com.

Please note that product support for Microsoft software and hardware is not offered through the previous addresses. For help with Microsoft software or hardware, go to *http://support.microsoft.com*.

We want to hear from you

At Microsoft Press, your satisfaction is our top priority, and your feedback our most valuable asset. Please tell us what you think of this book at:

http://aka.ms/tellpress

The survey is short, and we read every one of your comments and ideas. Thanks in advance for your input!

Stay in touch

Let's keep the conversation going! We're on Twitter: *http://twitter.com/MicrosoftPress*.

Preparing for the exam

Microsoft certification exams are a great way to build your resume and let the world know about your level of expertise. Certification exams validate your on-the-job experience and product knowledge. While there is no substitution for on-the-job experience, preparation through study and hands-on practice can help you prepare for the exam. We recommend that you round out your exam preparation plan by using a combination of available study materials and courses. For example, you might use this Exam Ref and another study guide for your "at home" preparation and take a Microsoft Official Curriculum course for the classroom experience. Choose the combination that you think works best for you.

Note that this Exam Ref is based on publicly available information about the exam and the author's experience. To safeguard the integrity of the exam, authors do not have access to the live exam.

CHAPTER 1

Implement and manipulate document structures and objects

Web developers today need to understand the complexities of the constructs involved in building interactive and dynamic applications with HTML and JavaScript. The introduction of HTML5 brought a new standard for defining the structure of your webpages as well as changes in how you interact with them via script.

This chapter demonstrates how to create HTML5 documents with the new HTML5 semantic markup. You'll explore the process of creating the code required to manipulate and interact with HTML5 markup and applying styles to HTML5 elements.

> **IMPORTANT**
> ### Have you read page xi?
> It contains valuable information regarding the skills you need to pass the exam.

> **NOTE   ELEMENTS VS. TAGS**
>
> HTML markup is referred to as both HTML *tags* and HTML *elements*. These terms are often used interchangeably. This book refers to the HTML markup as elements.

Objectives in this chapter:

- Objective 1.1: Create the document structure
- Objective 1.2: Write code that interacts with UI controls
- Objective 1.3: Apply styling to HTML elements programmatically
- Objective 1.4: Implement HTML5 APIs
- Objective 1.5: Establish the scope of objects and variables
- Objective 1.6: Create and implement objects and methods

Objective 1.1: Create the document structure

Writing an HTML page can be very easy or very daunting, depending on your objectives. Any HTML page renders in a browser even if it contains only plain text. But this type of web application might not be effective at delivering your intended message or at providing inter-activity to keep users coming back to the site for more. This is where HTML markup comes in handy.

HTML enables you to apply a fluid and organized structure to webpages. Paired with a powerful tool such as JavaScript, HTML5 lets you deliver highly interactive content that can pique your users' interest. This objective focuses on the semantic elements available to you in HTML5, which, along with JavaScript, allow you to create the rich end-user experience that modern web users want and have come to expect.

The purpose of a document's structure is to tell the browser how the content should be displayed. Without any declarative structure in your page, the browser won't detect any structure, so it will lay out your content according to the rules implemented by its render-ing engine. When using the HTML5 markup presented in this objective, you are telling the browser to take your semantics into account when displaying the page. Going forward, new releases of browsers will incorporate more and more of the HTML5 standards into their rendering engines.

The exam will test your ability to use HTML5 semantic markup to create webpages and your ability to optimize webpages for use on screen readers. The exam will also cover the effect that the HTML5 semantic markup will have on search engine optimization.

> **This objective covers how to:**
> - Use HTML5 semantic markup
> - Create a layout container in HTML
> - Optimize for search engines
> - Optimize for screen readers

Using HTML5 semantic markup

Table 1-1 lists the HTML5 semantic elements as defined by the specification. These elements make up the core of HTML5. As such, understanding the definition and proper usage of each element is critical to successful completion of the exam. In the following sections, you will use each of these semantic markup elements to create a complete document structure.

TABLE 1-1 HTML5 semantic markup

HTML5 element	Description
<article>	Defines self-contained areas on a page
<aside>	Defines smaller content areas outside the flow of a webpage
<figcaption>	Defines the caption of a figure element
<figure>	Defines content that contains a figure, such as an image, chart, or picture
<footer>	Defines the bottom of a section or page
<header>	Defines the top of a section or page
<hgroup>	Defines a group of headings (H1–H6 elements)
<mark>	Defines text that should be highlighted
<nav>	Defines navigation to other pages in the site
<progress>	Defines the progress of the task
<section>	Defines the distinct content of a document

> **NOTE   USE ONLY WHAT YOU NEED**
>
> When designing a webpage, you don't necessarily need to use every available element. Instead, use only the elements you need to get your job done.

Understanding the core structure of an HTML5 page

Although a browser can render any plain text file, to provide any structure to the document the page must contain the basic elements that you are about to learn. Although this book assumes you have a basic understanding of how webpages are structured, the following HTML code demonstrates the basic template of an HTML5 page:

```
<!DOCTYPE html>
<html>
<head>
    <meta charset="utf-8"/>
    <title></title>
</head>
<body>
<!-- page content goes here -->
</body>
</html>
```

This section elaborates on this basic structure as semantic markup is introduced throughout the objective. All content to be introduced to the page will go within the *<body>* element because that page section displays content in the browser. As it is now, this code would render nothing more than a blank page. To see some content as you work through the following sections for each semantic element, use the code in Listing 1-1.

LISTING 1-1 HTML5 semantic elements

```
<body>
    <header>
        <h1>Some fictional company Website</h1>
        <nav>
            <a href="Home.html">Document Structure</a>
            <a href="Blog.html">Writing Code</a>
            <a href="About.html">Styles</a>
        </nav>
    </header>
    <article>
        <header>
            <hgroup>
                <h1>Our first new Article</h1>
            </hgroup>
        </header>
        <section>
            <h1>Section 1</h1>
            <p>Some details about section 1</p>
            <aside>Did you know that 7/10 is 70%</aside>
        </section>
        <section>
            <h1>Section 2</h1>
        </section>
    </article>
    <article>
        <header>
            <hgroup>
                <h1>Second huge article</h1>
            </hgroup>
        </header>
        <p>Provide some useful information in the article</p>
    </article>
    <article>
        <header>
            <hgroup>
                <h1>Third huge article</h1>
            </hgroup>
        </header>
        <p>Provide some useful information in the third article</p>
        <figure>
            <img src="orange.jpg"  style="width:50px; height:50px;"/>
            <figcaption>Fig 1: A really juicy orange.</figcaption>
        </figure>
    </article>
</body>
```

Using the *<header>* and *<footer>* elements

Most webpage documents contain common content at the top and bottom of all pages. Although using the *<header>* and *<footer>* elements doesn't automatically provide this functionality, the elements do provide the ability to define the content in the header and footer of the website.

Typically, a webpage header contains content such as a company logo or banner. In some cases, it might also contain a navigation menu. (See the upcoming "Using the *<nav>* element" section for this.) Start the example page by adding the *<header>* element to your page:

```
<body>
    <header>
        <h1>Some fictional company Website</h1>
...
    </header>
</body>
```

This HTML code produces the output shown in Figure 1-1:

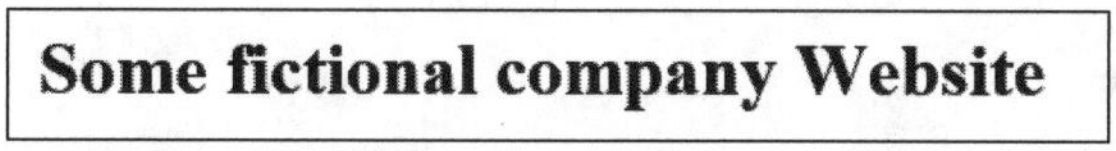

Some fictional company Website

FIGURE 1-1 A *<header>* element, which causes the browser to format the text within the element as a heading.

The *<header>* element isn't limited to only the start of your page—it provides a semantic way of declaring the header to any area of the webpage. You can use the *<header>* element as a header to a *<section>* element or to an *<article>* element. The *<header>* element is intended to hold an H1–H6 element as needed; however, you can populate a header with any markup that suits your needs to create the best header for that particular area of the site.

This HTML code produces the output shown in Figure 1-2:

```
<body>
...
    <header>
        <h1>Some fictional company Website</h1>
    </header>
    <article>
        <header>
            <h1>Our first new Article</h1>
        </header>
...
</body>
```

Some fictional company Website

Our first new Article

Section 1

FIGURE 1-2 The *<header>* element with a nested *<h1>* element

Using the *<nav>* element

Using the *<nav>* element in an HTML5 document provides users with navigation through the main elements of the web document or web application as a whole. These main navigation elements could be represented as a list of links across the top of the page to navigate the current website. It could also list your favorite websites along the side of the page, such as in a blog where you list other favorite blogs that you follow.

Typically, the list of links across the top, commonly known as the main menu of the web application, is contained in the header (but doesn't have to be). A list of favorite URLs would most likely be placed into an *<aside>* so that the list could be placed off to the side, away from the main content but readily accessible. For the current example, you create a main menu across the top of the page. This HTML code produces the output in Figure 1-3:

```
<body>
   <header>
      <h1>Some fictional company Website</h1>
      <nav>
         <a href="Home.html">Document Structure</a>
         <a href="Blog.html">Writing Code</a>
         <a href="About.html">Styles</a>
      </nav>
   </header>
   ...
</body>
```

Some fictional company Website

Document Structure Writing Code Styles

Our first new Article

Section 1

FIGURE 1-3 A navigation menu created using the *<nav>* element

The other main element commonly used under the *<header>* element is the rightfully named *<hgroup>*.

Using the *<hgroup>* element

The *<hgroup>* element is a semantic method that organizes headers and subheaders. This element typically contains the standard and familiar *<h1>* to *<h6>* elements. The *<hgroup>* element groups related headers in sequence. You can add a new *<hgroup>* element to your webpage to serve this purpose, like so:

```
<body>
    ...
    <article>
        <header>
            <hgroup>
                <h1>Our first new Article</h1>
            </hgroup>
        </header>
        <p>Provide some useful information in the article</p>
    </article>
</body>
```

This HTML code renders the output in Figure 1-4.

Some fictional company Website

Document Structure Writing Code Styles

Our first new Article

Section 1

Some details about section 1

FIGURE 1-4 Using the *<hgroup>* element to group headers

This code example effectively tells the renderer that the article has a main heading (*<h1>*). You could go on, adding *<h2>* to *<h6>* elements if required. How many of these (*<h1>* to *<h6>*) elements you use in your *<hgroup>* element obviously depends on the document structure you want to present.

Now that the page is starting to take shape, you can learn about the two main content elements: *<article>* and *<section>*.

Using the *<article>* element

An *<article>* element represents a whole and complete composition or entry. Examples of an *<article>* element could be a magazine article or a blog post, where the content can be redistributed independently and not lose its meaning. Each article is wholly contained within itself. You can have an article with subarticles; however, each subarticle must be a direct extension and related to the root article.

Now that you know about this new *<article>* element, you can go back to your sample document and organize it with articles:

```
<body>
...
    <article>
        <header>
            <hgroup>
                <h1>Our first new Article</h1>
            </hgroup>
        </header>
        <section>
            <h1>Section 1</h1>
            <p>Some details about section 1</p>
            <aside>Did you know that 7/10 is 70%</aside>
        </section>
        <section>
            <h1>Section 2</h1>
        </section>
    </article>
    <article>
        <header>
            <hgroup>
                <h1>Second huge article</h1>
            </hgroup>
        </header>
        <p>Provide some useful information in the article</p>
    </article>
    <article>
        <header>
            <hgroup>
                <h1>Third huge article</h1>
            </hgroup>
        </header>
        <p>Provide some useful information in the third article</p>
    </article>
</body>
```

This HTML code produces the output in Figure 1-5.

Some fictional company Website

Document Structure Writing Code Styles

Our first new Article

Section 1

Some details about section 1

Did you know that 7/10 is 70%

Section 2

Second huge article

Provide some useful information in the article

Third huge article

Provide some useful information in the third article

FIGURE 1-5 Using the *<article>* element to segment different articles on the page

You have expanded the document to include three articles. Clearly, you don't want to put the entire chapter into the sample HTML document, but you'll add enough to be able to demonstrate the function of each semantic element. Each article added to the document in this example represents an independent part of the document that can be wholly contained. Typically, the first element within the *<article>* element is a header element or header group. Closely related to the *<article>* element is the *<section>* element, which you explore next.

Using the *<section>* element

The *<section>* element subdivides pages into sections. You could continue to break down the sample page with additional *<article>* elements; however, the purpose of the *<article>* element isn't to break down a page into more granular details. This is where the *<section>* element becomes useful. Each *<article>* element contains zero or more *<section>* elements to denote the different content sections within the *<article>* element. Like an *<article>* element, the first element within a *<section>* element is typically a header or a header group.

Now you can expand the sample page with *<section>* elements to produce the output shown in Figure 1-6:

```
<body>
…
    <article>
        <header>
            <hgroup>
                <h1>Our first new Article</h1>
            </hgroup>
        </header>
        <section>
            <h1>Section 1</h1>
            <p>Some details about section 1</p>
        </section>
        <section>
            <h1>Section 2</h1>
        </section>
    </article>
    …
</body>
```

Some fictional company Website

Document Structure Writing Code Styles

Our first new Article

Section 1

Some details about section 1

Section 2

Second huge article

Provide some useful information in the article

Third huge article

Provide some useful information in the third article

FIGURE 1-6 Using the *<section>* element within an *<article>* element

When you view this page in the browser now, you might notice something quite interesting. The *<h1>* elements inside the *<hgroup>* elements are rendering differently from the previous *<h1>* elements in the same article. Considering that you haven't applied any styles to this page yet, you might expect that all *<h1>* elements would render in the same style (for example, the same font size) as the *<h1>* element in the *<article>* element. However, when you render the page in the browser, you can see that this isn't the case. This is because of the way the document parser in the browser works through the document to determine the implied hierarchy of the headings, also called the document outline. You see more of this when you learn about screen readers later in this lesson. For now, focus on the *<aside>* element.

Using the *<aside>* element

The *<aside>* element defines any content that doesn't fall within the main flow or main content of the current page—for example, a sidebar, a note, an alert, or an advertisement. The *<aside>* element doesn't place itself automatically to any particular side of the webpage; it merely serves as a way to semantically define a section of text or graphics as an aside. Later you will see how to position an aside using styles. For now, add the following *<aside>* element to your page for later use:

```
<body>
    ...
    <article>
        <header>
            <hgroup>
                <h1>Our first new Article</h1>
            </hgroup>
        </header>
        <section>
            <h1>Section 1</h1>
            <p>Some details about section 1</p>
            <aside>Did you know that 7/10 is 70%</aside>
        </section>
        <section>
            <h1>Section 2</h1>
        </section>
    </article>
...
</body>
```

This HTML code produces the output in Figure 1-7:

Some fictional company Website

Document Structure Writing Code Styles

Our first new Article

Section 1

Some details about section 1

Did you know that 7/10 is 70%

Section 2

Second huge article

Provide some useful information in the article

Third huge article

Provide some useful information in the third article

FIGURE 1-7 Using an *<aside>* element within an *<article>* element

As you can see in the browser output, the *<aside>* element isn't treated as special in any way compared to the other elements used to structure your page. However, a little later you can see how much more easily you can style the content by using semantic markup, such as the *<aside>* element.

Using the *<figcaption>* and *<figure>* elements

The *<figcaption>* and *<figure>* elements, new in HTML5, provide the semantic elements necessary for adding graphics and figures to webpages. These graphics and figures typically provide a visual representation of information in the textual content and referenced by the text. You often see such images in tutorials or textbooks in which the author directs the reader to a specific figure. As an example, I've added some HTML to the end of the previous example:

```
<body>
...
    <article>
        ...
        <figure>
            <img src="orange.jpg"  style="width:50px; height:50px;"/>
            <figcaption>Fig 1: A really juicy orange.</figcaption>
        </figure>
    </article>
</body>
```

This HTML code produces the output in Figure 1-8.

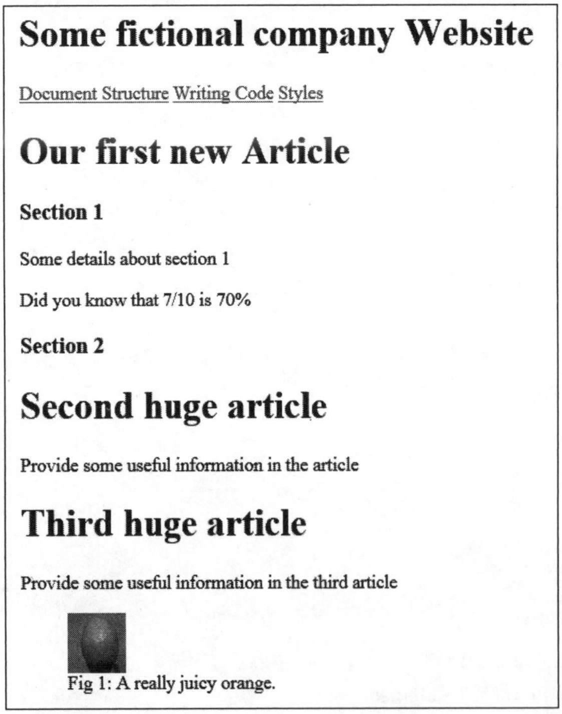

Some fictional company Website

Document Structure Writing Code Styles

Our first new Article

Section 1

Some details about section 1

Did you know that 7/10 is 70%

Section 2

Second huge article

Provide some useful information in the article

Third huge article

Provide some useful information in the third article

Fig 1: A really juicy orange.

FIGURE 1-8 Using the *<figure>* element to add a graphic or figure to the page

You need to replace the example image with one you already have to get the page to render correctly. However, the essence of what you achieve with the *<figcaption>* and *<figure>* elements should be clear.

Using the *<progress>* element

The *<progress>* element represents the progress of an objective or task. The two supported types of progress tasks are *determinate* and *indeterminate*.

Use a determinate progress task when you know in advance the amount of work to be completed; in other words, you know the starting and ending values. Sample scenarios for this case include downloading a file for which you know the exact size or displaying the progress of a fundraising effort. In both situations, you know the exact status of the task at any particular time, and you also know what the end goal is—either the number of bytes for the file download or the number of dollars for the fundraiser. In these determinate cases, you can specify HTML5 markup such as this:

```
<p>Our goal is to have 1000 users:</p>
<span>0</span>
<progress value="50" max="1000"></progress>
<span>1000</span>
```

The result of this HTML is the progress bar shown in Figure 1-9.

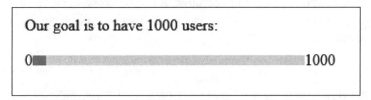

FIGURE 1-9 Using the *<progress>* element to show progress toward a total

As shown in the preceding code, the *<progress>* element has two attributes you need to know: *value* and *max*. The *value* attribute lets you specify the current value or position of the *<progress>* element at a specific point in time. The *max* attribute tells the browser what the maximum possible value is for the element. The browser uses these two values to determine how much of the element should be colored in. Usually, the *value* attribute updates dynamically using JavaScript. In Figure 1-10, you can see how the *<progress>* element's display changes when the *value* attribute is updated to 750.

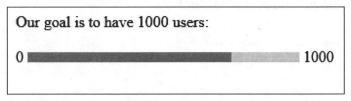

FIGURE 1-10 The effect of the *value* attribute on the *<progress>* element

You use indeterminate tasks when you don't know how long a task will take to complete but still want to show users that some work is occurring and that they should wait. You still use the *<progress>* element but remove the *value* attribute. When you don't specify the *value* attribute, the browser can infer that the *<progress>* element represents an indeterminate task. This might be useful for data received from a service where you have no control over or knowledge of how quickly the request will complete or how large the request results will be. The following HTML5 markup demonstrates an indeterminate task:

```
<p>Data download is in progress, please wait patiently:</p>
<progress max="5"></progress>
```

This code produces a progress display like the one shown in Figure 1-11:

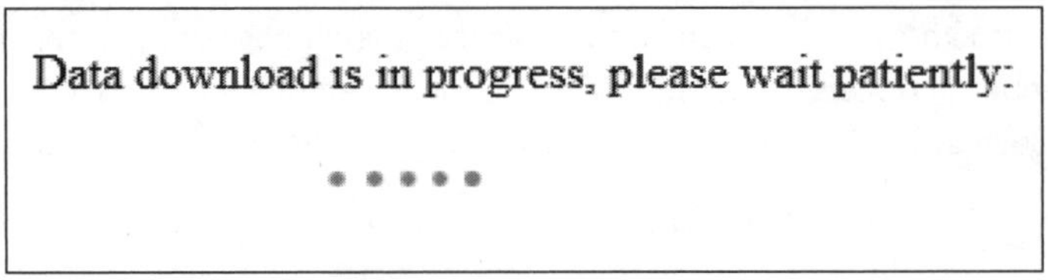

Data download is in progress, please wait patiently:

• • • • •

FIGURE 1-11 Showing indeterminate progress by using moving dots to demonstrate that work is occurring

In Figure 1-11, the blue dots replace the progress bar from the previous determinate example. This visual change to the progress indicator occurred by simply removing the *value* attribute from the *<progress>* element. In actuality, the dots are animated, as you would see if you run the code in a browser.

<mark> element

With the *<mark>* element, you can easily highlight important information or any text you want to emphasize. It has essentially the same function as a highlighter. By wrapping text in a *<mark>* element and providing a *background-color* attribute to its *style* element, you can get the desired highlight effect. The following HTML code demonstrates the *<mark>* element:

```
<p>Some very <mark style="background-color:red;">important</mark> information provided
here!</p>
```

Figure 1-12 shows the output of this HTML. The word "important" is highlighted as a result of the *<mark>* element being placed around it.

Some very important information provided here!

FIGURE 1-12 The effect on text placed inside the *<mark>* element

Using the *<div>* element

The new HTML5 semantic elements don't (with the exception of the *<progress>* element) necessarily provide any default or altered behavior. Instead, they provide a stronger semantic definition to your webpages. This, in turn, gives you a more reliable and maintainable way to structure your pages and style them consistently. The goal of these elements is to replace the older method of structuring pages—prior to HTML5—by using *<div>* elements and naming them according to their function. However, note that the *<div>* element is still part of HTML5 and still plays an important role. Use the new semantic elements as appropriate, but remember that the *<div>* element is still quite useful for styling content.

This section explored the new semantic elements in HTML5. In the next section, you learn how to create and work with layout containers.

Creating a layout container in HTML

You can lay out a webpage in various ways. An important aim here is to urge you to give serious thought to layout so that your page presentation is user friendly. If users can't find what they are looking for because the entire page is styled as a single *<p>* element inside the *<body>* element, they aren't likely to keep coming back. In this section, you look at a couple of layout options available in HTML. Chapter 4, "Use CSS in applications," explains how to use cascading style sheets (CSS) to implement your layouts.

The two most common methods of creating a layout in HTML involve using *<div>* and *<table>* elements. In either case, more than likely you will still use CSS to help with positioning and sizing. Chapter 4 goes into more detail about CSS; this section looks specifically at the layout, using only HTML.

Still the catchall container elements, the familiar *<div>*s are often used to divide the page into various sections to create the layout. For example, you might see this sort of HTML used to achieve layout:

```
<div id="PageHeader"></div>
<div id="LeftSide"></div>
<div id="RightSide"></div>
<div id="Footer"></div>
```

The rendering engine displays each *<div>* according to its rules. To position the divisions dynamically would require CSS.

The main issue with using *<div>* elements to structure the document is their inability to impart standard semantic meaning to each section. You'll revisit these examples later, when you explore creating layouts in CSS.

The *<div>* element allows for more dynamic capability in page layout. For a more static layout declared right in the HTML page, the *<table>* element is more appropriate. The following HTML defines a table that provides a common blog-site format, with a header section, a left sidebar, a content area, a right sidebar, and a footer area:

```
<table>
    <tr>
        <td colspan="3" id="Header"></td>
    </tr>
    <tr>
        <td rowspan="3" id="LeftBar"></td>
        <td rowspan="3" id="MainContent"></td>
        <td id="RightSideTop"></td>
    </tr>
    <tr>
        <td id="RightSideMiddle"></td>
    </tr>
    <tr>
        <td id="RightSideBottom"></td>
    </tr>
    <tr>
        <td colspan="3" id="Footer"></td>
    </tr>
</table>
```

The *<table>* element is very flexible. Additional elements such as *<thead>* and *<tfoot>* provide a more semantic approach to labeling the table cells. The concern with using the *<table>* element approach is the static nature of the structure. To change the overall structure of a site that uses tables for layout, you need to go to every page and make the changes. It's worth noting that some methods that make such changes easier have evolved over the years in response to the maintenance headache involved.

Optimizing for search engines

When a website is required to create an online presence, you have to ensure that it can be found among the millions of sites that already exist. Search engine optimization (SEO) is a technique used to make elements of the website easily discoverable and appropriately indexed by search engines, so that when users search for content related to your site, they find your pages. Search engines such as Bing and Google constantly scour the Internet for content. When they find webpages, they go through the HTML and index content such as page and image metadata. They use the indexed data to allow users to search for essentially anything on the Internet and receive relevant results. Clearly, then, a relationship exists between the content on your websites and how easily users can find your sites using a search engine. With the semantic HTML elements discussed in the previous objective in mind, you should note some additional things with respect to the logic search engines use to discover what's on websites. On the whole, the subject of SEO is far outside the scope of this book and exam; entire books are written on the subject. However, discussing how HTML5 impacts SEO and website design is relevant.

In the past (defined as pre-HTML5), web designers often used *<div>* elements to segment the page. These elements don't provide very much context as to what they are intended to contain. But with the semantic markup available in HTML5, you can use more descriptive elements for the page sections. As you saw in the blog-page layout example, the HTML elements alone make clear the intent of each segment of the page. As search engines scour webpages, they detect the markup and know what to take from it to properly index the page.

The *<article>* and *<section>* elements are the main ones used by the SEO algorithm. These elements are known to contain the main body of the page. That a page have more than one *<article>* and/or *<section>* element is acceptable; they all get indexed. Within each *<article>* element, the engine then seeks out elements such as *<hgroup>* or *<h1>* to get the main topic of the *<article>* element for relevant indexing. However, this doesn't mean that if a site doesn't have *<article>* or *<section>* elements, it won't get indexed and be searchable. This speaks only to the quality of indexing the search engines can conduct to make your site more searchable by end users.

SEO is a great technique to understand when designing websites. Creating a website just to leave it in the dark and hard to find doesn't serve much purpose. Being found is very important and, when the site is found, you don't want to limit your audience. Accessibility is also very important.

Next, look at how HTML5 affects the use of screen readers.

Optimizing for screen readers

Screen readers rely on the document outline to parse the structure and present information to the user. Screen-reader programs can read the text on the page and convert it to audio through a text-to-speech algorithm. This is helpful for users who might have difficulty viewing the webpage. As discussed earlier, the way the document gets outlined in HTML5 has changed. Here's a little more detail.

Prior to HTML5, a page was outlined using only the header elements (*<h1>* through *<h6>*). The relative position of each header element to the previous header element within the page created the hierarchy. Screen readers could use this information to present a table of contents to users. However, HTML5 introduced semantic elements to create new sections. This means that *<section>*, *<article>*, *<nav>*, and *<aside>* elements all define new sections. The introduction of the semantic elements changes how the document outline is created. For example, if the following HTML was going to be the hierarchy of the sample document, you could possibly lay it out like this:

```
<h1>Fruits and Vegetables</h1>
<h2>Fruit</h2>
<h3>Round Fruit</h3>
<h3>Long Fruit</h3>
<h2>Vegetables</h2>
<h3>Green</h3>
<h3>Colorful</h3>
```

This produces the expected outline, shown in Figure 1-13.

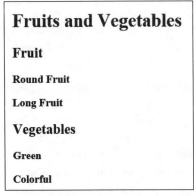

Fruits and Vegetables

Fruit

Round Fruit

Long Fruit

Vegetables

Green

Colorful

FIGURE 1-13 The output of a series of header elements to create a document structure

The outline shows the default styles of the different header elements as expected. The heading elements create implied sections and subsections within the document. This is still valid in HTML5. However, you shouldn't leave the page sectioning set to implied sectioning as presented by the header elements; rather, you should explicitly define the sections by using the appropriate semantics. Also recommended is that *<h1>* elements be used solely throughout an HTML5 document. To produce the same hierarchy in this fashion, you would need to change your HTML to be like the following:

```
<section>
    <h1>Fruits and Vegetables</h1>
    <section>
        <h1>Fruit</h1>
        <section>
            <h1>Round Fruit</h1>
        </section>
        <section>
            <h1>Long Fruit</h1>
        </section>
    </section>
    <section>
        <h1>Vegetables</h1>
        <section>
            <h1>Green</h1>
        </section>
        <section>
            <h1>Colorful</h1>
        </section>
    </section>
</section>
```

This HTML produces the same output as shown earlier in Figure 1-13. The difference is that now each *<section>* element creates a new page section rather than rely on the header elements to create the sections. Screen readers can parse the semantic elements to create the document outline and eventually can provide a much richer user experience because of how HTML5 allows webpage designers to lay out the pages.

Thought experiment
Converting a website to HTML5

In this thought experiment, apply what you've learned about this objective. You can find answers to these questions in the "Answers" section at the end of this chapter.

You have just been hired to convert an existing website to the new HTML5 semantic markup. Analyze the following HTML and determine what elements should be updated to fully leverage the HTML5 semantic markup:

```html
<html>
    <head>
        <title>Experimentations</title>
    </head>
    <body>
        <table>
            <tr>
                <td colspan="3">
                    <div id="header">
                        <h1>A Thoughtful Experiment</h1>
                    </div>
                </td>
            </tr>
            <tr>
                <td>
                    <a href="">Home</a>
                    <a href="">Page 1</a>
                    <a href="">Page 2</a>
                    <a href="">Page 3</a>
                </td>
                <td>
                    <div id="content">
                        <div id="anArticle">
                            <h1>An Article regarding thought is
                            presented here.</h1>
                            <h2>Thought as a provoking element.</h2>
                            ....................
                                <div id="moreInfo">Here are some
                                reference material.</div>
                        </div>
                    </div>
                </td>
```

```
            <td>
                <div id="profile">
                    .....
                </div>
            </td>
        </tr>
        <tr>
            <td>
                <div id="footer">
                    This page is copyright protected.
                </div>
            </td>
        </tr>
    </table>
</body>
</html>
```

Objective summary

- HTML5 introduced new semantic elements to more clearly define sections of an HTML page. These elements include *<section>*, *<article>*, *<nav>*, *<header>*, *<footer>*, *<aside>*, *<progress>*, *<mark>*, *<figure>*, and *<figcaption>*.

- Elements within an HTML page can have their layout controlled when they are included inside structures such as *<div>* elements and/or HTML tables.

- HTML5 semantic elements provide the mechanisms necessary to structure the page more easily for accessibility via screen readers.

- Search engines take advantage of HTML5 semantics by leveraging the *<article>* element to determine the purpose of the page.

Objective review

Answer the following questions to test your knowledge of the information in this objective. You can find the answers to these questions and explanations of why each answer choice is correct or incorrect in the "Answers" section at the end of this chapter.

1. Which of the following elements aren't introduced in HTML5?

   A. *<article>*

   B. *<footer>*

   C. *<hgroup>*

   D. *<input>*

2. Which element(s) does the *<hgroup>* element contain?

   A. *<h1>* to *<h6>*

   B. *<header>*

   C. *<nav>*

   D. All of the above

3. Which HTML5 element would you use to organize content so that the page maximizes a search engine's algorithm?

   A. *<div id="CompanyNews">*

   B. *<header>*Company News*</header>*

   C. *<article>*Company News*</article>*

   D. All of the above

4. Which HTML5 element should you use to create a more structured layout?

   A. *<div>*

   B. *<p>*

   C. *<table>*

   D. *<form>*

Objective 1.2: Write code that interacts with UI controls

In this objective, you review how to interact with webpages in the browser using code. Web browsers include a powerful environment in which you can control the behavior of webpages. And some new HTML5 elements provide improved interactivity for end users.

You also review how to modify the document object model dynamically, using JavaScript. You review how to implement video and audio in webpages and how to control them programmatically. Finally, you review how to render graphics dynamically or allow users to draw their own graphics.

> **This objective covers how to:**
> - Add or modify HTML elements
> - Implement media controls
> - Implement graphics with HTML5 canvas and SVG

Adding or modifying HTML elements

The ability to modify an HTML document at run time is very powerful. So far you've seen how to create your webpages, lay them out elegantly, and render them for users. In many cases, you should modify the layout of your webpages at run time depending on what your users do. This is where you can take advantage of the power of JavaScript. JavaScript provides the toolkit you need to write code that interacts with webpage elements after they are already rendered into the browser. Before you can start to modify the webpage, you need to know how to access or reference the elements so you can manipulate them.

Document Object Model

The Document Object Model (DOM) is a representation of the structure of your HTML page that you can interact with programmatically. As demonstrated earlier, an HTML page is a hierarchy. The browser produces an outline based on the HTML hierarchy presented to it and displays this in the browser to the user. Behind the scenes, unknown to the user, the browser constructs a DOM. The DOM's application programming interface (API) is exposed as objects with properties and methods, enabling you to write JavaScript code to interact with the HTML elements rendered to the page.

This notion is very powerful. You can add new elements to the page that didn't even exist in your original HTML page. You can modify elements to change their behavior, layout, appearance, and content. Theoretically, although this is rarely a recommended practice, you could render a blank HTML page to the browser, build the entire page using JavaScript, and produce the exact same results. Having that power over your webpages is very exciting, even after they are rendered. You start by selecting items in the DOM to get a reference to them.

Selecting items in the DOM

To manipulate the DOM, you need to know how to access it and to obtain references to the elements you want to manipulate. In the next section you look at altering the DOM, but first you need to get elements from the DOM so you can work with them.

> **NOTE   THE DOCUMENT OBJECT MODEL AS A FAMILY TREE**
>
> The DOM is essentially a collection of nodes arranged in a tree. All the nodes are related to each other. They are one big happy family of children, siblings, parents, grandparents, grandchildren, and so on. This essence of a family tree represents the hierarchy of the DOM and is important to understand as you manipulate the DOM through code.

You have a few choices when it comes to using JavaScript to access the DOM. You can access DOM elements through a global object provided by the browser, called *document*, or through the elements themselves after you obtain a reference to one. Table 1-2 outlines the core native methods used for selecting elements in the DOM.

TABLE 1-2 Methods available for selecting DOM elements

Method	Usage description
getElementById	Gets an individual element on the page by its unique id attribute value
getElementsByClassName	Gets all the elements that have the specified CSS class applied to them
getElementsByTagName	Gets all the elements of the page that have the specified tag name or element name
querySelector	Gets the first child element found that matches the provided CSS selector criteria
querySelectorAll	Gets all the child elements that match the provided CSS selector criteria

For the most part, the methods are straightforward to use. In this section, you begin with a simple HTML document structure that you will use in many other examples in this book to highlight various concepts. Create a webpage with the HTML markup in Listing 1-2 to proceed with the following examples.

LISTING 1-2 HTML source to work with the DOM

```html
<body>
    <div id="outerDiv">
        <p class='mainPara'>Main Paragraph</p>
        <ul>
            <li>First List Item</li>
            <li>Second List Item</li>
            <li>Third List Item</li>
            <li>Fourth List Item</li>
        </ul>
        <div id="innerDiv">
            <p class='subPara' id='P1'>Paragraph 1</p>
            <p class='subPara' id='P2'>Paragraph 2</p>
            <p class='subPara' id='P3'>Paragraph 3</p>
            <p class='subPara' id='P4'>Paragraph 4</p>
        </div>
        <table>
            <tr>
                <td>Row 1
                </td>
            </tr>
            <tr>
                <td>Row 2
                </td>
            </tr>
            <tr>
                <td>Row 3
                </td>
            </tr>
            <tr>
                <td>Row 4
                </td>
            </tr>
            <tr>
                <td>Row 5
                </td>
            </tr>
        </table>
        <input type="text"/><input type="submit" value="Submit"/>
    </div>
</body>
```

This sample page is very simple, but it serves the purpose of demonstrating various ways to access elements through code. To demonstrate this functionality, you need an entry point. Add the following script block to the head section of the webpage:

```html
<script>
    window.onload = function () {
        ...
    }
</script>
```

This should look familiar, but if it doesn't, you'll review the concepts later. For now, this code essentially tells the runtime to run your code after the window finishes loading. You can use your code to experiment with the various methods listed in Table 1-2 in this function, starting with *getElementById*.

The *getElementById* method returns the element in the page that matches the specific ID value you pass to it. It returns null if no element on the page has the specified ID. Each element on the page should have a unique ID. For example, if you want to reference the *<div>* element with the ID *outerDiv*, you would use the following code:

```
var element = document.getElementById("outerDiv");
alert(element.innerHTML);
```

The JavaScript *alert* method, which displays a message box, is used here to show whether you have actually accessed the DOM successfully. The *alert* isn't all that useful in the real world but it is for development purposes. When you run the page, notice the message box from the browser with all the *innerHTML* contents of the *<div>* you selected out of the DOM with your code (see Figure 1-14).

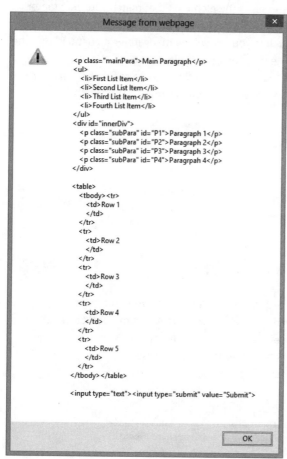

FIGURE 1-14 A JavaScript *alert* demonstrating successful access to the DOM

Now that you have successfully obtained a reference to your *<div>*, you can do anything you want to it dynamically—just as you could have defined or applied such changes to it statically. The *getElementById* method is great when you know the ID of a specific element in the page that you want to work with, but in other cases you might want to do something to all the elements of a particular type—for example, all paragraph elements. In this case, the *getElementsByTagName* method is more appropriate. You can use the following code to get a reference to all the *<p>* elements:

```
<script>
    window.onload = function () {
        var paragraphs = document.getElementsByTagName("p");
        alert(paragraphs.length);
    }
</script>
```

In this code, the object returned from the *getElementsByTagName* method is a little differ-ent; it's a special type that acts as a wrapper to all the elements that match your parameter, called a *NodeList*. This object isn't especially useful by itself. In fact, it doesn't really provide anything useful other than a length, which lets you know how many items it contains, and the ability to access each individual item. In the preceding example, the JavaScript *alert* displays how many items were returned in the list (*paragraphs.length*). You can see that the method returned all five of the *<p>* elements in the page, as shown in Figure 1-15.

FIGURE 1-15 A message showing the number of *<p>* elements

In the same way that you could use the *getElementsByTagName* method to get all elements of the same type, you can use the *getElementsByClassName* method to get all elements of the same CSS class. This is useful when you have many elements with the same style but perhaps want to modify them at run time. This method also returns a *NodeList*. The following snippet demonstrates the usage:

```
<script>
    window.onload = function () {
        var paragraphs = document.getElementsByClassName("subPara");
        alert("<p> elements with class subPara: " + paragraphs.length);
    }
</script>
```

Figure 1-16 shows the output of this script.

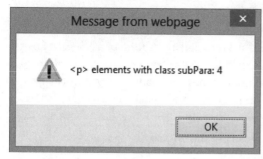

FIGURE 1-16 A message showing the number of *<p>* elements with the specified class name *subPara*

This example adds a little more text to the message box so that it looks different from the previous example, but the idea is the same. All *<p>* elements with the *subPara* class assigned to them were returned in a *NodeList*. You can see that the call returned four HTML elements. When selecting elements in the DOM by class name, the *NodeList* contains all elements whose class matches the specified class—not just elements of the same type. If, for example, you assigned the class *subPara* to one of your *<div>* elements and then ran the function again, the returned *NodeList* would contain the four *<p>* elements and the *<div>* element because they all have the same class. This is important when you intend to iterate over the elements and do something to them. In Figure 1-17, the same JavaScript code is run, but with an added *subPara* class attribute to a *<div>* element.

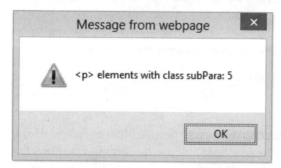

FIGURE 1-17 The same script run with a *<div>* assigned the class name *subPara*

This message box is now actually incorrect, because the *NodeList* contains a single *<div>* element and the four *<p>* elements. Keep this behavior in mind concerning the *getElementsByClassName* method.

All the methods you have looked at so far to find elements in the DOM provide a specific implementation for a specific purpose. If you want a single element by its unique ID, you use the *getElementById* method; if you want to find an element or all the elements of a specific CSS class, you use the *getElementsByClassName* method. Now look at some examples that use the much more flexible *querySelector* and *querySelectorAll* methods.

The *querySelector* and *querySelectorAll* methods allow you to achieve most of what you've already done with the other methods. Both methods take a parameter in the form of a CSS selector. The *querySelector* method returns the first element it finds that matches the selector criteria passed to it, whereas the *querySelectorAll* method returns all elements that match the selector criteria passed in. The elements are still returned in the form of a *NodeList* object. Both methods exist not only on the document itself, but also on each element. Therefore, when you have a reference to an element, you can use these methods to search its children without having to traverse the entire document. You can see some simpler examples in this section.

To find all the *<p>* elements on a page, you can use this syntax:

```
document.querySelectorAll("p");
```

To find an element by its unique ID, you can use this syntax:

```
document.querySelector("#outerDiv");
```

Put those two lines into your HTML file and try them out. You will explore much more advanced and interesting functionality in Chapter 4. For now, you can use what you've seen about finding elements in the DOM to apply that knowledge to adding or modifying the DOM through code.

EXAM TIP

jQuery is probably the most popular library available to date for simplifying and extending the core JavaScript capabilities. Although jQuery isn't a Microsoft technology, it's essentially an industry standard and fully supported by Microsoft. As such, web developers today are generally understood to have a grasp of using jQuery interchangeably with core JavaScript. The exam will expect that you can use jQuery effectively in place of the document object selector methods.

Altering the DOM

Having access to the DOM through JavaScript can be used to provide rich user experience when creating dynamic webpages. So far, all you've done is obtain references to the elements, which is not particularly useful by itself. The purpose of retrieving elements from the DOM is to be able to do something with them. In this section, you look at how to manipulate the DOM by using JavaScript code to add and remove items.

After you have a reference to a container element, you can add child elements to it dynamically. You can remove elements from it or simply hide elements. When you remove an element from the DOM, it is gone. So if you want to make something invisible to the user but be able to use it again later, you can simply hide it by using the appropriate CSS rather than remove it. Here's an example:

```
var element = document.getElementById("innerDiv");
alert(element.innerHTML);
document.removeChild(element);
var afterRemove = document.getElementById("innerDiv");
alert(afterRemove);
```

The first *alert* properly shows the *innerHTML* property of the *innerDiv*, but the code never reaches the second alert. Instead, the *getElementById* method throws an error because the element *id* specified no longer exists in the document.

Be aware of various methods when it comes to adding elements to and removing them from the DOM.

The first method to look at is *document.createElement*. You use this method of the *document* object to create a new HTML element. The method receives a single parameter—the element name of the element you want to create. The following code creates a new *<article>* element to use in your page:

```
var element = document.createElement("article");
element.innerText = "My new <article> element";
```

This new *<article>* element isn't visible to anyone at this point; it merely exists in the DOM for use within your page. Because you don't have much need to create elements but then not use them, next look at the methods available to get your new *<article>* element into your page. The first of these methods is *appendChild*. You use this method to add a new HTML element to the collection of child elements belonging to the calling container. The node is added to the end of the list of children the parent node already contains. The *appendChild* method exists on the document object as well as on other HTML container elements. It returns a reference to the newly added node. This example appends a new *<article>* element to the *outerDiv*:

```
var outerDiv = document.getElementById("outerDiv");
var element = document.createElement("article");
element.innerText = "My new <article> element";
outerDiv.appendChild(element);
```

Like most of the other methods explained in this section, the *appendChild* method returns a reference to the new element appended to the child elements. This is a good way to ensure that you always have a reference to an element for future use, especially when deleting elements. It also enables you to simplify or restructure the code. The following code achieves the same result:

```
var element = document.getElementById("outerDiv").appendChild(document.
createElement("article"));
element.innerText = "My new <article> element";
```

Figure 1-18 shows the output of this code.

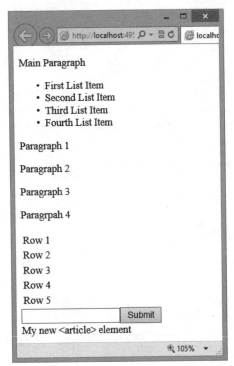

FIGURE 1-18 A new *<article>* element appended to the bottom of the page

You can see that the *<article>* element was put in at the end of your page. The *appendChild* method always adds the new element to the end of the parent element's child node list. To insert the new *<article>* element somewhere more precise, the *insertBefore* method could be more suitable. This method takes two parameters: the new element itself, and the node before which you want to append the new element. For example, to insert your new article before the *innerDiv* element, you could write the following code:

```
var element = document.getElementById("outerDiv").insertBefore(
              document.createElement("article"),
              document.getElementById("innerDiv"));
element.innerText = "My new <article> element";
```

This example uses the *getElementById* method to get a reference to the node before which you wanted to insert your *<article>* element in the DOM. You can use other tools to make this code simpler in some cases, depending on the document's structure. Each element or node has the properties listed in Table 1-3 to help get references to the more common nodes when working with the DOM.

TABLE 1-3 Properties available on a DOM element

Property	Description
childNodes	A collection of all child nodes of the parent element.
firstChild	A reference to the very first child node in the list of child nodes of the parent node.
lastChild	A reference to the very last child node in the list of the child nodes of the parent node.
hasChildNodes	A useful property that returns *true* if the parent element has any child nodes at all. A good practice is to check this property before accessing other properties, such as *firstChild* or *lastChild*.

For an example of these properties, you can change the preceding code to insert your *<article>* element as the first element in the *innerDiv* element:

```
var inner = document.getElementById("innerDiv");
var element = inner.insertBefore(document.createElement("article"),inner.firstChild);
element.innerText = "My new <article> element";
```

This code produces the output shown in Figure 1-19.

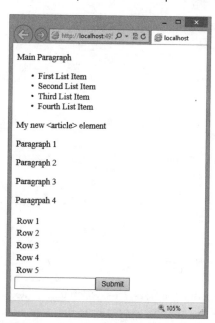

FIGURE 1-19 The new *<article>* element inserted as the first child of a *<div>* element

Your *<article>* element is now positioned as the first child element of the *innerDiv* element. Experiment with the other properties to become familiar with how they behave. Every element that can have child elements supports all this functionality; however, if you try to insert elements into a node that doesn't support child nodes—such as an *<img>*, for example—the interpreter throws a run-time error.

Just as you can add new elements to the DOM through code, you also can remove elements from the DOM using code. In this section you look at the methods available to do just this, named *removeChild* and *removeNode*.

The *removeChild* method removes a child node from the calling container. This method exists on the document object as well as other HTML container elements. The *removeChild* method returns a reference to the removed node. This is especially handy if you plan to return that node to the DOM—perhaps in response to some other user interaction with the page. Remember, however, that if you don't keep the returned reference to the removed node, you have no way to add the element back in without completely re-creating it. The following example removes the first <p> element from your *innerDiv* element:

```
var innerDiv = document.getElementById("innerDiv");
var p = innerDiv.removeChild(document.getElementById("P1"));
```

This code provides the output in Figure 1-20. You can see that the first <p> element has been removed. Because you captured the removed element into the variable *p*, you could use it later if you wanted to put the <p> element somewhere else.

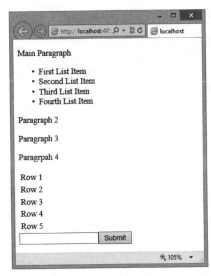

FIGURE 1-20 Removal of the first <p> element by the *removeChild* method

Another useful method for removing nodes or elements is *removeNode*, which takes one Boolean parameter. Setting the parameter as *true* tells the method to do a deep removal, which means that all children are also removed. The following code demonstrates this:

```
var innerDiv = document.getElementById("innerDiv");
innerDiv.removeNode(true);
```

Figure 1-21 shows that when this code is run in the browser, the *innerDiv* element has been removed.

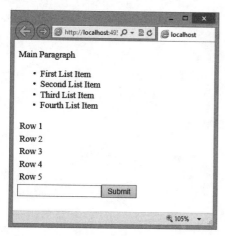

FIGURE 1-21 Using the *removeNode* method to remove the *<div>* node

Now, suppose that you want to change the content of the page more dramatically—perhaps even by rewriting all the HTML content. This is completely possible with the techniques you have seen so far, but you haven't tried some methods yet: *replaceNode* and *replaceChild*. These two methods operate in the same way as *removeNode* and *removeChild* in terms of the parameters they take and which elements they affect. The difference, however, is that you can replace the target element with a completely new element. The following code converts all your inner paragraphs to anchor elements and adds line breaks, because you don't get those automatically as you do from the *<p>* element:

```
var innerDiv = document.getElementById("innerDiv");
var newDiv = document.createElement("div");
for (var i = 0; i < innerDiv.childNodes.length; i++) {
    var anchor = newDiv.appendChild(document.createElement("a"));
    anchor.setAttribute("href", "http://www.bing.ca");
    anchor.text = innerDiv.childNodes[i].textContent;
    newDiv.appendChild(document.createElement("br"));
}
innerDiv.replaceNode(newDiv);
```

This code produces the browser output as shown in Figure 1-22.

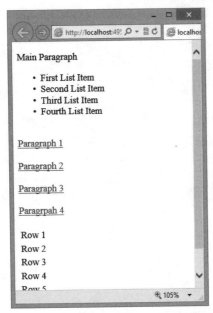

FIGURE 1-22 Converting all the *<p>* elements to *<a>* elements

All your plain-text paragraphs now display as hyperlinks. Your original *innerDiv* element is gone and no longer in the DOM. Your only reference to it is within the JavaScript code. You would need to hang on to that reference if you intended to swap it back into the DOM later. Further, because the code didn't assign the new *<div>* element a unique *id*, the only way to get a reference to it in the DOM is through your existing code reference. For this reason, a recommended practice is to always give your new elements a unique *id*. If the JavaScript variables go out of scope before you insert them into the document, you lose the references to your elements completely.

In this section, you saw how to access HTML elements by using JavaScript to manipulate the DOM in the browser. You now can retrieve references to the elements or nodes that make up your HTML document as well as modify, add, and remove elements in the HTML document. Next, you look at implementing media controls into your pages.

Implementing media controls

Embedding multimedia elements into webpages isn't a new concept. This capability has been around for a long time and has presented challenges in various situations. One key challenge has often been dependence on a third-party object integrated with the browser to render the media. In this section, you look at two new elements added to the HTML5 specification that work with multimedia natively in the web browser and with JavaScript. You also examine the *<video>* and *<audio>* elements.

Using the *<video>* element

Embedding video into a webpage has become very popular, and many websites now include a video element in their design. HTML5 has made including video in your webpages much easier than it was previously. Here, you learn about the new *<video>* element provided by the HTML5 standard and look at the available attributes and events you can use to control video either declaratively, through static HTML, or dynamically, using JavaScript.

Embedding a video in the page is as simple as adding the following markup:

```
<video src="samplevideo.mp4" autoplay> </video>
```

That's the bare minimum. However, you know that the bare minimum is rarely enough for a professionally designed website. You need to work with more properties and events. You also need to consider browser support for various video formats. First, you need to examine the key attributes available to use on the *<video>* element, as listed in Table 1-4.

TABLE 1-4 Attributes available on the *<video>* element

Attribute	Description
src	This attribute specifies the video to play. It can be a local resource within your own website or something exposed through a public URL on the Internet.
autoplay	This attribute tells the browser to start playing the video as soon as it loads. If this attribute is omitted, the video plays only when told to through player controls or JavaScript.
controls	This attribute tells the browser to include its built-in video controls, such as play and pause. If this is omitted, the user has no visible way to play the content. You would use *autoplay* or provide some other mechanism through JavaScript to play the video.
height/width	These attributes control the amount of space the video will occupy on the page. Omitting these causes the video to display in its native size.
loop	This attribute tells the browser to continuously play the video after it completes. If this attribute is omitted, the video stops after it plays through completely.
poster	This attribute specifies an image to show in the place allocated to the video until the user starts to play the video. Use this when you're not using *autoplay*. It's very useful for providing a professional image or artwork to represent the video. If it's omitted, the poster appears in the first frame of the video.

With all this new information about the available attributes, you can provide a bit more detail in your *<video>* element to control how you would like it to behave:

```
<video src="samplevideo.mp4" controls poster="picture.jpg" height="400" width="600">
</video>
```

The preceding *<video>* element specifies that it should initially display a poster image, sets the height and width parameters, and indicates that the default controls should be available. The absence of a *loop* attribute means that when the video is finished, it shouldn't repeat automatically. And the absence of an *autoplay* attribute tells the browser that you don't want the video to start playing automatically; instead, it should wait until the user invokes the play operation with the controls or until you invoke the play operation with JavaScript. When you do include the default controls, the user gets a basic set. Figure 1-23 shows what the default controls look like in Internet Explorer.

FIGURE 1-23 The default Internet Explorer media controls

From left to right, the default controls provide a play button that changes to a pause button while the video is playing. A timer shows the current video position and how much time remains in the video. A slider bar lets users navigate to a specific point in the video. The audio control button pops out a volume slider bar when pressed, and finally, at the far right, is a control that enables users to display the video at full-screen size.

So far, so good—for Internet Explorer users. But you also need to ensure that your video will play successfully in other browsers. The problem is that not all browsers support all video formats. Keep this in mind as you implement your *<video>* elements; what each browser supports can (and will) change as well. You need to ensure that you provide options to the browser so that it can choose which video format to play. If you don't have all the appropriate supported video formats and your page happens to get a visitor with a browser that can't play the video format you have, you also need to provide an alternative or at least the information that the user's browser doesn't support this video. The following code demonstrates this:

```
<video controls height="400" width="600" poster="picture.jpg">
    <source src="samplevideo.ogv" type="video/ogg"/>
    <source src="samplevideo.mp4" type="audio/mp4"/>
    <object>
        <p>Video is not supported by this browser.</p>
    </object>
</video>
```

This sample removed the *src* attribute from the *<video>* element and added child *<source>* elements instead. The *<video>* element supports multiple *<source>* elements, so you can include one for each video type. A browser goes through the *<source>* elements from top to bottom and plays the first one that it supports.

Notice that the example also has an *<object>* element to cover the possibility that the client browser has no support for the *<video>* element at all. In such cases, you could have a Flash version of the video to play; but if no other version of the video is available to play, you can just display a message that video isn't supported, as shown in the code snippet. Browsers that don't support the *<video>* element ignore the element altogether but show the *<object>* element that they do understand. This lets older browsers "fall back" to previous methods for displaying video, ensuring that you can reach as many users as possible.

Finally, the *<p>* element is a last resort to provide at least some information to users that a video is supposed to be playing here but that their browser doesn't support it.

EXAM TIP

If the browser supports the HTML5 video element, it doesn't show the fallback. In this case, make sure that you have the valid *<source>* element specified for that browser. If you don't, the video container shows an error in place of the control bar, saying that an invalid link or file is specified.

Sometimes having more control over things is nice, or perhaps you just don't like the look and feel of the default controls. This is where JavaScript comes in. You can create your own control bar and substitute your own control buttons to enable users to control the video. The following example adds a few custom image elements to the page and wires up some JavaScript to control the video:

```html
<head>
    <style>
        img:hover {
            cursor: pointer;
        }
    </style>
    <script>
        var video;
        window.onload = function () {
            video = document.getElementById("sampleVideo");
        }

        function play() {
            video.play();
        }
        function pause() {
            video.pause();
        }
        function back() {
            video.currentTime -= 10;
        }

    </script>
</head>
<body>
    <table>
        <tr>
            <td>
                <video height="400" width="600" id="sampleVideo">
                    <source src="samplevideo.mp4" type="audio/mp4"/>
                </video>
            </td>
            <td>
                <img id="backButton" src="backword.png" onclick="back();"/><br/>
                <img id="playButton" src="forward.png" onclick="play();"/><br/>
                <img id="PauseButton" src="pause.png" onclick="pause();"/><br/>
            </td>
        </tr>
    </table>
</body>
```

This HTML produces the media controls shown in Figure 1-24.

FIGURE 1-24 A custom media control bar

As you can see, the code has created a little custom control bar and positioned it to the right of the video frame. The *<video>* element offers many methods. Table 1-5 outlines the more common ones.

TABLE 1-5 Methods and properties on the *<video>* object

Method/property	Description
play()	Plays the video from its current position.
pause()	Pauses the video at its current position.
volume	Allows the user to control the volume of the video.
currentTime	Represents the current position of the video. Increase or descrease this value to move forward or backward in the video.

You've learned all about how to display video in your webpages. Now turn your attention to playing sounds using the *<audio>* element.

Using the *<audio>* element

The *<audio>* element is essentially identical to the *<video>* element. It has all the same attributes and the same methods. The only real difference is how it displays in the browser. Because no video is available to show, the *<audio>* element occupies no screen space. However, you can show the default controls—or you can again choose not to show the default controls and to create your own mechanism to control the audio, either through custom user interface elements or behind the scenes in JavaScript. Here is an example of what an *<audio>* declaration looks like in your webpage:

```
<audio controls>
    <source src="sample.mp3" type="audio/mp3"/>
    <source src="sample.ogg" type="audio/ogg"/>
    <p>Your browser does not support HTML5 audio.</p>
</audio>
```

This HTML provides the output in Internet Explorer shown in Figure 1-25.

FIGURE 1-25 The default audio controls in Internet Explorer

Figure 1-25 shows the output of the *<audio>* element when you opt to use the built-in controls. From left to right, you get a pause/play button, the counter, a progress bar, the total time in the audio, and a volume slider bar. Because no other screen space is required as in the video samples, the *<audio>* element has no height or width properties available. If you don't like the built-in audio control bar, you can choose not to include it in your declaration and instead create a custom control bar that suits your needs.

The *<audio>* and *<video>* elements are very similar. The key point regarding these elements is that they provide a standardized way to represent media in HTML pages to simplify reading the HTML code and know exactly what the page is supposed to be doing.

Now that you know how to use audio and video in your webpages, you can turn your attention to the use of graphics.

Implementing graphics with HTML5 *<canvas>* and SVG

HTML5 provides a new mechanism to work with graphics in your webpages. The HTML5 specification introduces the *<canvas>* webpage element, which provides a blank canvas on which you can draw dynamically. You can draw lines, text, and images on the canvas and manipulate them with JavaScript.

Adding a canvas to your page is as simple as declaring one in the HTML. The *<canvas>* element is similar to the *<div>* element. However, it's a container for graphics as opposed to text-based elements. Here is the markup for a *<canvas>* element:

```
<canvas id="drawingSurface" width="600" height="400">
Your browser does not support HTML5.
</canvas>
```

The HTML is very straightforward. You simply need to define a *<canvas>* and specify a size. Also, if the user's browser doesn't support the *<canvas>* element, you can place fallback text inside the *<canvas>* element to be displayed in its place. When you run this HTML in the browser, you should notice absolutely nothing! This is because—just like with a *<div>* element or any other container—the *<canvas>* element has no default visibility; in other words, it's visible, but it's white with no borders, and thus it's invisible on a blank HTML page. The next example adds a simple style to your *<canvas>* element so that you can see its borders:

```
<style>
  canvas {
        border: 1px solid black;
     }
</style>
```

Now you can see your canvas, which should look Figure 1-26.

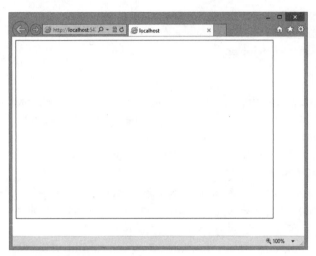

FIGURE 1-26 A blank *<canvas>* element

A blank canvas isn't terribly exciting yet. But now that you have a basic canvas up and running, you can work through all the various methods to create graphics on the canvas. To do that, you should create an onload event for your window (as you have in previous examples) to encapsulate your code and cause the graphics to render when the page is loaded. To draw on the canvas, you need to understand the coordinate system that the canvas uses.

The canvas provides a fixed (x,y) coordinate system in which the top-left corner of the canvas is (0,0). In this case, the bottom-left corner of the canvas is (0,400), the top-right corner is (600,0), and the bottom-right corner is (600,400). You should be fairly used to this type of system because it matches the browser window coordinate system, with (0,0) in the top-left corner. However, the position of the canvas in the browser window is irrelevant to the drawing methods you use to draw on the canvas. The coordinates for drawing on the canvas are always based on the coordinates within the canvas itself, where the top-left pixel is (0,0).

As with any HTML element, to work with it through code you need to get a reference to it in your JavaScript. Begin by writing the following code in your page:

```
window.onload = function () {
        var drawingSurface = document.getElementById("drawingSurface");
        var ctxt = drawingSurface.getContext("2d");
    }
```

In the preceding code, you get a reference to your canvas element followed by a reference to a "2d" context. The context is an object that provides the API methods you use to draw on the canvas. Now, *<canvas>* supports only a 2d context, but you can expect to see a 3d context in the future.

Having acquired a reference to the context, you can now start to look at the various methods for drawing on your canvas.

Drawing lines

At the most basic level, you can draw lines on the canvas with the 2d context object you are referencing. The context object provides the following methods for drawing lines, as listed in Table 1-6.

TABLE 1-6 Methods for drawing lines

Method	Description
beginPath	Resets/begins a new drawing path
moveTo	Moves the context to the point set in the *beginPath* method
lineTo	Sets the destination end point for the line
stroke	Strokes the line, which makes the line visible

With that information, in its simplest form, you can draw a line across your canvas like this:

```
ctxt.beginPath();
ctxt.moveTo(10, 10);
ctxt.lineTo(225, 350);
ctxt.stroke();
```

This code produces the line on the canvas shown in Figure 1-27.

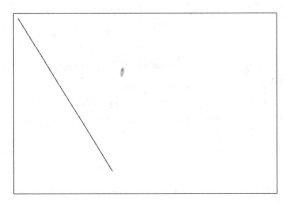

FIGURE 1-27 A line drawn on the canvas

At the point where the line ends, you can continue drawing more lines by adding more *lineTo* methods, as in the following example:

```
ctxt.beginPath();
ctxt.moveTo(10, 10);
ctxt.lineTo(225, 350);
ctxt.lineTo(300, 10);
ctxt.lineTo(400, 350);
ctxt.stroke();
```

Run this code and look at the output. You get a graphic that resembles Figure 1-28. You might use straight lines in this way when plotting connected points on a line graph, for example.

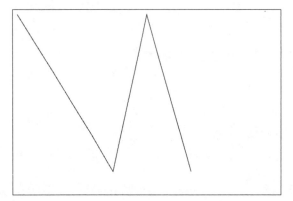

FIGURE 1-28 A polyline drawn on the canvas

Exploring the *stroke* method in more depth is worth the effort. If you were creating a chart or a graph, you might want to change the color of your lines so that they stand out from the axis. You might want to change the thickness. You do this by changing some properties on the context object before calling the *stroke* method:

```
ctxt.lineWidth = 5;
ctxt.strokeStyle = '#0f0';
```

The *lineWidth* property accepts a value that determines the line width. The *strokeStyle* property lets you change the line color. This property accepts all the common style formats for specifying colors in HTML, including hexadecimal values or named colors. These changes produce a new, more attractive output, as shown in Figure 1-29.

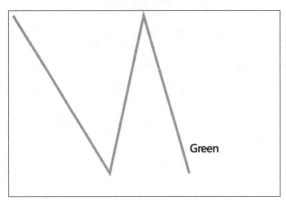

Green

FIGURE 1-29 The polyline rendered with a different color

You also can experiment with the *lineCap* property, which accepts a few values that control how the end of the line will render. For example, you can set the *lineCap* property to round to give the line a rounded cap. Applying a cap affects the length of the line. The cap is added to the end of line, and its length matches what you have set for the line's width. In this example, the line has a width of 5. With a round cap set on the line, the total line length would be extended by 5.

You've seen all you need to know about working with straight lines. Now turn your attention to curves.

Drawing curves

Drawing curves is a little more involved because you have more parameters to consider. Table 1-7 lists the methods used when working with curves on the HTML5 canvas.

TABLE 1-7 Methods for drawing curves

Method	Description
arc	A standard arc based on a starting and ending angle and a defined radius
quadradicCurveTo	A more complex arc that allows you to control the steepness of the curve
bezierCurveTo	Another complex arc that you can skew

Each drawing method can have styles applied to it, just like the line examples. You can control the *lineWidth*, *strokeStyle*, and *lineCap* properties to change how your curves display. Start off by creating some basic arcs on your canvas. The *arc* method takes the parameters listed in Table 1-8.

TABLE 1-8 Parameters required to draw an arc

Parameter	Description
X, Y	The first two parameters are the X and Y coordinates for the center of the circle.
radius	The third parameter is the radius. This is the length of the distance from the center point of the circle to the curve.
startAngle, endAngle	The fourth and fifth parameters specify the starting and ending angles of the arc to be drawn. This is measured in radians, not in degrees.
counterclockwise	The final parameter specifies the drawing direction of the arc.

Add the following code to your page:

```
ctxt.beginPath();
ctxt.arc(150,100,75,0,2 * Math.PI, false);
ctxt.lineWidth = 25;
ctxt.strokeStyle = '#0f0';
ctxt.stroke();

ctxt.beginPath();
ctxt.arc(450, 100, 75, 1.5 * Math.PI, 2 * Math.PI, false);
ctxt.lineWidth = 25;
ctxt.strokeStyle = 'blue';
ctxt.stroke();

ctxt.beginPath();
ctxt.arc(150, 300, 75, 1 * Math.PI, 1.5 * Math.PI, false);
ctxt.lineWidth = 25;
ctxt.strokeStyle = '#0ff';
ctxt.stroke();

ctxt.beginPath();
ctxt.arc(450, 300, 75, .5 * Math.PI, 1 * Math.PI, false);
ctxt.lineWidth = 25;
ctxt.strokeStyle = '#f00';
ctxt.stroke();
```

This code sample draws four arcs: a full circle followed by three quarter circles, each with a different style. Notice that some math formulas are specified in the parameters to the arc. This math is necessary to get the value in radians because the parameters for *startAngle* and *endAngle* are specified in radians, not in degrees. The code produces the drawing shown in Figure 1-30.

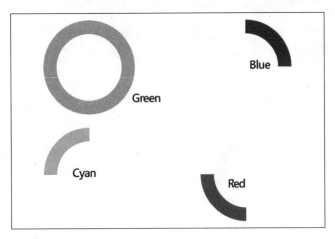

FIGURE 1-30 Drawing arcs on the canvas in different colors

The previous example demonstrated a simple arc. Now look at the next arc method, the *quadraticArc*. The curve of a quadratic arc is evenly distributed from one end to the other in terms of its distance from the center point. The *quadraticCurveTo* method allows you to specify some additional parameters to alter the "steepness" of the curve—in other words, to change the distance from the center point along the curve. Drawing a quadratic curve is somewhat like drawing a straight line but then pinching it in the middle and pulling it away to create a curve where the starting and ending points of the line stay fixed. The farther away you pull the center point, the steeper the curve becomes. Here's an example:

```
ctxt.beginPath();
ctxt.moveTo(10,380);
ctxt.quadraticCurveTo(300,-250,580,380);
ctxt.lineWidth = 25;
ctxt.strokeStyle = '#f00';
ctxt.stroke();
```

You first need use the *moveTo* method to tell the context where you want your curve to start. Then, you pass the four parameters described in Table 1-9 to the *quadraticCurveTo* method.

TABLE 1-9 Parameters required for the *quadraticCurveTo* method

Parameter	Description
controlX, controlY	These parameters define the control point, relative to the top left of the canvas, that is used to "stretch" the curve away from the line formed by the start and end points.
endX, endY	This is the point where the curve should end.

The code sample produces the image in Figure 1-31.

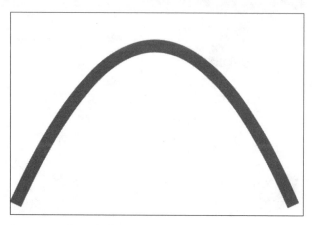

FIGURE 1-31 A quadratic curve output onto a canvas

As the control point moves farther away from the line formed by the start and end points, you get a steeper curve. This example used a negative number to indicate that the control point should be above the top of your canvas to stretch the curve to where you want it.

The final curve to look at is the Bezier curve. A Bezier curve is similar to the quadratic curve except that it has two control points instead of just one. Having two points allows the Bezier curve to create more complex curves. In both examples you have seen so far, the curve was created around the context of a single point. The Bezier curve changes that. It's easiest to see in an example, and then I'll explain the parameters. Create the following code:

```
ctxt.beginPath();
ctxt.moveTo(125, 20);
ctxt.bezierCurveTo(0, 200, 300, 300, 50, 400);
ctxt.lineWidth = 5;
ctxt.strokeStyle = '#f00';
ctxt.stroke();
```

The *bezierCurveTo* method follows a *moveTo* method call in the same way that the *quadraticCurveTo* method did. You need to pass three sets of coordinates to the *bezierCurveTo* method, as listed in Table 1-10.

TABLE 1-10 Parameters required for the *bezierCurveTo* method

Parameter	Description
controlX, controlY	The first two parameters specify the first control point that is used to stretch out the curve.
Control2X, control2Y	The second two parameters specify the second control point that is used to stretch out the curve.
endX, endY	The final two parameters specify the end point for the curve.

The code sample produces the output shown in Figure 1-32. You can see that this curve is skewed because of the two control points.

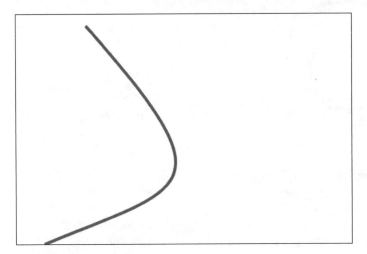

FIGURE 1-32 A Bezier curve drawn on a canvas

In the next section, you learn about using path methods to combine everything you've looked at so far.

Using *path* methods

When using the context object to draw, you always need a starting point and an ending point. The ending point for one stroke also can become the starting point for the next stroke. You do this by calling the *beginPath* method on the context object and then drawing all your lines before calling either the *closePath* method (which ends the line) or the *beginPath* method (which starts a new line) again. Recall that the first arc example called the *beginPath* method before drawing each arc. Had the code not done that, the line would have continued across the canvas from one arc to the next. But by calling the *beginPath* method again, you reset the path's starting point. So essentially, you can string together all the calls to the various drawing methods to create a complex stroke. The stroke—no matter how simple or complex—is called a *path*. Run the following code and see what kind of image you end up with:

```
ctxt.beginPath();
ctxt.arc(300, 200, 75, 1.75 * Math.PI, 1.25 * Math.PI, false);
ctxt.lineTo(150, 125);
ctxt.quadraticCurveTo(300, 0, 450, 125);
ctxt.lineTo(353, 144);
ctxt.strokeStyle = "blue";
ctxt.lineCap = "round";
ctxt.lineWidth = 10;
ctxt.stroke();
```

This code produces the output shown in Figure 1-33.

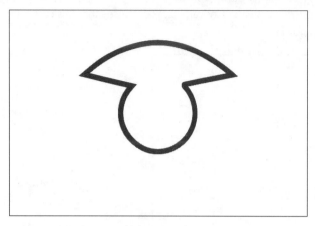

FIGURE 1-33 A custom path drawn on the canvas

Although this is still a simple example, you can get creative and put together images quite nicely. Depending on your math skills, you can create some very complex graphics using these methods.

Next, look at the other methods that exist for drawing shapes.

Using the *rect* method

Earlier, you saw how to draw circles using the *arc* method. And as you saw in the previous section, you can draw custom shapes of any sort and size by using the *beginPath* method and stringing together a series of drawing methods. But you don't always need to do that; some shapes are built in. In this section, you look at the built-in functionality to build rectangles. Then you look at the functionality to fill your drawn shapes with colors and patterns. The context object to which you have a reference has a method called *rect*. The *rect* method takes the parameters listed in Table 1-11.

TABLE 1-11 Parameters required for drawing rectangles

Parameter	Description
x,y	The x-coordinate and y-coordinate define the starting position of the rectangle. This is the top-left corner of the rectangle.
width	This defines the width of the rectangle.
height	This defines the height of the rectangle.

A simple call to the *rect* method, as in the following code, draws a rectangle:

```
ctxt.beginPath();
ctxt.rect(300, 200, 150, 75);
ctxt.stroke();
```

This code draws a rectangle as shown in Figure 1-34.

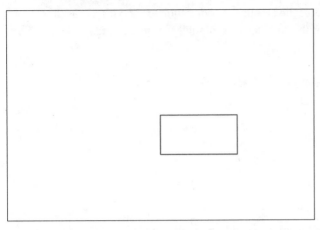

FIGURE 1-34 A rectangle drawn on the canvas using the *rect* method

Notice that although the parameters passed in for the top-left corner were (300,200), which is the center of your canvas, the rectangle is off center. To center your rectangle, you would need to do a bit of math to calculate the center based on the size of your canvas as well as the size of your desired rectangle. The following code should center your rectangle:

```
ctxt.beginPath();
var x, y;
x = 150;
y = 75;
ctxt.rect(300-(x/2), 200-(y/2), x, y);
ctxt.stroke();
```

Now that you can draw shapes and rectangles, you can look at how you would go about filling your shapes with colors or patterns.

Using the *fill* method

In this section you examine how you can fill your shapes. You have drawn various types of shapes, but so far they have been empty. Here you'll see how to fill them with colors, gradients, and patterns.

Filling a shape with a color is as simple as setting the *fillStyle* property to a color and calling the *fill* method. Inserting the following code before calling the *stroke* method fills your shape with a blue color:

```
ctxt.fillStyle = "blue";
ctxt.fill();
```

With respect to the *rect* method, you get a special *fill* method specifically for *rect* called *fillRect*. With this method, you can create and fill your rectangle in one call:

```
ctxt.fillStyle = "blue";
ctxt.fillRect(300-(x / 2), 200-(y / 2), x, y);
```

Using the *fillRect* method reduces the amount of code required. And it's just as simple to fill nonrectangular shapes, such as the complex *Path* graphic that you created earlier, with a single call to the *fill* method:

```
ctxt.beginPath();
ctxt.arc(300, 200, 75, 1.75 * Math.PI, 1.25 * Math.PI, false);
ctxt.lineTo(150, 125);
ctxt.quadraticCurveTo(300, 0, 450, 125);
ctxt.lineTo(353, 144);
ctxt.strokeStyle = "blue";
ctxt.lineCap = "round";
ctxt.lineWidth = 10;
ctxt.fillStyle = "Green";
ctxt.fill();
ctxt.stroke();
```

You can see in Figure 1-35 that the logic of coloring in this complex shape is completely handled by the browser.

FIGURE 1-35 Using the *fill* method to color in a complex object

That's all it takes to fill a shape with a solid color. Filling shapes with a gradient requires a few extra steps.

Creating a gradient involves using a new *CanvasGradient* object. You first call the *createLinearGradient* method available on the context object to get a *CanvasGradient* object. On that *CanvasGradient* object, you define the color stops that you want to blend to create the gradient effect. Then you assign your *CanvasGradient* object to the *fillStyle* property of the context. The following code creates and fills a rectangle with a linear gradient:

```
var ctxt = drawingSurface.getContext("2d");
ctxt.lineWidth = 3;
ctxt.rect(150, 150, 200, 125);
var gradient = ctxt.createLinearGradient(150, 150, 200, 125);
gradient.addColorStop(0, "Black");
gradient.addColorStop(0.5, "Gray");
gradient.addColorStop(1,"White");
ctxt.fillStyle = gradient;
ctxt.fill();
ctxt.stroke();
```

This code creates the *CanvasGradient* object by passing in the start and end points of a gradient line. You then add three color stops. The *addColorStop* method takes two parameters. The first is a value from 0 to 1, where 0 is the starting point of the gradient line and 1 is the ending point. The second parameter is the color to start filling with at that stop. This example has three stops, so the gradient transitions through three colors. The gradient output is displayed in Figure 1-36.

FIGURE 1-36 The *<canvas>* element colored with a linear gradient

You can also create a radial gradient using the *createRadialGradient* method. This method takes six parameters, which specify the center point and radius of two circles and the color transitions through the stops along the cone formed by the two circles. The following code produces a radial gradient in which the cone is pointed toward the viewer:

```
var ctxt = drawingSurface.getContext("2d");
ctxt.lineWidth = 3;
ctxt.rect(150, 150, 250, 175);
var gradient = ctxt.createRadialGradient(200, 200,5, 250, 250,100);
gradient.addColorStop(0, "Red");
gradient.addColorStop(.5, "Orange");
gradient.addColorStop(1, "Blue");
ctxt.fillStyle = gradient;
ctxt.fill();
ctxt.stroke();
```

Figure 1-37 shows the output of this gradient:

FIGURE 1-37 A radial gradient colored on a canvas

The last fill option to look at involves using a fill pattern. You need an external image, which is applied as a pattern throughout the shape. For example, you can use a texture that you created as a background to your canvas by using the following code:

```
var ctxt = drawingSurface.getContext("2d");
ctxt.lineWidth = 3;
ctxt.rect(150, 150, 200, 125);
var img = new Image();
img.src = "texture.png";
img.onload = function () {
    var pat = ctxt.createPattern(img, "repeat");
    ctxt.fillStyle = pat;
    ctxt.fill();
    ctxt.stroke();
}
```

Figure 1-38 shows the output of this code.

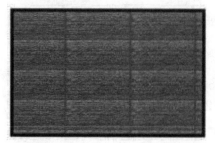

FIGURE 1-38 The canvas filled with a pattern drawn on it

The preceding code calls the *createPattern* method and passes it a reference to an Image object and a repeat pattern. The repeat pattern can be *no-repeat*, *repeat-x*, or *repeat-y*, but it defaults to *repeat* if you don't specify anything. You need to assign an event handler to the onload event of the Image object to ensure that you draw the pattern only after the image loads. Otherwise, the code could run before the picture is rendered, and the pattern won't display.

This section has covered a lot about how to work with shapes and fill them. All your graphics have been created by using code to manually draw shapes. Next, you see how to draw existing graphics from external files on your canvas, and then you look at drawing text.

Drawing images

Drawing images on a canvas is just as straightforward as the other drawing methods you've seen. To draw an image on a canvas, you use the *drawImage* method of the context object. This method takes an Image object and some (x,y) coordinates to define where the image should be drawn. Just like with the rectangle, the image's top-left corner is drawn at the specified (x,y). The default size of the image is the actual image size, but as you will see right after, you can also resize the image as you draw it. To simply draw the image, create the following code:

```
var drawingSurface = document.getElementById("drawingSurface");
var ctxt = drawingSurface.getContext("2d");
var img = new Image();
img.src = "orange.jpg";
img.onload = function () {
    ctxt.drawImage(img, 0, 0);
    ctxt.stroke();
}
```

This code produces a *<canvas>* element with the image drawn on it, as shown in Figure 1-39.

FIGURE 1-39 An image drawn on a canvas

If you want to resize the image, you can replace the *drawImage* method call with the following line:

```
ctxt.drawImage(img, 0,0,img.width * .5, img.height * .5);
```

This reduces the image size by 50 percent.

Now look at how you can draw text on your canvas.

Drawing text

Drawing text on the canvas involves adding a few additional tools to your chest from the context object, using the *strokeText* method and the *font* property. You see how to apply color to your text and, finally, how to manage its alignment.

In its simplest form, drawing text requires only the following code:

```
ctxt.strokeText("1. Text with default font", 100, 100);
```

Remember that you need to make sure the window has finished loading and you need to get a context object. Here's the full code for this example:

```
window.onload = function () {
    var drawingSurface = document.getElementById("drawingSurface");
    var ctxt = drawingSurface.getContext("2d");
    ctxt.strokeText("1. Text with default font", 100, 100);
}
```

That's it. The *strokeText* call draws the specified text into the specified coordinates on the canvas. The parameters specify what text to draw, and the (x,y) coordinates specify where drawing should begin. The *strokeText* method draws in the default font style. You can easily change the *font* property of the context object to enhance the appearance of your text. For example, running the following code changes the font size to 24 and the font family to Arial:

```
ctxt.font = "24px arial";
ctxt.strokeText("2. Text with altered font", 100, 125);
```

To color your text, you could add this code:

```
ctxt.font = "24px arial";
ctxt.strokeStyle = "Red";
ctxt.strokeText("3. Text with altered colored font", 100, 160);
```

When you run the preceding code, notice that your text is outlined. This is the default behavior when you increase the font size; it's drawn as outlined. To draw solid-colored text, add the following code, which sets the *fillStyle* property and calls the *fillText* method instead of the *strokeStyle* and *StrokeText* methods:

```
ctxt.font = "24px arial";
ctxt.fillStyle = "Red";
ctxt.fillText("4. Text with altered colored font", 100, 185);
```

You can also set the alignment of your text within the canvas. For example, to ensure your text is centered, add this code:

```
ctxt.font = "24px arial";
ctxt.textAlign = "center";
ctxt.fillStyle = "Red";
ctxt.fillText("5. Text with altered colored font Centered.", drawingSurface.width / 2,
drawingSurface.height / 2);
```

By setting the *textAlign* property to the value *center*, you are telling the context to consider the specified (x,y) coordinate as the center point of the string instead of the beginning point of the string. So, you divide the canvas width and height by two to get the center point of the canvas, and you get a string centered horizontally and vertically.

Figure 1-40 shows the progression of your text:

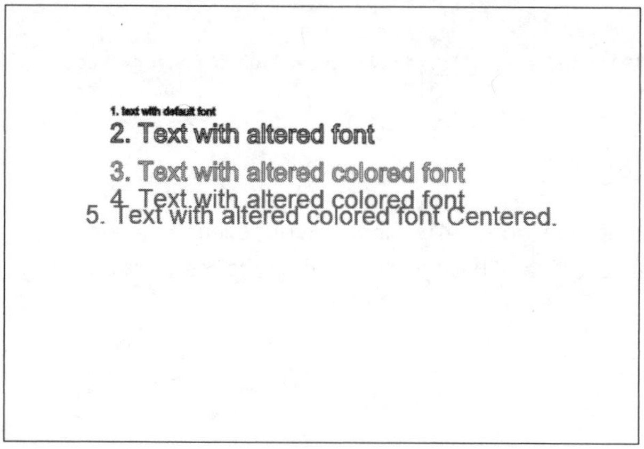

1. text with default font
2. Text with altered font
3. Text with altered colored font
4. Text with altered colored font
5. Text with altered colored font Centered.

FIGURE 1-40 Progression of text with changing styles

The canvas is a strong utility for presenting graphics dynamically in the browser. However, it's not the only graphical tool available. In the next section, you look at using Scalable Vector Graphics.

Scalable Vector Graphics (SVG)

Scalable Vector Graphics (SVG) is an XML-based language for creating two-dimensional graphics. It's implemented by using tags defined by the SVG XML namespace and embedded in HTML5 documents within opening and closing *<svg>* elements.

SVG objects don't lose any quality as users zoom in or out. You can access SVG objects via the DOM, and—similar to HTML elements—SVG elements support attributes, styles, and event handlers. The *<svg>* element provides a container in which to render graphics; SVG renders inline with the page's layout. Here's an example of an SVG graphic with event handlers:

```
<!DOCTYPE html>
<html>
    <head>
        <title>Test Web Page</title>
        <script language="javascript">
            function Red(evt) {
                var circle = evt.target;
                circle.setAttribute("style", "fill: red");
            }

            function Green(evt) {
                var circle = evt.target;
                circle.setAttribute("style", "fill: green");
            }
        </script>
    </head>
```

```
<body>
    <svg>
        <circle id="Circle" cx="50" cy="50" r="50" fill="green" onmouseover="Red(evt)"
            onmouseout="Green(evt)"/>
    </svg>
</body>
</html>
```

This code produces the output shown in Figure 1-41. The JavaScript event handlers turn the circle red when the mouse hovers over it and back to green when the mouse is moved out of the circle.

FIGURE 1-41 A circle drawn using SVG

All the shape-drawing and line-drawing functionality you saw in the *<canvas>* element discussion exists for SVG as well, although the syntax is different, of course. The following code produces a slightly more elaborate graphic.

```
<svg>
    <rect id="lightStandard"  x="100" y="100" width="60" height="200" fill="black"/>
    <circle id="redLight" cx="129" cy="145" r="25"  fill="red"/>
    <circle id="amberLight" cx="129" cy="205" r="25"  fill="yellow"/>
    <circle id="greenLight" cx="129" cy="265" r="25"  fill="green"/>
</svg>
```

The image in Figure 1-42 shows the output of this code:

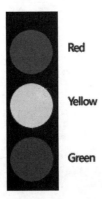

FIGURE 1-42 Multiple shapes drawn using SVG

In this example, the *<rect>* element was used to create the background rectangle, and a series of *<circle>* elements were used to create the lights. Each SVG shape requires the same types of parameters as their canvas counterpart, and the same rules apply. The *<rect>* element needs an (x,y) coordinate to establish where it should be drawn, along with a width and height to establish the size. The same is true for each circle, except that you specify the radius for the size. The *fill* attribute sets the color to be used to fill the shape.

SVG also supports the same basic shape-drawing functions as the canvas context. The following code segment shows the use of the polyline, polygon, line, and ellipse and produces the output shown in Figure 1-43:

```
<svg>
    <polygon points="10,15 30,35 10,85 100,85, 70,35,100,15" fill="purple"/>
    <polyline points="10,150 30,170 50,132 62,196 78,165 96,170"

            style="stroke:orange; fill:none; stroke-width:5;"/>
    <line x1="150" y1="100" x2="150" y2="150" style="stroke:blue;stroke-width:3"/>
    <ellipse cx="250" cy="150" rx="30" ry="55" fill="green"/>
    <text x="10" y="10" style="stroke: black;stroke-width:1;">

            Examples of SVG Shapes and Text</text>
</svg>
```

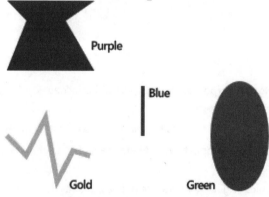

FIGURE 1-43 Text, a line, a polygon, an ellipse, and a polyline drawn in different colors

---

EXAM TIP

In some cases, using SVG graphics is simpler than using the *<canvas>* element. As the examples have shown, you can create SVG images declaratively directly within the HTML itself. However, as you increase the number of objects in an SVG rendering, performance can become a concern. In cases where performance is a consideration, using the *<canvas>* element is a preferable approach.

SVG also supports rendering existing graphics in the form of external image files, as shown here:

```
<svg id="mySVG">
    <image href="orange.jpg" width="250" height="100"/>
</svg>
```

Thought experiment

Creating a game

In this thought experiment, apply what you've learned about this objective. You can find answers to these questions in the "Answers" section at the end of this chapter.

You were hired to create a game. For the first stage of the game, you must make a ball move from the left side of the screen to right side. How can you achieve this with the HTML5 *<canvas>* element? How about with SVG? You demonstrate this stage to stakeholders, and they love it. For the next stage, when the ball is clicked, it must split into two balls. As the number of balls increases due to being clicked, what considerations need to be taken into account? Would using SVG or the *<canvas>* element be the better solution for this game?

Objective summary

- JavaScript is a powerful tool that enables developers to manipulate the DOM programmatically in the browser.
- HTML5 supports rich media controls to incorporate video by using the *<video>* element and audio by using the *<audio>* element.
- The *<video>* element supports multiple media formats by using the *<source>* element.
- The HTML5 *<canvas>* and *<svg>* elements support a rich API to create both simple and complex graphics in the browser.
- Both the *<canvas>* and *<svg>* graphics engines can draw text, lines, shapes, fonts, fills, and gradients.
- The *<canvas>* element is drawn on via JavaScript by getting a reference to the context.
- The *<svg>* element renders graphics by using a declarative syntax.

Objective review

Answer the following questions to test your knowledge of the information in this objective. You can find the answers to these questions and explanations of why each answer choice is correct or incorrect in the "Answers" section at the end of this chapter.

1. Which of the following JavaScript methods can't be used to select an element in the DOM?

   A. *getElementById*

   B. *querySelector*

   C. *getElementByClassName*

   D. *queryAll*

2. Which line of JavaScript successfully retrieves only the image element with the ID *myDog* from the following HTML? Choose all that apply.

   ```
   <form>
       <div id="main" class="mainStyle">
           <p id="dogs">
               This is a web page about dogs. Here is my dog picture:
               <img src="dog.jpg" id="myDog" class="thumb"/>
               Here is a picture of my friend's dog:
               <img src="dog.jpg" id="myfriendsDog" class="thumb"/>
           </p>
       </div>
   </form>
   ```

   A. document.getElementbyId("myDog");

   B. <p>.getChildNode("img");

   C. document.getElementbyId("dogs").querySelector ("thumb");

   D. document.querySelectorAll("thumb");

3. To hide an element in the DOM and still be able to add it back later, what should you do?

   A. Nothing, because the DOM is always available in a static form.

   B. Keep a reference to the removed node to be able to add it back.

   C. Call the *document.restoreNodes* method.

   D. You can't add an element back after it's removed.

4. When implementing the HTML5 video element, how do you ensure that the rendering of the element can function in different browsers?

   A. You need to do nothing, because HTML5 is now a standard specification.

   B. Specify all the source video types in the *src* attribute of the video element.

   C. Include the *<source>* element for each video type so that each browser can play the version that it supports.

   D. Include the *<object>* element for each video type so that the browser can play the version that it supports.

5. When drawing on the HTML5 *<canvas>* element, what method is used on the context to begin drawing at a new point?

   A. *moveTo*

   B. *lineAt*

   C. *beginPath*

   D. *stroke*

6. When performance is critical for an HTML5 graphics application, what should you use?

   A. *<canvas>* using a declarative syntax to create the graphics

   B. *<svg>* using a declarative syntax to create the graphics

   C. *<canvas>* using JavaScript to create the graphics

   D. *<svg>* and *<canvas>* combination to leverage the best performance of both

Objective 1.3: Apply styling to HTML elements programmatically

The section covers applying styles to the HTML elements on the page dynamically, using JavaScript. When you retrieve element references by using methods such as *getElementById*, you can then manipulate those elements, including their styles.

This objective covers how to:

- Change the location of an element
- Apply a transform
- Show and hide elements

Changing the location of an element

By using the methods to retrieve an element from the DOM in JavaScript, you can apply styles dynamically through code that can change the element's position on the page. How elements are laid out on the page can affect how elements behave when they are repositioned.

A few options determine how HTML elements are positioned on a webpage. By default, all HTML elements flow statically from left to right in the same order that they are declared in the HTML page. However, CSS provides a mechanism to specify some advanced options in element position. You can position elements by using *absolute positioning* or *relative positioning*. With absolute positioning, the element is placed in the exact location specified, relative to its container's borders. However, with relative positioning, the element is positioned relative to its immediate left sibling's coordinates. You can apply four properties individually or in combination to control the position of an element: *Top*, *Left*, *Right*, and *Bottom*. Each property takes a distance parameter that specifies the relative distance of the object from a reference point based on the positioning attribute specified. When using absolute or relative positioning, the default border or margin settings are ignored because the object is positioned where the positioning attributes direct the element to be.

The code in Listing 1-3 demonstrates this.

LISTING 1-3 HTML and JavaScript to illustrate positioning

```
<!DOCTYPE html>
<html lang="en" xmlns="http://www.w3.org/1999/xhtml">
    <head>
        <meta charset="utf-8"/>
        <title></title>
        <style>
            html, body {
                height: 100%;
                width: 100%;
            }
            img {
                height: 150px;
                width: 225px;
            }
        </style>
        <script>
            window.onload = function () {
                var top = document.getElementById("topText");
                var left = document.getElementById("leftText");
                var pos = document.getElementById("positioning");
                document.getElementById("btnPosition").onclick = function () {
                    var img = document.getElementById("orange2");
                    img.style.position = pos.value;
                    img.style.left = left.value + "px";
                    img.style.top = top.value + "px";
                }
            }
        </script>
    </head>
```

```
<body>
    <table style="width: 100%; height: 100%; border: 1px solid black;">
        <tr>
            <td style="vertical-align: top; width: 80%">
                <img id="orange1" src="orange.jpg"/>
                <img id="orange2" src="orange.jpg"/>
            </td>
            <td style="vertical-align: top;">Left:
                <input type="text" id="leftText"/><br/>
                Top:
                <input type="text" id="topText"/><br/>
                Position:
                <select id="positioning">
                    <option>relative</option>
                    <option>absolute</option>
                </select><br/>
                <input type="button" id="btnPosition" value="Update"/>
            </td>
        </tr>
    </table>
</body>
</html>
```

When the code is rendered in the browser, the default position is in effect, as shown in Figure 1-44.

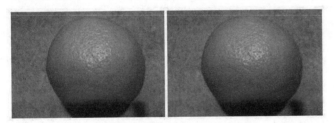

FIGURE 1-44 The default position of two images

All positioning attributes that have been discussed are available declaratively in the style attribute of the HTML element but can also be accessed programmatically and manipulated via JavaScript. The webpage is enhanced to provide some end-user functionality to control the positioning of the two images. The code in Listing 1-3 provides an HTML page with the two images and some input controls to control the positioning of the second image. You can enter the *top* and *left* positions as well as whether to position relative to the first orange picture or to position as absolute to the parent table element.

When *top* and *left* are set to 50px and positioning is relative, you'll see the result shown in Figure 1-45.

FIGURE 1-45 Positioning the second image relative to its neighboring element

Keeping the values the same but changing the positioning to absolute changes the positioning of the elements, as shown in Figure 1-46.

FIGURE 1-46 Positioning the second image absolute to its parent element.

You can employ yet another mechanism to change the appearance of an HTML element: transforms, which you examine next.

Applying a transform

Applying transforms is a way to change an object on the webpage. Transforms enable you to change an element's appearance. You can make an element larger or smaller, rotate it, and so on. Quite a few transform methods are available. To add a transform to an element, you declare it in the CSS for the element by adding the *transform* property as follows:

```
.rota {transform: rotate(90deg);}
```

This code applies the *rotate* method to an object when you add the *.rota* CSS class to the object's styles collection. As mentioned, various transform methods are available, and you'll examine each in turn. Use the following code for all the examples in this section:

```
<!DOCTYPE html>
<html lang="en" xmlns="http://www.w3.org/1999/xhtml">
    <head>
        <meta charset="utf-8"/>
        <title></title>
        <style>
            #orange1 {
                height: 150px;
                width: 225px;
            }
            .trans {
                transform: scale(1) ;
            }
        </style>
        <script>
            window.onload = function () {
                document.getElementById("orange1").onclick = function () {
                    this.classList.add("trans");
                }
            }
        </script>
    </head>
    <body>
        <img id="orange1" src="orange.jpg" style="position:relative"/>
    </body>
</html>
```

This code creates a single image object to which you'll apply the transformations; however, the transformations can work successfully against any HTML element. The image also is assigned an event handler for the *click* event. This suffices for demonstration purposes. You can use any supported event to trigger a transformation. In the examples that follow, you'll need to replace the *.trans* CSS class in the preceding code with the appropriate transform methods to demonstrate them. You'll be prompted to replace the code when needed.

Using the *rotate* method

The *rotate* transform method enables you to rotate an object by a specified number of degrees. The method accepts a single parameter that specifies the number of degrees. In the previous code used for the scale transformation, replace the transform method with the following:

```
transform: rotate(90deg);
```

Now, run the webpage in the browser. Click the image to see the transform take effect. In this case, the image is rotated clockwise by 90 degrees (see Figure 1-47). If you instead want to rotate the image counterclockwise, you can specify a negative number of degrees.

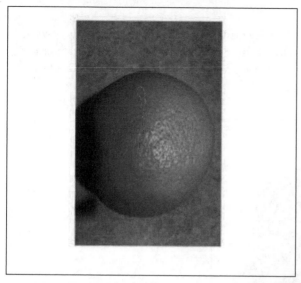

FIGURE 1-47 The effect of the *rotate* transformation on an image

The transform also supports the *rotateX* and *rotateY* methods, which accept a single parameter in degrees to specify an angle around the x-axis or y-axis in which to rotate. You can, for example, use these methods to flip an element vertically or horizontally by specifying *180deg* as the parameter. In this case, the element rotates 180 degrees along the specified axis—which essentially results in the image being flipped or mirrored along that axis.

Using the *translate* method

The *translate* method lets you move an HTML element by changing its relative X and Y position on the page. You implement the *translate* method by specifying the *translate* method on the *transform* property. In the example listing, replace the transform method with the following:

```
transform: translate(50px,0px);
```

The *translate* method moves the HTML element to which it's applied by 50 pixels in the X direction and 0 pixels in the Y direction relative to where it now resides (see Figure 1-48). Again, *translateX* and *translateY* methods are available if the desired effect is to move the object around the x-axis or y-axis.

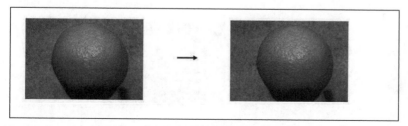

FIGURE 1-48 The effect of the *translate* method applied to an image

Using the *skew* method

You can skew an HTML element using the *skew* method of the *transform* property. Skewing slants the object so that it's not parallel to the vertical or horizontal axis. In the example code, replace the *transform* property with the following code line. Figure 1-49 shows the effect

```
transform: skew(10deg, 10deg);
```

FIGURE 1-49 The effect of the *skew* method on an image

Using the *scale* method

The *scale* method enables you to resize elements by a specified ratio. The *scale* method takes one parameter: a decimal value that represents the percentage to scale. Specifying a value greater than 1 makes the object larger; specifying a value less than 1 but greater than 0 makes the object smaller. Specifying a value of –1 flips the object over its horizontal axis. In the sample code, replace the *transform* property with the following:

```
transform: scale(1.5);
```

This *scale* transform increases the size of the element by 50 percent, essentially multiplying the existing height and width values by 1.5. The object scales out from its absolute center so that it expands in all directions; it doesn't just extend down and to the right. Figure 1-50 shows the result of a *scale* transform.

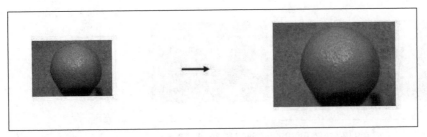

FIGURE 1-50 The effect of the *scale* transform on an image

Combining transformations

Transformations individually lend great flexibility to what you can accomplish by changing the appearance of HTML elements, but the transform style isn't limited to specifying a single transformation method. You can combine the methods to apply multiple effects to the element. In the sample code, change the *transform* property to the following code:

```
transform: translate(50px,0px) scale(1.5) skew(10deg, 10deg);
```

In this code, three effects are applied. Order matters. The effects are applied in the order that they are specified in the *transform* property. In this case, the *translate* property is applied first, and then the translated object is scaled. Finally, the resulting object is skewed. The effect on the HTML element is that it is moved 50 pixels along the x-axis, scaled by 50 percent, and then skewed 10 degrees.

Showing and hiding elements

You can show and hide elements declaratively in the HTML markup or programmatically by modifying the object's CSS properties through JavaScript. You can create the CSS properties that show or hide an element directly in an object's *style* property or in a CSS style, and it is added to the element's style collection. This section's examples use the code from Listing 1-2, updated as follows:

```
<html lang="en" xmlns="http://www.w3.org/1999/xhtml">
    <head>
...

        <script>
            window.onload = function () {
                document.getElementById("btnHideAnElement").onclick = function () {
                    if (document.getElementById("innerDiv").style.display == 'inline') {
                        document.getElementById("innerDiv").style.display = 'none';
                    }
                    else {
                        document.getElementById("innerDiv").style.display = 'inline';
                    }
                }
            }
        </script>
...

            <button type="button" id="btnHideAnElement" >Show/Hide Element</button>
        </form>
    </body>
</html>
```

This code modifies the script block and adds a new button to the bottom of the page. The button is connected to an onclick event after the window finishes loading. In this event, you modify programmatically the visibility of the HTML elements.

The *innerDiv* element defaults to *hidden* when the page is loaded. When the button is clicked, the code evaluates the state of the *display* CSS property to determine whether the element is now visible or hidden. Depending on the result, the property is toggled. The *display* property accepts two possible values. A value of *inline* tells the browser to show the item, while a value of *none* means the browser should hide the item.

The second property available for controlling element visibility is called *visibility*. This property accepts four possible values, as outlined in Table 1-12.

TABLE 1-12 Values available for the *visibility* property

Value	Effect
visible	Sets the property to *visible* to show the element
hidden	Hides the element
collapse	Collapses the element where applicable, such as in a table row
inherit	Inherits the value of the *visibility* property from the parent

Some of these values have interesting behaviors. When you use the *display* CSS property and set it to the value of *none*, the HTML element is hidden. But hiding the element in this way also removes it from the layout. All the surrounding elements realign themselves as though the element was not there at all. When *display* is set to *inline*, the element is shown again and all the surrounding elements move out of the way, back to where they were originally.

The *visibility* CSS property behaves slightly differently. Setting the *visibility* property to *hidden* hides an element, but the hidden element's surrounding elements act as though it's still there. The space that the element occupied is maintained intact, but the element's content is hidden. When the property is set back to *visible*, the element reappears exactly where it was, without affecting any surrounding elements. The *collapse* value, on the other hand, acts more like the *display* property. If you specify *collapse* on something such as a table row, the table rows above and below collapse and take over the space that the collapsed row was occupying. When you set the *visibility* property back to *visible*, the surrounding elements move out of the way to show the element. This is useful for situations where you want to have content that can be collapsed or displayed one item at a time to preserve space, such as on an FAQ, where the answer to a question is shown when a user clicks the question but then collapsed when the user clicks a different question.

EXAM TIP

If you need to preserve the page layout when altering visibility, use the *visibility* property with the *hidden* value. If you don't need to preserve the layout, you can either set the *display* property to *none* or set *visibility* to *collapse*.

Thought experiment
Creating a dynamic survey

In this thought experiment, apply what you've learned about this objective. You can find answers to these questions in the "Answers" section at the end of this chapter.

You have been tasked with building a webpage that requires a user to answer a series of questions. However, the questions are dynamic, based on the user's answer to a previous question. The user should see only relevant questions. Take the following question flow as the rules for this page:

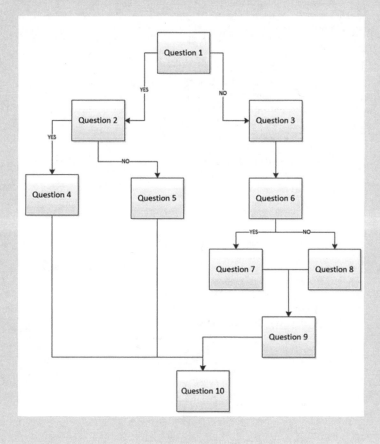

And the following HTML5 page:

```html
<html>
    <head>
        <meta charset="utf-8"/>
        <title></title>
    </head>
    <script>
        ...
    </script>
    <body>
        <header>
            A dynamic Questionnaire.
        </header>
        <section>
            <article>
                <hgroup>
                    <h1>Questionnaire</h1>
                    <h2>Answer the questions in order as they
                        appear.</h2>
                </hgroup>
                <div id="Question1">
                    1. ....
                </div>
                <div id="Question2">
                    2. ....
                </div>
                <div id="Question3">
                    3. ....
                </div>
                <div id="Question4">
                    4. ....
                </div>
                <div id="Question5">
                    5. ....
                </div>
                <div id="Question6">
                    6. ....
                </div>
                <div id="Question7">
                    7. ....
                </div>
                <div id="Question8">
                    8. ....
                </div>
                <div id="Question9">
                    9. ....
                </div>
                <div id="Question10">
                    10. ....
                </div>
            </article>
        </section>
```

```
        </body>
    </html>
```

Create all the JavaScript necessary to show and hide the required elements, depending on the answer to each question. Assume that the answer to each question is a radio button selection with only Yes/No options.

Objective summary

- You can use CSS to define transformation effects.
- You can apply transformations via JavaScript to manipulate the DOM with effects such as rotate, skew, scale, and translate.
- The *visibility* property provides options to control an element's visibility within the page.

Objective review

Answer the following questions to test your knowledge of the information in this objective. You can find the answers to these questions and explanations of why each answer choice is correct or incorrect in the "Answers" section at the end of this chapter.

1. Absolute positioning positions an object relative to what?

    A. The top-left corner of the browser window.

    B. The top-left corner of its parent element.

    C. Centered inside the window.

    D. Centered inside its parent element.

2. Which transformation enables you to change the size of an element?

    A. *rotate*

    B. *skew*

    C. *translate*

    D. *scale*

3. Which syntax preserves the layout of the page when hiding an element in the DOM?

    A. display='hidden'

    B. display='inline'

    C. visibility='none'

    D. visibility='hidden'

Objective 1.4: Implement HTML5 APIs

JavaScript APIs have provided some new powerful functionality, such as the ability to store more data locally and make that data available to the webpage through the Web Storage API. The AppCache API allows you to take web applications offline. The Geolocation API provides methods to work with global positioning within the application.

This objective covers how to:

- Use the storage API
- Use the AppCache API
- Use the Geolocation API

Using the storage API

WebA Storage is a new API for storing webpage data locally. Web Storage, described in this section, replaces the concept of cookies.

NOTE **BROWSER SUPPORT**

Of course, you must consider your audience's browser support for HTML5 and Web Storage before you choose to use it exclusively.

Two forms of Web Storage exist: *local* and *session* storage. Local storage is persistent; data stored in local storage is available to the webpage even if the user closes the browser completely and then reopens it to your site. Session storage is available only for the duration of the current session, so if the user closes the browser, session storage is automatically cleaned up and is no longer available. The Web Storage API is available as a global object. To access local storage, use the *localStorage* object; to access session storage, use the *sessionStorage* object.

EXAM TIP

The *localStorage* and *sessionStorage* objects provide exactly the same API. All the examples shown in this section work exactly the same with either object. The only difference is the lifetime of the storage. Remember that *sessionStorage* is cleared when the session is closed, whereas *localStorage* is still be accessible after a session closes and a new session opens.

Table 1-13 lists the API methods and their usage. Web Storage is implemented as name value pairs and stored as strings. Any data that you can put into a string format can be stored in Web Storage. This isn't as limiting as it sounds. You'll see some examples of storing complex objects.

TABLE 1-13 Methods available on storage objects

Method	Description
setItem	Adds a key/value pair into storage. If no item with the specified key exists, the item is added; if that key does exist, its value is updated.
getItem	Retrieves data from storage based on a specified key value or index.
clear	Clears all storage that has been saved. Use this method to clear out the storage as needed.
key	Retrieves the key at a specified index. You can use the resultant key to pass as a parameter to one of the other methods that accepts a key.
removeItem	Removes the specified key/value pair from storage.

In addition to the methods described in Table 1-13, the storage objects expose a length property which returns the number of key/value pairs in storage. Use the sample code in Listing 1-4 to explore the Web Storage API.

LISTING 1-4 Exploring the Web Storage API

```
<html lang="en" xmlns="http://www.w3.org/1999/xhtml">
    <head>
        <meta charset="utf-8"/>
        <title></title>
        <style>
            section {
                margin-top: 15px;
            }
        </style>
        <script>
            window.onload = function () {
                document.getElementById("btnAdd").onclick = function () {
                }

                document.getElementById("btnRemove").onclick = function () {
                }

                document.getElementById("btnClear").onclick = function () {
                }

                function LoadFromStorage() {
                }
            }
        </script>
    </head>
    <body>
        <section>
            Key:
            <input type="text" id="toStorageKey"/>
            Value:
            <input type="text" id="toStorageValue"/><br/>
        </section>
```

```
                <section>
                    <button type="button" id="btnAdd">Add To Storage</button>
                    <button type="button" id="btnRemove">Remove from Storage</button>
                    <button type="button" id="btnClear">Clear Storage</button>
                </section>
                <div id="storage">
                    <p>Current Storage Contents</p>
                </div>
            </body>
</html>
```

The code in Listing 1-4 creates text boxes to accept a key and a value, respectively. Buttons let you add items to storage, remove an item, or completely clear the storage. Each capability is implemented in turn. To display the contents of the storage, the page contains a *div* that shows the contents of the storage appended to it. The *LoadFromStorage* method is called for each operation to refresh the page with the data available in the storage. All the following examples use local storage, but again, they would work the same way with session storage. If you want to test these examples using session storage, simply replace the *localStorage* reference with a reference to *sessionStorage*.

You first need to implement the *LoadFromStorage* method so that when the page loads, you can see any items that have already been placed into storage. Enter the following code into the *LoadFromStorage* function in the script block:

```
window.onload = function () {
    LoadFromStorage();
    document.getElementById("btnAdd").onclick = function () {
...
function LoadFromStorage() {
    var storageDiv = document.getElementById("storage");
    var tbl = document.createElement("table");
    tbl.id = "storageTable";
    if (localStorage.length > 0) {
        for (var i = 0; i < localStorage.length; i++) {
            var row = document.createElement("tr");
            var key = document.createElement("td");
            var val = document.createElement("td");
            key.innerText = localStorage.key(i);
            val.innerText = localStorage.getItem(key.innerText);
            row.appendChild(key);
            row.appendChild(val);
            tbl.appendChild(row);
        }
    }
    else {
        var row = document.createElement("tr");
        var col = document.createElement("td");
        col.innerText = "No data in local storage.";
        row.appendChild(col);
        tbl.appendChild(row);
    }
```

```
    if (document.getElementById("storageTable")) {
        document.getElementById("storageTable").replaceNode(tbl);
    }
    else {
        storageDiv.appendChild(tbl);
    }
}
```

Notice that this code added a call to the *LoadFromStorage* method to the top of the *window.onload* event, so that *localStorage* is checked after the page loads. The *LoadFromStorage* method takes any available elements in local storage and displays them in an HTML table. This code takes advantage of the *length* property to determine whether any local storage values need to be displayed. If not, the page displays a message about no data in local storage. Add the following code to the button onclick events to start manipulating *localStorage*:

```
document.getElementById("btnAdd").onclick = function () {
  localStorage.setItem(document.getElementById("toStorageKey").value,
             document.getElementById("toStorageValue").value);
  LoadFromStorage();
}
document.getElementById("btnRemove").onclick = function () {
  localStorage.removeItem(document.getElementById("toStorageKey").value);
  LoadFromStorage();
}
document.getElementById("btnClear").onclick = function () {
  localStorage.clear();
  LoadFromStorage();
}
```

The preceding code implements each button's onclick event. A user can now add items to local storage and see what's in storage. The user can continue adding to local storage in this application until the storage is full. Availability of local storage is limited, and the storage available isn't consistent across browsers. As of this writing, the documentation states that Microsoft Internet Explorer 10 supports up to about 10 MB of storage. However, that could change and may not be the same in other browsers; some now support only 5 MB of storage. Keep this in mind when designing web applications that take advantage of the Web Storage API.

Run the preceding example and add the following items to *localStorage*:

```
("Red","FF0000"), ("Green","00FF00"), ("Blue","0000FF").
```

Figure 1-51 shows the output on the screen after adding these items to the local storage.

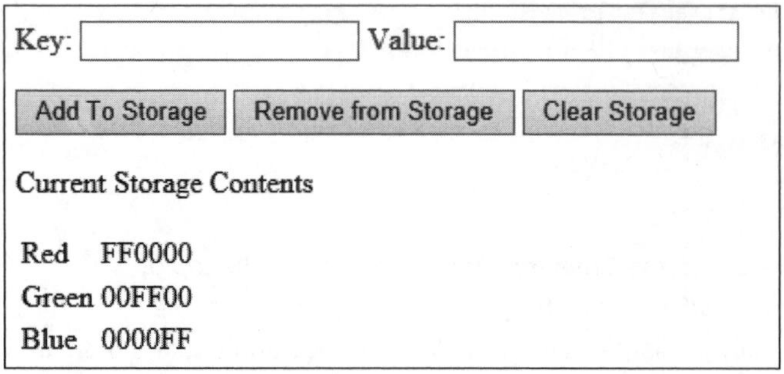

FIGURE 1-51 Storing items in and retrieving them from web storage

Now, if you close the browser and then reopen your page, the items are still available in local storage. Try replacing all uses of *localStorage* with *sessionStorage*. This time notice that closing the browser automatically clears out any data in the storage.

The benefit to using the Web Storage API instead of cookies is that the data resides locally and stays local. The data doesn't get sent back and forth to and from the server, as is the case with cookies. Data stored in web storage is organized by *root domain*. The space allotment is available on a per–root domain basis. For example, domains such as *localhost* or *microsoft.com* each get their own secure web storage space.

As defined by the API, web storage allows storage only of key/value pairs where the key and the value component are stored as a string. If you need to store more complex objects in web storage, you can use a few techniques. For example, add the following code right before the first call to *LoadFromStorage* in the *onload* event:

```
var customer = new Object();
customer.firstName = "Rick";
customer.lastName= "Delorme";
customer.shirtSize = "XL";
localStorage.setItem("cart1", JSON.stringify(customer));
LoadFromStorage();
```

This code creates a custom object to represent a customer browsing the site and sets that customer's shirt size. This information is to be kept and used locally, so it doesn't need to be posted to the server. Local storage is a great solution for this. However, to store the custom object in local data, you need a method to convert the custom object to a string that matches the local storage model. This is where JavaScript Object Notification (JSON) can come in handy. You can serialize the object into a JSON string, give it a key, and then store it in web storage. When you run this application now, it shows the customer object represented as a JSON string in Figure 1-52.

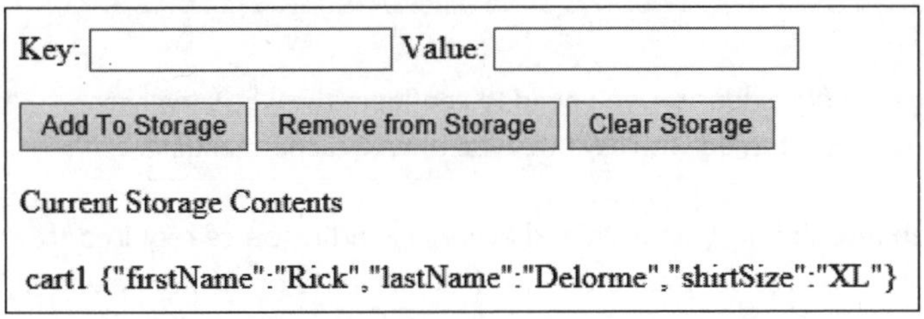

FIGURE 1-52 Web storage contents

The availability of local web storage can improve both end-user experience and performance of your web applications by saving round trips to the server to retrieve or store temporary data. You must consider the local web storage as *temporary*. Even when you're using *localStorage* as opposed to *sessionStorage*, you should think of the storage as temporary and design your applications so that they can fall back on default values and behavior if the user purges the web storage. Web storage provides a way to make data available locally and even persist across browser sessions. These techniques work with a live connected website. If you want to make an application available offline, in a disconnected way, you can use the AppCache API, which is covered next.

Using the AppCache API

The ability to continue to work with web applications when disconnected from an Internet source has become particularly important in today's mobile world. This section talks about how to create an application that works when disconnected by using the Application Cache API, also commonly called the AppCache API.

The AppCache API makes content and webpages available even when a web application is in offline mode. AppCache stores files in the application cache in the browser. Just as with Web Storage, the amount of data the browser can store locally is limited for offline use. Two components make up the AppCache API: the manifest file and a JavaScript API to support it.

Using AppCache manifest

Specifying that a page should be available for offline use is as easy as adding an attribute to the HTML element in the page. Here's an example:

```
<html manifest="webApp.appcache">
...
</html>
```

The manifest attribute on the *html* element tells the browser that this webpage needs to be available offline. The value of the manifest attribute points to a manifest file. The name of the file is a convention more than a requirement; you can name the file anything, but the file extension is usually *.appcache*.

EXAM TIP

If you really want to change the file extension, you need to configure the web server so that your chosen file extension is returned with a MIME type of text/cache-manifest.

The application cache manifest file must list each and every file and resource required to be stored for offline use. When the browser parses the manifest attribute of the *html* element, it downloads the manifest and stores it locally. It also ensures that it downloads all the files listed in the manifest so that they are available offline. The manifest file contains three sections: *CACHE*, *NETWORK*, and *FALLBACK*. Each section might appear just once, multiple times in the file, or not at all. Each serves a specific purpose in how application caching functions when dealing with the resources in specific scenarios. A typical manifest file looks like this:

```
CACHE MANIFEST
# My Web Application Cache Manifest
# v.1.0.0.25
#
#Cache Section. All Cached items.
CACHE
/pages/page1.html
/pages/page2.html

#Required Network resources
NETWORK:
login.html

#Fallback items.
FALLBACK:
login.html   fallback-login.html
```

The first line in a manifest file must be *CACHE MANIFEST*. The manifest file, as with any code file, can have comment lines added to it for additional explanations, as denoted by the # symbol. The *CACHE* section lists all the resources that must be cached offline. This must include all CSS files, JPG files, video and audio files, and any other resource required for the page to function correctly. If you omit an item from the manifest file, it won't be cached, which can result in unexpected behavior when the application is run offline.

The *NETWORK* section declares any resources that *must* be available from the Internet. These items can't be cached. Anything that the page requires from the Internet, such as embedded third-party elements, must be listed here. If such a resource isn't listed here, the browser won't know to check on the Internet for it when in offline mode. When the browser is in offline mode, it doesn't attempt to go to the Internet for anything unless it's listed in the *NETWORK* section.

The *FALLBACK* section enables you to provide fallback instructions to the browser in the event that an item isn't available in the cache and the browser is in offline mode. In the example file, if *login.html* isn't available in the cache, render *fallback-login.html*. You can use shortcuts in the *FALLBACK* section to provide more general redirects, such as the following:

```
/resources /resource.jpg
```

This tells the browser that if the browser is offline and can't access anything in the resources folder, it should replace any references to items in the resources folder with *resource.jpg*. Note that *resource.jpg* is cached because it's specified in the *FALLBACK* section. You don't need to also specify *resource.jpg* in the *CACHE* section.

Using the AppCache API

As with Web Storage, the application cache is available in JavaScript as a global object. The following code gets a reference to the AppCache global object:

```
var appCache = window.applicationCache;
```

When you're using the application cache to make pages available offline, one of the more useful things you can do when the page is loaded is verify its status. You achieve this by evaluating the *status* property of the AppCache object. The *status* property could be one of the values listed in Table 1-14.

TABLE 1-14 The application cache *status* property

Status	Description
Uncached	The web application isn't associated with an application manifest.
Idle	The caching activity is idle, and the most up-to-date copy of the cache is being used.
Checking	The application manifest is being checked for updates.
Downloading	The resources in the application manifest are being downloaded.
UpdateReady	The resources listed in the manifest have been successfully downloaded.
Obsolete	The manifest can no longer be downloaded, so the application cache is being deleted.

After you know the cache status, two methods on the AppCache object can be useful. Table 1-15 lists these.

TABLE 1-15 Methods available with the *applicationCache* object

Method	Description
swapCache	Indicates that the cache be replaced with a newer version.
update	Tells the browser to update the cache if an update is available.

When the *update* method is called, an update to the cache is prepared. When that's ready to download, the status of the application cache changes to *UpdateReady*. When this is set, a call to the *swapCache* method tells the application to switch to the most recent cache.

EXAM TIP

The call to the *update* method is asynchronous. Therefore, you must handle the *onupdateready* event to determine when the update has completed the download process.

In addition to the properties and methods, the AppCache object can raise a series of events that you can handle. The application cache typically operates in the background, and you won't need these events. However, in some cases handling some of the events and forcing an update can be useful. Table 1-16 lists the available events.

TABLE 1-16 Events available from the *applicationCache* object

Event	Description
onchecking	The browser is checking for an update to the application manifest, or the application is being cached for the first time.
onnoupdate	The application manifest has no update available.
ondownloading	The browser is downloading what it has been told to do per the manifest file.
onprogress	Files are being downloaded to the offline cache. This event fires periodically to report progress.
oncached	The download of the cache has completed.
onupdateready	The resources listed in the manifest have been newly redownloaded, and the *swapCache* method might be called.
onobsolete	A manifest file is no longer available.
onerror	An error has occurred. This could result from many things. Appropriate logging is necessary to get the information and resolve.

Most of these events might not be used often, if at all. The most common scenario is to handle the *onupdateready* method and then make a call to the *swapCache* method, as in this example:

```
window.onload = function () {
    var appCache = window.applicationCache;
    appCache.oncached = function (e) { alert("cache successfully downloaded."); };
    appCache.onupdateready = function (e) { appCache.swapCache(); };
}
```

Using the application cache is more about configuration than about coding. However, it's important that you're aware the API is available for advanced scenarios where you need more control over the process, or when you need to receive timely information about the process, such as by handling the *onprogress* event.

Using the Geolocation API

Location services have become a large part of most people's lives. From routing and navigation to just finding nearby points of interest or checking into their favorite social community sites, more and more people are using some form of location services. Location services depend on the Global Positioning System (GPS), IP addresses, and other device characteristics. You can take advantage of geolocation in web applications by leveraging browsers that support the Geolocation API.

You can get a reference to the Geolocation API from the *window.navigator* property, as follows:

```
var geoLocator = window.navigator.geolocation;
```

This code saves a reference to the Geolocation API in a variable to provide shorthand access to the API during future use. A good practice is to ensure that the client's browser supports the Geolocation API by making sure that the reference is actually present.

The Geolocation API supports three key methods that you use to interact with it: *getCurrentPosition*, *watchPosition*, and *clearWatch*.

Using the *getCurrentPosition* method

Here's an example of using the *getCurrentPosition* method:

```
getCurrentPosition(positionCallback, [positionErrorCallback], [positionOptions])
```

You use *getCurrentPosition* to get exactly what its name indicates—the current position of the user or the device in which the application is running. This method takes one required parameter and two optional parameters. The first parameter is a callback method that the API calls after the current position is determined. The second parameter is optional, but it's also a callback function called when an error occurs. The callback method you specify here should handle any errors that can occur when trying to get the current position. The last optional parameter is a special object called *PositionOptions*, which lets you set some special options that control how the *getCurrentPosition* method behaves. Table 1-17 lists the possible values.

TABLE 1-17 Properties available on the *PositionOptions* object

Property	Description
enableHighAccuracy	This causes the method to be more resource intensive if set to true. The default is false. If true, the *getCurrentPosition* method tries to get as close as it can to the actual location.
timeout	This specifies a timeout period for how long the *getCurrentPosition* method can take to complete. This number is measured in milliseconds and defaults to zero. A value of zero represents infinite.

Property	Description
maximumAge	If this is set, the API is being told to use a cached result if available, rather than make a new call to get the current position. The default is zero, so a new call is always be made. If *maximumAge* is set to a value and the cache isn't older than the allowable age, the cached copy is used. This value is measured in milliseconds.

Listing 1-5 shows the *getCurrentPosition* method in use, with all parameters specified.

LISTING 1-5 Using the *getCurrentPosition* method

```
<html lang="en" xmlns="http://www.w3.org/1999/xhtml">
    <head>
        <meta charset="utf-8"/>
        <title></title>
        <script>
            window.onload = function () {
                var geoLocator = window.navigator.geolocation;
                var posOptions = {enableHighAccuracy: true,timeout: 45000};
                geoLocator.getCurrentPosition(successPosition, errorPosition,
                posOptions);
            }
            function successPosition(pos) {
                alert(pos);
            }
            function errorPosition(err) {
                alert(err);
            }
        </script>
    </head>
    <body>
        <div id="geoResults">
            <p>Current Location is:</p>
        </div>
    </body>
</html>
```

When the code runs in the browser, some interesting things can happen. First, browser security starts; users are asked whether they want to allow this application to determine their location. In Internet Explorer, the message looks like the image in Figure 1-53.

FIGURE 1-53 The security warning presented by Internet Explorer when accessing the Geolocation API

If the user chooses to allow the application to proceed, everything is great. Otherwise, the method throws an exception.

For purposes of demonstrating the code, select Allow For This Site from the drop-down list so that the page can proceed. It might take a few seconds, but the call returns and shows a message box that a position object exists as passed to the success callback method.

Both the success and error callback methods receive one parameter from the Geolocation API. The success method receives a position object, whereas the error method receives an error object. The position object exposes two properties: *coords* and *timestamp*. The *timestamp* property indicates the time at which the *coords* were received. The *coords* property is itself a coordinates object that contains the latitude, longitude, altitude, heading, and speed of the device's current position and/or relative to the last position acquired. The *positionError* object contains two properties: one for the code and one for the message. You can use these objects in Listing 1-5 by adding the following fragments:

```
<script>
    function successPosition(pos) {
        var sp = document.createElement("p");
        sp.innerText = "Latitude: " + pos.coords.latitude +
                       " Longitude: " +  pos.coords.longitude;
        document.getElementById("geoResults").appendChild(sp);
    }
    function errorPosition(err) {
        var sp = document.createElement("p");
        sp.innerText = "error: " + err.message; + " code: " + err.code;
        document.getElementById("geoResults").appendChild(sp);
    }
</script>
```

Figure 1-54 shows the output from running this code successfully.

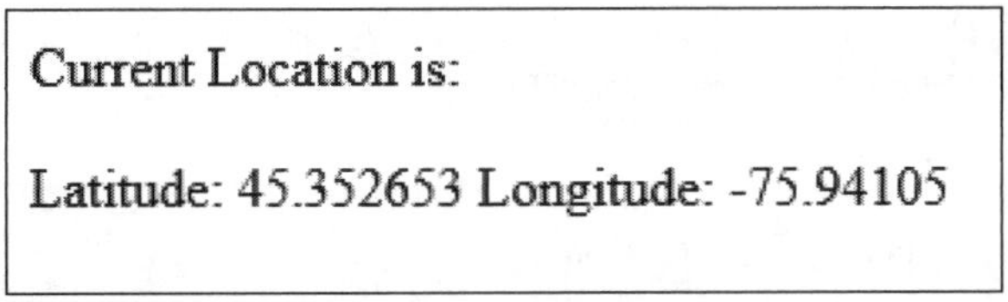

Current Location is:

Latitude: 45.352653 Longitude: -75.94105

FIGURE 1-54 Displaying current location as retrieved by the Geolocation API

Using the *watchPosition* method

The second method available on the geolocation object is the *watchPosition* method, which provides a built-in mechanism that continuously polls for the current position. Here's an example of using the method:

```
geoLocator.watchPosition(successCallBack,errorCallback,positionOptions)
```

The *watchPosition* method takes the same set of parameters as the *getCurrentPosition* method but returns a *watchPosition* object:

```
var watcher = geoLocator.watchPosition...
```

After running this code, the watcher variable holds a reference to the *watchPosition* instance being invoked, which can be useful later. The method calls the success callback method every time the Geolocation API detects a new location. The polling continues forever unless it you stop it. This is where the watcher object comes in handy; you can cancel polling by calling the *clearWatch* method. You could call this method in either the success or the error callback—for example, to cancel polling when you have captured enough position information or when you want to pause polling for a period of time:

```
geoLocator.clearWatch(watcher);
```

Listing 1-6 shows the full solution code for the *watchPosition* example.

LISTING 1-6 Using the Geolocation API to monitor position

```
var watcher;
var geoLocator;
window.onload = function () {
    geoLocator = window.navigator.geolocation;
    var posOptions = {enableHighAccuracy: true,timeout: 45000};

    watcher = geoLocator.watchPosition(successPosition, errorPosition, posOptions);
}
function successPosition(pos) {
    var sp = document.createElement("p");
    sp.innerText = "Latitude: " + pos.coords.latitude + " Longitude: "
    + pos.coords.longitude;
    document.getElementById("geoResults").appendChild(sp);
    geoLocator.clearWatch(watcher);
}

function errorPosition(err) {
    var sp = document.createElement("p");
    sp.innerText = "error: " + err.message; + " code: " + err.code;
    document.getElementById("geoResults").appendChild(sp);
}
```

Figure 1-55 shows the output of this code on a mobile device.

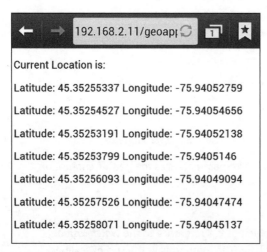

FIGURE 1-55 Multiple positions being recorded by the *watchPosition* method

Thought experiment

Combining the JavaScript APIs

In this thought experiment, apply what you've learned about this objective. You can find answers to these questions in the "Answers" section at the end of this chapter.

Consider an application such as a running or walking utility that measures the distance traveled. One feature of this application is to play back a completed route to users if they so choose. How would you use the Geolocation API and Web Storage API in combination to save the data points as users travel the route so the application can play them back later? (Assume that you're interfacing with map software on which to draw the lines.)

Objective summary

- The new Web Storage API enables you to store data locally on the client computer.
- Web Storage supports both *localStorage* and *sessionStoroage*.
- Data in Web Storage is stored as name and value pairs.
- The AppCache API provides a way to make webpages available when users are offline.
- The AppCache manifest defines what's available offline.
- The Geolocation API provides a way to integrate location services into a webpage.
- The Geolocation API provides two methods: *getPosition* and *watchPosition*.

Objective review

Answer the following questions to test your knowledge of the information in this objective. You can find the answers to these questions and explanations of why each answer choice is correct or incorrect in the "Answers" section at the end of this chapter.

1. When using the Web Storage API, where should you store data to ensure that it's cleared when the user closes the browser?

    A. *localStorage*

    B. *cookieStorage*

    C. *sessionStorage*

    D. A hidden input element

2. What do you need to do to designate a page as available offline?

   A. Specify in JavaScript as document.offLine=true.

   B. Specify the manifest attribute on the form element.

   C. Specify the manifest attribute on the HTML element.

   D. Tell users to switch to offline mode using their browser. No code is required.

3. Which of the following aren't valid sections of the AppCache manifest?

   A. Cache manifest

   B. Session manifest

   C. Network manifest

   D. Fallback manifest

4. Which event is fired by the AppCache object when the cache download is complete?

   A. *oncached*

   B. *onupdateready*

   C. *ondownloading*

   D. *onchecking*

5. When using the Geolocation API, how do you configure the ability to use cached data?

   A. Set the *enableCache* property to true on the *PositionOptions* object.

   B. Set the *maximumAge* property to a non-zero value on the *PositionOptions* object.

   C. Set the timeout property of the *PositionOptions* object.

   D. Using the cache is always on to save bandwidth, so no configuration is required.

Objective 1.5: Establish the scope of objects and variables

A key component of any programming language is how it uses variables, and JavaScript is no exception. To use variables effectively, you must understand their scope and lifetime. Declaring variables and instantiating objects consumes resources. The primary system resource used for variables is memory. The more memory an application uses, the greater the potential that usage of other resources will increase also—such as battery power to support the additional memory use. When applications drain the battery, users are less likely to use those applications.

Establishing the lifetime of variables and variable scope

Variables begin their life with a declaration. The remainder of their life within the application depends on where the variables are declared.

To declare a variable in JavaScript, you use the *var* keyword.

```
var myVariable;
```

You can declare many variables concurrently. For example, the following code declares three variables:

```
var x, y, z;
```

You can also initialize your variables inline with the declaration, giving them immediate nondefault values:

```
var x =0.0, y=0.0, z=0.0
```

Until a variable is initialized, it's not really "alive"—it has a value of undefined. After a variable is available for use, it's considered to be "in scope." The duration over which the variable remains in scope depends on where the variable is declared. A variable that has global scope is available throughout the webpage. A variable with local scope is available only within a specified context, as Listing 1-7 shows.

LISTING 1-7 An example to demonstrate variable scope

```
<html lang="en" xmlns="http://www.w3.org/1999/xhtml">
    <head>
        <meta charset="utf-8"/>
    <style>
        div {
            width: 100px;
            height: 100px;
            border: 1px solid black;
        }
    </style>
        <script>
            var globalVar = "global";
            window.onload = function () {
                var localVar = "local";
                document.getElementById("Div1").onclick = function () {
                    var insideDiv1Click;
                    //Do some logic here...
```

```
        };
        document.getElementById("Div2").onclick = function () {
        };
        document.getElementById("Div3").onclick = function () {
        };
        function AFunction() {
            var x;
        }
        function BFunctionWithParam(p) {
        }
        }
    </script>
    </head>
    <body>
        <div id="Div1"></div>
        <div id="Div2"></div>
        <div id="Div3"></div>
    </body>
</html>
```

In Listing 1-7, notice that the *<script>* block creates a section of script available to the entire page. The first line in the script section is the variable *globalVar*, which is considered global to the entire page. Any JavaScript anywhere on this page could access this variable. At the next level, the code implements a *window.onload* event handler. Inside this event handler, the first line declares a variable called *localVar*, which is local to the *onload* event handler. Inside the *onload* event handler, the code has access to the *globalVar* variable.

Now things start to get interesting.

The *onload* event handler accesses the DOM to wire up some other event handlers. Inside these event handlers, the code has access to both *localVar* and *globalVar* variables. The *localVar* variable is local to the *onload* event, but because the other event handlers are declared within the *onload* event handler, they also have access to local variables declared in the *onload* event handler. Update the *Div1 onclick* handler to this code:

```
document.getElementById("Div1").onclick = function () {
    var insideDiv1Click = "insideDiv1";
    alert(globalvar);
    alert(localVar);
    alert(insideDiv1Click);
};
```

When this code runs and a user clicks the *Div1* element, all three alerts successfully display the value of each variable, which means they are all in scope.

Now, update the *Div2 onclick* handler with this code, the same as was placed into *Div1*:

```
document.getElementById("Div2").onclick = function () {
    alert(globalVar);
    alert(localVar);
    alert(insideDiv1Click);
};
```

When you run this code and click *Div2*, the *globalVar* variable is in scope, the *localVar* variable is in scope, but the *insideDiv1Click* variable isn't in scope. That variable lives only within the *Div1 onclick* handler, so it's in scope only while that function runs. This example raises an undefined exception when it tries to access the *insideDiv1Click* variable.

As a final example, update the code for *Div3* and other functions as follows:

```
document.getElementById("Div3").onclick = function () {
    var insideDiv3 = "Div3";
    AFunction();
    BFunctionWithParam(insideDiv3);
};
function AFunction() {
    var x;
    alert(insideDiv3);
}
function BFunctionWithParam(p) {
    alert(p);
    alert(localVar);
}
```

In this code, the variable *insideDiv3* is local to the *onclick* event handler for *Div3*. The *onclick* event handler has access to the *globalVar* and *localVar* variables just like the other event handlers did. The event handler for *Div3* also calls the *AFunction* and *BFunctionWithParam* methods. The *AFunction* method attempts to access the *insideDiv3* variable. Unfortunately, that variable lives only within the scope of the *Div3 onclick* handler. The functions called from the *Div3* click event function don't inherit or have access to the local variables of the *Div3* method. To access the local variables declared in the *Div3* event handler from another function, you need to pass them as parameters to those functions.

You can also see an illustration of passing a local variable as a parameter to another function in the code. After the call to the *AFunction* method, the event handler calls the *BFunctionWithParam* method. This function expects a single parameter named *p*. The *onclick* event handler passes the value of the *insideDiv3* variable to the method. Now, the *p* variable is a local variable to the *BFunctionWithParam* method, so it can show the value of the *insideDiv3* variable. This is the only way to make a local variable from one function accessible to another function—by passing a parameter.

Next, the *BFunctionWithParam* method attempts to access the *localVar* variable. It assumes it would have access, but it doesn't for the same reason the *AFunction* method doesn't have access to the *insideDiv3* variable. The *localVar* variable is accessible only to code within the *onload* event handler in which it's declared. For functions outside that scope to have access to it, you need to pass it as a parameter. One more thing to consider with respect to the lifetime and scope of variables is *hierarchy*.

If you plan to use the values of *globalVar* or *localVar* variables in the *onclick* event handlers for the various div elements, you must not declare any variables at the local level with the same name. Locally scoped variables override higher-level scoped variables of the same name. Note that they don't over*write* them, they over*ride* them—meaning that you can't access the overridden values. The following code demonstrates this point:

```
window.onload
…
var scaleX = 0.0;
…
    document.getElementById("Div4").onclick = function () {
        var scaleX = -3;
        alert(scaleX);
    }
function scaleDiv() {
    //code to scale the Div by a factor of scaleX
}
```

In this code, if your intention is to use the *scaleX* variable declared globally within the *scaleDiv* function, the results should be unexpected. That's because the function assigned to the *onclick* event handler also declares a variable named *scaleX*. The value in the *alert* window within the *onClick* function is –3, not 0.0, and when the *scaleDiv* function accesses the *scaleX* variable, the value is 0.0. Scoping problems such as these highlight why you must always provide meaningful names to variables. Meaningful names can help prevent accidentally naming variables the same thing.

Avoiding using the global namespace

The global namespace is where all the native JavaScript libraries live. In Internet Explorer, the *window* object references the global namespace. Everything this object exposes is global. The global namespace has far more functionality than this book can cover; however, you've already seen some examples of the objects in the global namespace used in this chapter, including the Web Storage API and the Geolocation API. The global namespace includes other nested namespaces, such as Math, WebSocket, and JSON.

The global namespace is available to *all* code within an application session. With the increasing number of third-party libraries in use, and as applications become more complex and require the use of such libraries, the potential for naming conflicts increases. Names of classes within a namespace must be unique. If multiple developers define a namespace with the same name, the JavaScript runtime can't identify which namespace they intended to use. This is why keeping your objects out of the global namespace is important.

One strategy to avoid name collisions is to create your own namespaces for your JavaScript libraries. One pattern to consider using to create unique namespace names is the name of the domain in reverse, such as *com.microsoft*. Because domain names are unique, this pattern helps reduce the possibility of naming collisions. The following code demonstrates this strategy to create a namespace for a library developed for a bookstore:

```
var com = {};
com.Bookstore = {};
com.Bookstore.Book = {
    title: 'my book',
    genre: 'fiction'
};
com.Bookstore.Author = {
    firstName: 'R',
    lastName: 'D'
}
```

By creating the objects in this way, you can be reasonably certain that if another developer creates a useful library to manage books that you want to include in your site, you won't have to worry about a naming collision between your *Book* and *Author* objects and those provided by the other library. When developing reusable JavaScript libraries, never implement your objects in the global namespace.

Leveraging the *this* keyword

The keyword *this* is a special term that allows JavaScript developers to reference the containing object directly. The following code snippet demonstrates the context of the *this* keyword:

```
<script>
    //Here, "this" references the global namespace
    this.navigator.geolocation
    window.onload = function () {
        //Here, "this" references the window object
        this...
        document.getElementById("aDiv").onclick = function()
        {
            //Here, "this" references the DIV element
          this…
        }
    }
</script>
```

In this code snippet, the first *this* reference is in the global namespace—so it provides a direct reference to the global namespace. As you move down through the code, the context of the *this* keyword changes. In the onload event for the window, *this* refers to the *window* object (yes, that's in the global namespace, but keep reading). Within the *onclick* function, the *this* keyword refers to the *div* element returned from the *getElementById* method. The *this* keyword always refers to the object that contains the currently running code. That is its context.

Objective summary

- Variables are undefined until they are initialized.
- Variables are scoped and accessible depending on where they are declared. If they are inside a function, for example, they are local to the function.
- Passing parameters is the only way to make a local variable available in another function.
- The global namespace shouldn't be used because it's shared by all.
- You should apply a namespace to custom objects to prevent conflicts in the global namespace.
- The *this* keyword provides direct access to the object that raised the event.

Objective review

Answer the following questions to test your knowledge of the information in this objective. You can find the answers to these questions and explanations of why each answer choice is correct or incorrect in the "Answers" section at the end of this chapter.

1. In JavaScript, how do you determine the scope of a variable?

   A. The scope of a variable is global within the context of the page.

   B. The scope of a variable depends on where inside the script it's declared.

   C. The scope of a variable changes depending on the type it represents.

2. Why is it important to avoid creating custom JavaScript objects in the global namespace?

   A. The global namespace is reserved for the browser.

   B. The global namespace is available to all applications in the session, and using it could result in a naming conflict.

   C. The global namespace creates a security risk to users' systems.

3. What JavaScript keyword in an event handler can be easily used to reference the object that raised the event?

   A. The *it* keyword provides a reference to the object.

   B. The *document.current* property provides a reference to the object.

   C. The *this* keyword provides a reference to the object.

   D. No way is available other than to use a selector query to retrieve the object from the DOM.

Objective 1.6: Create and implement objects and methods

JavaScript is an object-oriented programming language, which means that to develop applications in JavaScript effectively, you must understand how to work with objects. Essentially, two types of objects exist in JavaScript:

- Native JavaScript objects, which are provided with JavaScript itself
- Custom objects, which developers create to represent their own data constructs and behaviors

In some cases, creating an entirely new object isn't necessary. You can base objects on other objects (if they are a subtype of that object) by using object inheritance, in which one object inherits all the attributes and behaviors of another object but can also implement additional aspects that are unique to it.

Objects encapsulate functionality and state information that is relevant for them. The functionality is provided in the form of methods, whereas state information is provided in the form of properties. This objective examines working with objects in JavaScript.

> **This objective covers how to:**
> - Implement native objects
> - Create custom objects and custom properties for native projects using prototypes and functions
> - Implement inheritance
> - Implement native methods and create custom methods

Implementing native objects

Native objects are available to developers directly through JavaScript. JavaScript provides a large number of objects that provide functionality to make developers' lives easier. Although covering every native object in JavaScript is out of scope for this book and this exam, you will be expected to be able to create and work with native JavaScript objects.

Some native objects are available statically, which means you don't need to create an instance of them. Others require you to create an instance. You can find both types among objects in the global namespace. One example of a static object is *Math*, which is available in the global namespace and provides a great deal of functionality without you having to create an instance:

```
var squareValue = Math.sqrt(144);
```

Other objects, such as *Array* shown in the following code, require you to create an instance to work with them:

```
var listofPrimeNumbers = new Array(1, 2, 3, 5, 7, 11, 13, 17, 19, 23);
```

This code introduces the *new* keyword, which you use to instantiate an object. This tells the runtime to allocate a new object of the type specified. In this case, a new *Array* object is being requested. The list after the *Array* object type is called the object's constructor. This information can be passed into the object as parameters to construct the initial state of the object. Some objects have many constructors to choose from, with differing sets of parameters. The addition of multiple constructors is called an *overloaded constructor*.

JavaScript also provides wrapper objects. These wrap up native types, for example. Native types are defined as integer, string, char, and so on. When a variable is declared like this,

```
var txt = "my long string";
var num = 5;
```

you can access method on the variable like this:

```
var index = txt.indexOf("long",0);
var exp = num.toExponential(5);
```

The underlying types for string and integer don't natively have methods or functionality; however, the JavaScript runtime creates a wrapper object for them dynamically so that some useful methods are available. For example, you could create the following string and number variables with the *new* keyword, but that's not very common.

```
var txt = new String("my long string");
var num = new Number(5);
```

The syntax reviewed thus far applies to both native objects and custom objects. Custom objects are created by the developer, whereas native objects are provided by core JavaScript.

Creating custom objects

Creating custom objects is standard practice when working with information in custom applications. Because JavaScript is an object-oriented language, you should apply proper object-oriented practices when developing JavaScript applications. In almost all cases, this involves creating custom objects to encapsulate functionality within logical entities.

For example, the following code creates a *book* object. This is a dynamic object, meaning that it's created inline with a variable declaration.

```
var book = {
    ISBN: "55555555",
    Length: 560,
    genre: "programming",
    covering: "soft",
    author: "John Doe",
    currentPage: 5
}
```

The object created represents a book. It provides a way to encapsulate into a single object the properties that apply to a book—in this case, a book entity. The code specifies five properties. When using the *book* variable, you can access all the properties just as with any other property; if desired, you could output to the screen by placing the values into the DOM. The properties of an object represent its state, whereas the methods of an object provide its behavior. At this point, the *book* object has only properties. To give the *book* object some behavior, you can add the following code:

```
var book = {
    ISBN: "55555555",
    Length: 560,
    genre: "programming",
    covering: "soft",
    author: "John Doe",
    currentPage: 5,
    title: "My Big Book of Wonderful Things",
    flipTo: function flipToAPage(pNum) {
        this.currentPage = pNum;
    },
    turnPageForward: function turnForward() {
        this.flipTo(this.currentPage++);
    },
    turnPageBackward: function turnBackward() {
        this.flipTo(this.currentPage--);
    }
}
```

In the *book* object, three methods have been added: *turnPageForward*, *turnPageBackward*, and *flipTo*. Each method provides some functionality to the *book* object, letting a reader move through the pages. The interesting parts of this code are the function declarations them-selves. For example, when you look at the code for the *flipTo* function, you might think that the function is called *FlipToAPage* because that's what was declared. However, this isn't the case. The methods are called using the *alias* property that assigned the function. When using the code, the runtime knows that it's a method, not a property, and it expects the method to be called with parentheses:

```
//This line throws an exception because the object does not support this method
book.FlipToAPage(15);
//This line works because this is what the method has been named.
book.flipTo(15);
```

Creating objects inline as the *book* object is in the previous code sample is useful only when it is used in the page where it's defined, and perhaps only a few times. However, if you plan to use an object often, consider creating a *prototype* for it so that you can construct one whenever you need it. A prototype provides a definition of the object so that you can construct the object using the new keyword. When an object can be constructed, such as with the *new* keyword, the constructor can take parameters to initialize the state of the object, and the object itself can internally take extra steps as needed to initialize itself. The following code creates a prototype for the *book* object:

```
function Book() {
    this.ISBN = "55555555";
    this.Length = 560;
    this.genre= "programming";
    this.covering = "soft";
    this.author = "John Doe";
    this.currentPage = 5,
    this.flipTo = function FlipToAPage(pNum) {
        this.currentPage = pNum;
    },
    this.turnPageForward = function turnForward() {
        this.flipTo(this.currentPage++);
    },
    this.turnPageBackward = function turnBackward() {
        this.flipTo(this.currentPage--);
    }
}
var books = new Array(new Book(), new Book(), new Book());
books[0].Length
…
```

 EXAM TIP

JavaScript consists of objects. Everything in JavaScript is an object. Each object is based on a prototype. Whenever you create a new instance of an object, that instance is based on the object's prototype.

In the preceding code, the *Book* object is constructed so that you can create one with default properties set. Then, the code creates an *Array* containing a list of books. You can access each element of the array to initialize each *Book* object as it's needed.

Accessing each *Book* element to provide initialization values isn't terribly efficient. It would be more convenient if the *Book* object supported more than one constructor. That way, you could create a blank book or create one with specific unique properties. This is where proto-typing comes in handy. The following code creates a prototype containing two constructors that support the needs of any users of the *Book* object:

```
function Book()
{
    //just creates an  empty book.
}

function Book(title, length, author) {

    this.title = title;
    this.Length = length;
    this.author = author;

}

Book.prototype = {
    ISBN: "",
    Length: -1,
    genre: "",
    covering: "",
    author: "",
    currentPage: 0,
    title: "",

    flipTo: function FlipToAPage(pNum) {
        this.currentPage = pNum;
    },

    turnPageForward: function turnForward() {
        this.flipTo(this.currentPage++);
    },

    turnPageBackward: function turnBackward() {
        this.flipTo(this.currentPage--);
    }
};

var books = new Array(new Book(), new Book("First Edition",350,"Random"));
```

With this new code, you can create an empty *Book* object by using the constructor with no parameters, or you can create a *Book* object by using specific parameters to initialize some fields.

Objects can contain other objects as needed. In this example, the *Author* property could easily be factored into a new prototype, making it more extensible and encapsulating the information related to an author. Add the following code to the *Book* prototype:

```
Book.prototype = {
    ISBN: "",
    Length: -1,
    genre: "",
    covering: "",
    author: new Author(),
    currentPage: 0,
    title: "",

    …
}
function Author(){
}
function Author(firstName, lastName, gender)
{
    this.firstName = firstName;
    this.lastName = lastName;
    this.gender = gender;
}
Author.prototype = {
    firstName:"",
    lastName:"",
    gender:"",
    BookCount: 0
}
var books = new Array(new Book(),
        new Book("First Edition",350, new Author("Random","Author","M"))
    );
```

Now, the book's *Author* is a custom object instead of just a string. This provides for more extensibility in the design. If you later decide that you need to add information about the author, you can simply add the property or properties to the *Author* prototype.

EXAM TIP

You can add properties to a prototype dynamically rather than use the preceding method. The following code achieves the same outcome. Using such code is just a matter of preference.

```
Book.prototype.ISBN = "";
Book.prototype.Length = 350;
Book.prototype.genre  = "";
Book.prototype.covering  = "";
Book.prototype.author  = new Author();
Book.prototype.currentPage  = 0;
Book.prototype.title  = "";
```

Implementing inheritance

In object-oriented programming, inheritance is a fundamental concept. In standard object-oriented programming, classes are created in a relational hierarchy, so that the attributes and functionality of one entity can be reused within another entity without having to re-create all the code. In object-oriented parlance, if an entity satisfies the "is-a" relationship question, it's a candidate for inheritance. For example, an organization is made up of employees, in which an employee entity has certain attributes (properties) and behaviors (methods). Management, executives, and staffers are all types of employees. A staffer "is-a" employee. So in an object-oriented design, a staffer object would inherit from an employee. This type of inheritance is quite easy to build in full-fledged object-oriented languages. However, JavaScript is a special situation because it doesn't use classes. As you saw in the previous sections, everything is an object; a custom object is made up of properties where some properties are native types and some properties are assigned to functions to implement methods. This section examines object inheritance as it works in JavaScript.

Building on the code used in the previous section, this section explains object inheritance. In the preceding code sample, you created an object called *Book*. But many types of books exist. To extend the definition of *Book*, you must separate the differences in functionality between, for example, pop-up books and other books. Pop-up books have some extra functionality, such as displaying the pop-up on the current page and perhaps playing a sound. In other words, while a pop-up book "is-a" type of book, it also has this extra functionality that doesn't apply to all books. In this case, it would be useful to inherit from *Book* so that all the basic attributes and behaviors of a book are available without you having to re-create them. Then you could add the specific functionality for pop-up books.

You can extend the *Book* object in a couple of ways. (Extending is another way of thinking about inheritance—an object is extended into another object.) Here's the first way to extend an object:

```
var popupBook = Object.create(Book.protoType,{ hasSound: {value:true},
    showPopUp:{ value: function showPop() {
                            //do logic to show a popup
                        }
            }
});
```

Object.create is a method available from the *Object* class in the global namespace. The create method takes two parameters: the object you want to create and a list of property descriptors.

The first parameter expects to receive the prototype of the object to create or null. If null is specified, the object uses only those functions or properties specified in the second parameter. If an object prototype is specified, as in the case *Book.prototype*, the object is created with all the properties and functions declared on that object prototype. This is another reason designing code in a proper object-oriented way is important—so that you can leverage this type of functionality to keep code more readable and maintainable.

The second parameter enables you to add properties or behaviors to the object being created. Essentially, you define this additional prototype information inline with the object creation. This example adds the property *hasSound,* which has a default value specified as *false.* You could also specify additional information here, such as whether the property is read-only and whether it's enumerable. Creating objects this way is similar to the inline example in the beginning of the earlier section on custom objects. Again, such an approach isn't very modular or reusable. For every instance of a pop-up book, you'd need to declare the additional property and method. So again, for objects that you might want to reuse often, extending the *Book* prototype is better.

Extending the *Book* prototype is much the same as creating a new prototype. You need only one line of code to tell JavaScript to inherit the functionality and attributes of another object. You do this by initializing the prototype to the parent object:

```
function PopUpBook() {
    Book.call(this);
}
PopUpBook.prototype = Book.prototype;
PopUpBook.prototype.hasSound = false;
PopUpBook.prototype.showPopUp = function ShowPop() { };
```

In this way, *PopUpBook* now extends the implementation of the *Book* object and adds its own functionality for reuse. The function *PopUpBook* makes a method call to *Book.call(..).* This is a call to the constructor of the super class (the class being inherited from). If the super class has a constructor that takes parameters, this method would enable you to pass the parameter values to the super-class constructors for object initialization.

 Thought experiment
Creating synergy between custom objects and native objects

In this thought experiment, apply what you've learned about this objective. You can find answers to these questions in the "Answers" section at the end of this chapter.

In this objective you've seen the use of native objects and custom objects. How would you bring those two worlds together? In JavaScript, inheriting from native objects is not fully supported. However, what if you wanted to add functionality to native objects by extending them? How would you go about doing this?

Objective summary

- Everything in JavaScript is an object—even functions.
- JavaScript supports native objects and custom objects.
- Objects are created with the *new* keyword.
- Access methods and properties on objects with the dot notation: *object.method* or *object.property.*
- You can create custom objects dynamically or by using prototypes.
- Prototypes provide for object definition reuse, whereas dynamic objects require attributes and methods defined for each use.
- Inheritance is achieved in JavaScript through the extension of prototypes.

Objective review

Answer the following questions to test your knowledge of the information in this objective. You can find the answers to these questions and explanations of why each answer choice is correct or incorrect in the "Answers" section at the end of this chapter.

1. In JavaScript, which of the following isn't a native object?

   A. Function

   B. Array

   C. Integer

   D. Person

2. Which of the following snippets shows the correct way to create a custom book object?

   A. var book = "Title: 'My book about things'" + "Author: 'Jane Doe'" + " Pages: 400";

   B. var book = {Title: "My book about things", Author: "Jane Doe", Pages: 400};

   C. var book = (Title= "My book about things", Author= "Jane Doe"= Pages: 400);

   D. var book = new {Title: "My book about things", Author: "Jane Doe", Pages: 400};

3. Inheritance is accomplished in JavaScript through the use of which construct?

   A. *inherits* keyword

   B. *implements* keyword

   C. *this* keyword

   D. Prototypes

Answers

This section contains the solutions to the thought experiments and answers to the objective review questions in this chapter.

Objective 1.1: Thought experiment

The following HTML shows the conversion of the page to HTML5:

```
<html>
    <head>
        <title></title>
    </head>
    <body>
        <table>
            <tr>
                <td colspan="3">
                    <header>
                        <h1>A Thoughtful Experiment</h1>
                    </header>
                </td>
            </tr>
            <tr>
                <td>
                    <nav>
                        <a href="">Home</a>
                        <a href="">Page 1</a>
                        <a href="">Page 2</a>
                        <a href="">Page 3</a>
                    </nav>
                </td>
                <td>
                    <section>
                        <article>
                            <hgroup>
                                <h1>An Article regarding thought is presented here.</h1>
                                <h2>Thought as a provoking element.</h2>
                            </hgroup>
                            ....................
                                <aside>Here are some reference materials.</aside>
                        </article>
                    </section>
                </td>
                <td>
                    <section id="profile">
                        .....
                    </section>
                </td>
            </tr>
            <tr>
                <td>
                    <footer>
                        This page is copyright protected.
                    </footer>
```

```
            </td>
          </tr>
        </table>
      </body>
    </html>
```

Objective 1.1: Review

1. **Correct answer:** D

    A. **Incorrect:** The *<article>* element is a new HTML5 semantic element.

    B. **Incorrect:** The *<footer>* element is a new HTML5 semantic element.

    C. **Incorrect:** The *<hgroup>* element is a new HTML5 semantic element.

    D. **Correct:** The *<input>* element isn't new in HTML5. However, new input types have been introduced to the specification.

2. **Correct answer:** A

    A. **Correct:** The *<hgroup>* element is expected to contain any or all of the *<h1>* to *<h6>* elements.

    B. **Incorrect:** The *<header>* element is used separately to define the header section of an *<article>* element or a *<section>* element.

    C. **Incorrect:** The *<nav>* element is used to define a menu structure. It wouldn't be included inside an *<hgroup>* element.

    D. **Incorrect:** The *<hgroup>* element is expected to contain only the *<h1>* to *<h6>* elements.

3. **Correct answer:** C

    A. **Incorrect:** The *<div>* element doesn't provide any additional context to a search engine.

    B. **Incorrect:** The *<header>* element is contained inside an *<article>* element and will help but isn't the main element to provide search engine optimization.

    C. **Correct:** The *<article>* element tells the search engine that specific content in this area is relevant to what users are searching for. This element provides for the best search engine optimization.

    D. **Incorrect:** The *<article>* element is specifically used for SEO.

4. **Correct answer:** C

   A. **Incorrect:** *<div>* elements flow left to right and top to bottom and don't provide any structure.

   B. **Incorrect:** The *<p>* element denotes a paragraph. This element doesn't provide any layout structure to the page.

   C. **Correct:** You use the *<table>* element to provide a structured layout, using its rows and columns elements as needed to create the desired layout.

   D. **Incorrect:** The *<form>* element is used to denote an area where the user can submit data. The *<form>* element doesn't provide any mechanism to control layout.

Objective 1.2: Thought experiment

This thought experiment speaks directly to performance. As the number of balls increases, the demand on the graphics engine and local resources such as CPU and memory becomes more intense. The *<canvas>* element is better designed to perform this duty. From a coding perspective, this experiment provides insight into capturing events from the canvas, calculating the location of the click in relation to the balls on the screen, and creating new balls dynamically as they get clicked. These computations need to occur quickly as the graphics are redrawn. The implementation of such a game would be too involved for the scope of this book. However, the notion of performance is an important concept to be clear on with respect to graphics rendering.

Objective 1.2: Review

1. **Correct answer:** D

   A. **Incorrect:** The *getElementById* method retrieves an element by its unique *id*.

   B. **Incorrect:** The *querySelector* method retrieves a single element that matches the specified selector.

   C. **Incorrect:** The *getElementsByClassName* method retrieves all the elements that have the specified CSS class assigned to them.

   D. **Correct:** The *queryAll* method isn't available to search the DOM.

2. **Correct answer:** A

   A. **Correct:** document.getElementbyId("myDog"); retrieves only the single image with the ID *myDog*.

   B. **Incorrect:** <p>.getChildNode("img"); isn't a valid syntax.

   C. **Incorrect:** document.getElementbyId("dogs").querySelector ("thumb"); fails because the page has no element named "dogs".

   D. **Incorrect:** document.querySelector.querySelectorAll("thumb"); is incorrect because it returns all the elements on the page with the specified class name.

3. **Correct answer:** B

   A. **Incorrect:** The DOM is dynamic and changes physically when items are removed from it.

   B. **Correct:** When an element is removed and needed again, a reference to the removed node must be kept to be able to add it back.

   C. **Incorrect:** No such method exists.

   D. **Incorrect:** A node can be added back to the DOM if a reference was kept. This is accomplished by using the various methods available to insert nodes in the DOM.

4. **Correct answer:** C

   A. **Incorrect:** Different browsers support different media formats. Use the *<source>* element to provide the media in the various formats.

   B. **Incorrect:** The *src* attribute allows you to specify only one source video. This doesn't work across multiple browsers unless the video format is supported across the browsers.

   C. **Correct:** The *<source>* elements specify multiple video formats so that the browser can choose the correct one.

   D. **Incorrect:** The *<object>* element is supported to provide a fallback mechanism in the event that the browser doesn't support the HTML5 *<video>* element.

5. **Correct answer:** C

   A. **Incorrect:** The *moveTo* method moves the current context to a new point but doesn't begin a drawing.

   B. **Incorrect:** The *lineAt* method draws a line within the current positional context.

   C. **Correct:** The *beginPath* method tells the context to start a new drawing from its current point.

   D. **Incorrect:** The *stroke* method tells the context to draw the graphics that are applied to the context.

6. **Correct answer:** C

   A. **Incorrect:** The *<canvas>* element doesn't support any declarative elements.

   B. **Incorrect:** The *<svg>* element has poorer performance than the *<canvas>* element when a lot of graphic refresh is required.

   C. **Correct:** The *<canvas>* element provides superior performance compared to the *<svg>* element.

   D. **Incorrect:** The *<canvas>* and *<svg>* elements combined don't provide better performance. The *<canvas>* element provides superior performance when the graphics require a lot of refreshing.

Objective 1.3: Thought experiment

To complete this thought experiment, you must get a reference to the DOM via JavaScript and set up events for the click to each radio button. When an event is created for notification of the selection of each radio button, the questions can be shown/hidden as needed. Setting the display CSS attribute of the elements so that the questions present in flow is key. The desired effect is for the surrounding elements to behave as though the element is no longer part of the DOM. Setting display=none achieves this effect.

Objective 1.3: Review

1. **Correct answer:** B

   A. **Incorrect:** The element isn't positioned relative to the browser window.

   B. **Correct:** Absolute positioning positions the element relative to its parent element.

   C. **Incorrect:** The element doesn't center within the window.

   D. **Incorrect:** Absolute positioning doesn't center an element.

2. **Correct answer:** D

   A. **Incorrect:** The *rotate* transform spins an object clockwise or counterclockwise.

   B. **Incorrect:** The *skew* transform slants an object.

   C. **Incorrect:** The *translate* transform moves an object.

   D. **Correct:** The *scale* transform changes the size of an object.

3. **Correct answer:** D

   A. **Incorrect:** Display='hidden' isn't a valid option.

   B. **Incorrect:** Display='inline' shows an object that previously wasn't showing.

   C. **Incorrect:** Visibility='none' isn't a valid option.

   D. **Correct:** Visibility='hidden' hides an element, and its surrounding elements remain in place as though the element was still there.

Objective 1.4: Thought experiment

This is a simple example of the power available when combining the HTML5 APIs. You can use the Web Storage API to store the location points as they occur from the Geolocation API by using the *watchPosition* method. The following code demonstrates the storage of the data:

```
<script>
        var watcher;
        var geoLocator;
        var positions = 0;
        window.onload = function () {
            geoLocator = window.navigator.geolocation;
            var posOptions = { enableHighAccuracy: true, timeout: 45000 };
            watcher = geoLocator.watchPosition(successPosition, errorPosition,
posOptions);
        }
        function successPosition(pos) {
            //on each position, store it into local storage sequentially.
            //Then it can be retrieved sequentially
            //in order to redraw the route on a map.
            var p = "Lat: " + pos.coords.latitude + " Long: " + pos.coords.longitude;
            localStorage.setItem(position, p);
        }
        function errorPosition(err) {
            var sp = document.createElement("p");
            sp.innerText = "error: " + err.message; + " code: " + err.code;
            document.getElementById("geoResults").appendChild(sp);
        }
</script>
```

Objective 1.4: Review

1. **Correct answer:** C

    A. **Incorrect:** *localStorage* is persistent even after the session closes.

    B. **Incorrect:** *cookieStorage* doesn't exist in the Web Storage API.

    C. **Correct:** *sessionStorage* clears when the session closes.

    D. **Incorrect:** A hidden input element isn't a valid solution to meet the requirement.

2. **Correct answer:** C

    A. **Incorrect:** The *offLine* property isn't a valid JavaScript option.

    B. **Incorrect:** You wouldn't specify the manifest on the *<form>* element.

    C. **Correct:** Specifying the manifest attribute on the HTML element is the correct action.

    D. **Incorrect:** The browser's offline option doesn't invoke the AppCache API.

3. **Correct answer:** B

   A. **Incorrect:** Cache manifest lists all resources that must be cached offline.

   B. **Correct:** Session manifest isn't a valid option.

   C. **Incorrect:** Network manifest specifies any resources that must be available from the Internet.

   D. **Incorrect:** Fallback manifest enables you to tell the browser what to do when resources aren't available offline.

4. **Correct answer:** A

   A. **Correct:** The *oncached* event is fired when the download completes.

   B. **Incorrect:** The *onupdateready* event is fired when items in the manifest are newly downloaded and the *swapCache* method can be called.

   C. **Incorrect:** The *ondownloading* event is fired when the browser is downloading.

   D. **Incorrect:** The *onchecking* event is fired when the browser is checking for updates.

5. **Correct answer:** B

   A. **Incorrect:** The *enableCache* property doesn't exist.

   B. **Correct:** Set the *maximumAge* property to a non-zero value on the *PositionOptions* object.

   C. **Incorrect:** The *timeout* property specifies how long to wait for a response before firing the *timeout* event.

   D. **Incorrect:** The cache *maximumAge* defaults to 0, so caching is off by default.

Objective 1.5: Thought experiment

In this experiment, you took a look at a real-world scenario where the addition of JavaScript libraries could potentially conflict with other libraries already in use. This is a case for using namespaces to scope the library with a unique fully qualified name to ensure that it's distinct from any other. Review the objective on the use of the global namespace to ensure that you understand this concept for the exam.

Objective 1.5: Review

1. **Correct answer:** B

   A. **Incorrect:** Variables are global only if declared in the global space.

   B. **Correct:** The scope of a variable depends on where inside the script it's declared.

   C. **Incorrect:** A variable's type doesn't affect its scope.

2. **Correct answer:** B

   A. Incorrect: The global namespace isn't reserved for the browser.

   B. Correct: Because the global namespace is available to all applications in the session, using it could result in a naming conflict.

   C. Incorrect: The global namespace doesn't create a security risk to the user's system.

3. **Correct answer:** C

   A. Incorrect: The *it* keyword doesn't exist.

   B. Incorrect: The *document.current* keyword doesn't provide the reference.

   C. Correct: The *this* keyword provides a reference to the object.

   D. Incorrect: The *this* keyword provides a direct shortcut to the element that raised the event.

Objective 1.6: Thought experiment

To extend a native object, you must add functionality to its prototype. This isn't ideal object orientation in all cases; however, it does provide another avenue to achieve the desired results. JavaScript objects are dynamic, meaning that the prototype can be modified to add functionality to them. In this example, you extend the *Array* object to provide a *sum* method that returns the sum of all the elements in the array.

For this type of example, type safety is a concern. Arrays can hold any type of data. True inheritance would allow you to create a special type of array to hold only numbers. In this code, you can add validation to ensure that the values in the array are numeric or add only the numeric values. However, for the sake of demonstrating the extension of the object, this sample omits that validation. The following code shows how you can extend the *Array* object to support a *sum* method by adding a new method to its prototype:

```
Array.prototype.sum = function () {
    var res = 0;
    for (var i = 0; i < this.length; i++)
        res += this[i];
    return res;
};
var x = new Array(2);
x[0] = 5;
x[1] = 6;
document.write(x.sum());
```

Objective 1.6: Review

1. **Correct answer:** D

   A. **Incorrect:** Functions are objects in JavaScript.

   B. **Incorrect:** Arrays are objects in JavaScript.

   C. **Incorrect:** Integers are objects in JavaScript.

   D. **Correct:** People aren't native JavaScript objects.

2. **Correct answer:** B

   A. **Incorrect:** This code segment produces a string.

   B. **Correct:** This code segment creates a dynamic object.

   C. **Incorrect:** This segment is incorrect because (..) was used instead of {}, along with = instead of :.

   D. **Incorrect:** The *new* keyword isn't used when creating a dynamic object.

3. **Correct answer:** D

   A. **Incorrect:** The *inherits* keyword isn't a JavaScript construct.

   B. **Incorrect:** The *implements* keyword isn't a JavaScript construct.

   C. **Incorrect:** The *this* keyword doesn't provide inheritance.

   D. **Correct:** Prototypes are used to create inheritance trees in JavaScript.

Implement program flow

Being able to manipulate the Document Object Model (DOM), create animations, and use the various application programming interfaces (APIs) provided by the JavaScript library is a great skill to have. To leverage the power of the user experience fully, however, you need to provide users with certain website functions only under certain conditions, a concept known as *program flow*. Without program flow, JavaScript programs would process from top to bottom in the order in which the code was written. This is useful in some cases, but in most situations in which a dynamic user experience is required, logic needs to be processed conditionally. Program flow can be conditional, iterative, or behavioral:

- *Conditional* program flow is based on evaluating state to make a decision as to which code should run.

- *Iterative* flow is the ability to process lists or collections of information systematically and consistently.

- *Behavioral* flow can be defined as an event or callback in which specific logic should be applied based on user engagement with the web application or the completion of another task.

Flow can—and almost always will—include a combination of all three.

Another special type of program flow involves *exception handling*. Exception handling constructs provide the ability to run specific logic in the case of an error in the program.

Objectives in this chapter:

- Objective 2.1: Implement program flow
- Objective 2.2: Raise and handle an event
- Objective 2.3: Implement exception handling
- Objective 2.4: Implement a callback
- Objective 2.5: Create a web worker process

Objective 2.1: Implement program flow

For the exam, you need to understand both conditional and iterative program flow. Conditional program flow enables an application to examine the state of an object or variable to decide which code path to process. The commands you use to apply the concept of conditional flow are the *if...else* statement, the *switch* statement, and the ternary operator.

This objective covers how to:

- Evaluate expressions, including using *switch* statements, *if/then* statements, and operators
- Work with arrays
- Implement special types of arrays
- Use advanced array methods
- Implement iterative control flow

Evaluating expressions

To use a conditional flow statement, you must evaluate some data against some condition, which you do by using conditional operators. You can use logical operators to combine conditional operators. Combining operators is useful when more than one condition must be met—or at least one condition from a set of conditions must be met—before processing specific logic. Table 2-1 outlines the available operators.

TABLE 2-1 Conditional and logical operators

Operator	Type	Description
>	Conditional	Evaluates whether the value on the left is greater than the value on the right
<	Conditional	Evaluates whether the value on the right is greater than the value on the left
>=,<=	Conditional	Evaluates the same as > or < but with the additional logic that the values can also be equal
!=	Conditional	Evaluates whether the values aren't equal
==	Conditional	Evaluates whether the values are equal independent of the underlying data type
===	Conditional	Evaluates whether the values are equal both in value and underlying data type
&&	Logical	The AND logical operator, in which the expressions on both sides must evaluate to true
||	Logical	The OR logical operator, in which at least one expression on either side must evaluate to true

Use these operators to evaluate data and to make decisions. For example, if a website requires that its users be a minimum age to sign up for an account, the logic on the sign-up page might include something like this:

```
if(users age >= minimum age)
{
  //allow sign-up.
}
```

Using *if* statements

Use the *if* statement to evaluate state to control the direction in which the code will run. The *if* statement can stand alone, as shown in the preceding snippet, or be combined with *else* to form more complex constructs:

```
if(exp1, exp2, exp3…expn){
    //true logic
}else {
    //false logic
}
```

This *if* statement starts on a new line with the keyword *if*. In parentheses following the *if* statement is a series of one or more expressions, separated by logical operators when more than one expression is provided. The code block immediately following the *if* statement conditional expression runs only when the expression evaluates to true. When the expression evaluates to false, the block immediately following the *else* keyword runs.

The *else* keyword is optional. An *if* statement can exist as a standalone statement when no logic is available to run when the expression evaluates to false.

EXAM TIP

Two conditional operators are available for checking equality: == (equality operator) and === (identity operator). Checking for equality with the == operator will ignore the underlying data type, whereas the === identity operator will consider data type. Look at the following example:

```
var n = 2000, s = '2000';
alert(n == s);
alert(n === s);
```

The first expression, which uses the equality operator, evaluates to true because the string is cast to a number for the purpose of the evaluation. The second expression, which uses the identity operator, evaluates to false because the string '2000' isn't equal to the integer 2000.

Conditional statements such as the *if* statement can be nested, like in the following example:

```javascript
var userAge = 10, gender = 'M';
var minimumAge = 11;
if (userAge > minimumAge) {
    if (gender == 'M') {
        //do logic for above age male
    }
    else {
        //do logic for above age female.
    }
} else if (gender == 'M') {
    //do logic for underage male
} else {
    //do logic for underage female.
}
```

In this example, the logic tests whether a user is older than a specified age. If the user is over the specified age, the logic in the true branch runs. At that point, another *if* statement evaluates the user's gender. If the user's age is younger than the required minimum, the false branch is processed. Here an *else if* statement performs additional conditional processing on the false branch based on the gender. Again, the code processes a specific branch depending on whether the user is male or female.

You aren't limited in how deeply you can nest *if* statements, but nesting them too deeply can make the code quite messy and difficult to read.

The following example examines the background color of an element and processes specific behavior based on the color:

```javascript
var canvas = document.getElementById("canvas1");
if (canvas.style.backgroundColor == 'green') {
    alert('proceed');
} else if (canvas.style.backgroundColor == 'yellow') {
    alert('slow down/safely stop');
} else if (canvas.style.backgroundColor == 'red') {
    alert('stop');
}
```

This code retrieves a reference to a page element called *canvas1* and then evaluates that element's background color to determine an appropriate action to take. In some places, whether by law or preference, yellow sometimes means "proceed faster." In that case, the code could be adapted to use the OR logical operator:

```javascript
var canvas = document.getElementById("canvas1");
if (canvas.style.backgroundColor == 'green' || canvas.style.backgroundColor == 'yellow')
{
    alert('proceed');
} else if (canvas.style.backgroundColor == 'red') {
    alert('stop');
}
```

This code provides the "proceed" instruction when the color is green OR yellow.

> **EXAM TIP**
>
> When using the logical OR operator in an *if* statement, the JavaScript engine knows that it can proceed if any of the statements are true. As such, it evaluates the expressions from left to right until it finds one that's true. As soon as it does, it won't evaluate any further expressions but will immediately jump into the true code block. In the preceding example, if the background is green, the check for whether the background is yellow would never be evaluated.

Structuring code this way is syntactically correct. However, lengthy *if* statements can prove difficult to read and even harder to maintain. If your *if* statements are becoming quite long—for example, if the previous code example had to test for 15 different colors—a *switch* statement might be more appropriate.

Using *switch* statements

The *switch* statement provides a construct in which you can test a list of values for equality (as with the == operator). The following example demonstrates a *switch* statement:

```
switch (canvas.style.backgroundColor) {
    case 'yellow':
        alert('slow down');
        break;
    case 'green':
        alert('proceed');
        break;
    case 'red':
        alert('stop');
        break;
    default:
        alert('unknown condition');
        break;
}
```

The *switch* statement consists of several parts. The first is the *switch* keyword itself, followed by parentheses surrounding an expression to evaluate. This particular example evaluates the background color of the canvas element.

Following the *switch* line is a series of *case* statements enclosed in braces. The *case* statement provides the values to evaluate against. This example provides three cases to evaluate: one for each of the possible red, green, and yellow background colors.

Each *case* statement contains a required *break* keyword. This keyword denotes the end of that particular *case* statement. Only the first case that evaluates to true in a *switch* statement will be processed. Omitting the *break* keyword will cause unexpected behavior.

The last piece of the *switch* statement is the optional *default* keyword, which serves as a failsafe. If none of the case statements evaluate to true, the *default* statement provides a way to handle the situation. You might not want to take any action when none of the case statements evaluates to true—in which case you can omit the *default* statement. However, it does enable you to handle the scenario where one of the conditions should have been reached but wasn't, possibly due to bad data being passed into a method or a valid case being missed. Including a default to account for both of those scenarios is good practice.

You can't force logical flow in a *switch* statement to move from one case to the next by omitting the *break* keyword; in other words, only one conditional block is processed within a *switch* statement. This means that logically, you can't use the AND logical operator. However, you can leverage the OR logical operator. The following code demonstrates a case in which you want the same code to run for both the green and yellow background conditions:

```
switch (canvas.style.backgroundColor) {
    case 'yellow':
    case 'green':
        alert('proceed');
        break;
    case 'red':
        alert('stop');
        break;
    default:
        alert('unknown condition');
        break;
}
```

In this code, multiple *case* statements are stacked onto each other. If any of the stacked *case* statements evaluates to true, the code block following that *case* statement is processed, thus implying a logical OR. You don't need to explicitly use the logical OR operator (||) to leverage logical OR semantics.

> **IMPORTANT A VALID *SWITCH* STATEMENT**
>
> The values used in the *case* statement for the purposes of the evaluation must be expressed as a constant. For example, switching on an integer value to determine whether it's divisible by another number won't work because the case would require an expression instead of a constant value. For example, *case x / 10:* would be an invalid *case* statement. However, the *switch* statement itself can accept an expression to evaluate against all cases inside the switch block.

Using ternary operators

The ternary operator is essentially a shorthand mechanism for an *if* statement. The syntax of the ternary operation is

```
<expression> ? <true part>: <false part>
```

When the expression evaluates to true, the true part runs; otherwise, the false part runs. This code demonstrates using the ternary operator to check the background color of the canvas:

```
canvas.style.backgroundColor == 'green' ? document.write('proceed') :
document.write('stop');
```

Working with arrays

Arrays are JavaScript objects and are created just like any other JavaScript object, with the *new* keyword:

```
var anArray = new Array();
var anArray = new Array(5);
var anArray = new Array('soccer', 'basketball', …, 'badminton');
```

This code example shows an *Array* object being instantiated and demonstrating the three available constructors. The first line creates an empty *Array* object without a default size. The second line creates an *Array* object with a default size. Each value in the array is undefined because nothing is assigned to it yet. The last example creates an array initialized with data. In addition to the object constructors, you can create an array as follows:

```
var anArray = ['soccer', 'basketball', …,'badminton'];
```

Under the hood, JavaScript converts the *anArray* variable to the *Array* object type. After creating an array, you can access its elements by using square brackets following the variable name, as shown in this example:

```
var anArray = new Array(5);
anArray[1] = 'soccer';
alert(anArray[1]);
```

You access elements within an array by their indexed position. This example accesses the element at index position 1 and assigns a value to it. Arrays in JavaScript are *zero-based*, which means that the first element in the array is at index zero, not at index one. The last element is at index *Array.length –1*—in the preceding example, 5–1=4. Hence, the array element indexes are 0, 1, 2, 3, and 4.

EXAM TIP

Sizing arrays is very dynamic. In the preceding example, even though the array is initially declared to have a length of 5, if you try to access the 10th element, the array automatically resizes to accommodate the requested length. The following example demonstrates this concept:

```
var anArray = new Array(5);
alert(anArray.length);
anArray[9] = 'soccer';
alert(anArray.length);
```

A multi-dimensional array can contain other arrays. The following code demonstrates this:

```
var multiArray = new Array(3);
multiArray[0] = new Array(3);
multiArray[1] = new Array(3);
multiArray[2] = new Array(3);
```

This example creates a two dimensional 3 × 3 array. Each array isn't required to be the same size; this example was just coded that way. Accessing the elements of a two-dimensional array is much the same as accessing a one-dimensional array, but you use two indexes:

```
multiArray[1][2] = 'ball sport';
```

This example assigns a value to the first index of the first dimension and the second index of the second dimension, as illustrated in Figure 2-1.

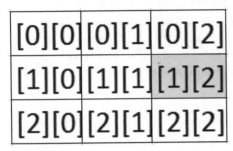

FIGURE 2-1 Layout of a two-dimensional array

Because arrays are objects, they expose a number of powerful methods to make working with them easier. The following sections explain each available method and property.

Using the *length* property

The *length* property provides information on how long the array is—that is, how many elements the array has allocated at the time the property is evaluated. This property is useful for situations in which you need to iterate over an array or to show users how many items are in the array at a specific point in time, such as in a queue. The following example shows how to access the *length* property:

```
var anArray = new Array(5);
alert(anArray.length);
```

Many functions enable you to manipulate array contents quickly and easily.

EXAM TIP

Some array methods affect the *Array* object directly, whereas other methods return a new *Array* object. For the exam, you must understand when each case is applicable.

Using the *concat* method

The *concat* method combines two or more arrays into one array:

```
var sports = new Array( 'football', 'cricket', 'rugby', 'tennis', 'badminton');
var moreSports = new Array('soccer', 'basketball', 'hockey');
var combinedSports = sports.concat(moreSports);
```

The array returned by the *concat* method and stored in the *combinedSports* variable contains all the elements from both arrays in sequence. The contents of the *moreSports* array appear after the elements of the *sports* array in this example.

Using the *indexOf* and *lastIndexOf* methods

The *indexOf* method provides a way to find the index of a known element. The following code sample demonstrates this:

```
var sports = new Array('soccer', 'basketball', 'hockey', 'football', 'cricket', 'rugby',
'tennis', 'badminton');
var index = sports.indexOf('football', 0);
```

This example calls the *indexOf* method to determine the index of the element 'football'. The *indexOf* method accepts two parameters: what to search for and the index at which to begin searching. This example searches the entire array, so the search starts at index 0. The result from this call to the *indexOf* method is *3*, because the element is found in the fourth position. If the element being sought isn't found, the method returns a value of *–1*.

The *indexOf* method uses the identity operator to check for equality, which means that if an array contains strings such as '1', '2', and '3' and you're searching for the integer 3, the result is –1 because the equality operation returns false for all elements in the array. The *indexOf* method searches in ascending index order. To search in descending order—that is, to search from the end of the array to the beginning—use the *lastIndexOf* method, which accepts the same parameters.

Using the *join* method

The *join* method joins all the elements in an array into a single string separated by a specified string separator. For example, to convert an array of strings into a comma-separated list, you could use the following code:

```
var sports = new Array('soccer', 'basketball', 'hockey', 'football', 'cricket', 'rugby',
'tennis', 'badminton');
var joined = sports.join(',');
```

The *join* method accepts a string as a parameter, which is the string used as a delimiter to separate the values in the array. The result is a string of all the elements separated by the string passed into the *join* method.

Using the *reverse* method

The *reverse* method reverses the sequence of all elements in the array. This example reverses the *sports* array:

```
var sports = new Array('soccer', 'basketball', 'hockey', 'football', 'cricket', 'rugby',
'tennis', 'badminton');
sports.reverse();
```

The method reverses all the items so that 'soccer' becomes the last item in the array and 'badminton' becomes the first item.

Using the *sort* method

The *sort* method sequences the items in the array in ascending order. In the *sports* array, the sort would be alphabetical, as shown in the following example:

```
var sports = new Array('soccer', 'basketball', 'hockey', 'football', 'cricket', 'rugby',
'tennis', 'badminton');
alert(sports.indexOf('soccer'));
sports.sort();
alert(sports.indexOf('soccer'));
```

The result is that the *sports* array is now sorted. The alert boxes show the index of the 'soccer' element before and after the sort, demonstrating that the element has moved from position 0 to position 6 in the array.

Using the *slice* method

The *slice* method takes out one or more items in an array and moves them to a new array. Consider the following array with the list of sports:

```
var sports = new Array('soccer', 'basketball', 'hockey', 'football', 'cricket', 'rugby',
'tennis', 'badminton');
var someSports = sports.slice(1, 2);
```

The *slice* method takes two parameters: the indexes where the slice operation should begin and end. The ending index isn't included in the slice. All copied elements are returned as an array from the *slice* method. In this example, because 'basketball' is at index 1 and the ending index is specified at index 2, the resulting array *someSports* contains only one element: 'basketball'.

Using the *splice* method

The *splice* method provides a way to replace items in an array with new items. The following code demonstrates this:

```
var sports = new Array('soccer', 'basketball', 'hockey', 'football', 'cricket', 'rugby',
'tennis', 'badminton');
var splicedItems = sports.splice(1, 3, 'golf', 'curling', 'darts');
```

The *splice* method returns an array containing the items that are spliced out of the source array. The first parameter is the index in the array where the splice operation should start. The second parameter is the number of items to splice, starting from the index specified in the first parameter. The optional last parameter lists items that are to replace the items being spliced out. The list doesn't have to be the same length as the items being spliced out. In fact, if the last parameter is omitted, the spliced items are simply removed from the array and not replaced. In this example, three items are replaced, starting at index 1. So, 'basketball', 'hockey', and 'football' are replaced with 'golf', 'curling', and 'darts'.

Implementing special types of arrays

JavaScript doesn't natively provide a custom object to represent specialized collections or arrays. Instead, methods are provided on the *Array* object that allows you to implement various types of specialized collections such as a queue or a stack.

A queue is essentially a first-in-first-out type of collection. Whenever items are added to the list, they should go at the end of the line. In contrast, a is a last-in-first-out type of collection in which the last item put on the stack is the first item you can take out of the stack. The array methods that facilitate this type of behavior are *pop*, *push*, *shift*, and *unshift*.

Using the *pop* and *push* methods

The *pop* and *push* methods provide stack functionality. The *push* method appends the specified items to the end of the array. The *pop* method removes the last item from the array. The following code demonstrates the *push* method:

```
var sports = new Array();
sports.push('soccer', 'basketball', 'hockey');
sports.push('football');
```

This code creates an *Array* object, and then inserts (pushes) three items into the array. The items are added to the stack in the same order in which they appear in the parameter list. Next, the code pushes one additional item onto the stack. The *pop* method removes and returns the last item in the array:

```
var nextSport = sports.pop();
```

When this code runs, the *nextSport* variable holds the value 'football' because that was the last value added to the array.

> **NOTE**   **USING *PUSH* AND *POP* ON ANY ARRAY**
>
> You can use the *pop* and *push* methods in any context to add and remove items from the end of an array. The stack concept is useful but isn't a confining mechanism that limits use of these methods to just stack arrays.

Using the *shift* and *unshift* methods

The *shift* and *unshift* methods work in the exact opposite way from the *pop* and *push* methods. The *shift* method removes and returns the first element of the array, whereas the *unshift* method inserts new elements at the beginning of the array. The following code uses the *shift* and *unshift* methods:

```
var sports = new Array();
sports.unshift('soccer', 'basketball', 'hockey');
sports.unshift('football');
var nextSport = sports.shift();
```

The net result of this code is exactly the same as for the *pop* and *push* code, except the operations occur at the front of the array instead of the end. In other words, this example still illustrates the stack functionality of "last in, first out."

Taken together, the two concepts you've just seen (*pop/push* and *shift/unshift*) can be combined to create the concept of a first-in-first-out queue. The following code demonstrates using a queue in which the front of the line is the beginning of the array and the end of the line is the end of the array:

```
var sports = new Array();
sports.push('soccer');
sports.push('basketball');
sports.push('hockey');
var get1 = sports.shift();
sports.push('golf');
var get2 = sports.shift();
```

This code first pushes some items into the array. This means that each item is added to the end of the array. When an item is needed from the array, the *shift* method gets the first item out of the beginning of the array—the item at index 0. You can easily implement the opposite mechanism by using the *unshift* and *pop* methods, which would achieve the same results but enter and retrieve items from the opposite ends of the array from this example.

Using advanced array methods

This section examines some of the more advanced array methods. These methods all involve the use of a *callback*, which you'll examine in more detail in Objective 2.4, "Implement a callback." If callbacks are a new concept to you, you should study that objective before completing this section.

The *Array* object exposes methods that enable you to process custom logic on every single element in the array. The following sections demonstrate each method.

Using the *every* method

The *every* method lets you process specific logic for each array element to determine whether any of them meet some condition. Look at following code:

```
var evenNumbers = new Array(0, 2, 4, 6, 8, 9, 10, 12);
var allEven = evenNumbers.every(evenNumberCheck, this);
if (allEven) {
    …
} else {
…
}
function evenNumberCheck(value, index, array) {
    return (value % 2) == 0;
}
```

In this code, assume that the evenNumber array is created with a list of what you expected to be all even numbers. To validate this, you can use the *every* method.

The *every* method takes two parameters:

- The name of the function that should be processed for each element
- An optional reference to the array object

The *evenNumberCheck* function called for each item in the array returns *true* or *false* for each item, depending on whether it meets the desired criteria. In this example, the value is tested to ensure that it's an even number. If it is, the function returns *true*; otherwise, it returns *false*. As soon as the *every* method gets the first *false* result for any item in the array, it exits and returns *false*. Otherwise, if all elements in the array return *true*, the *every* method returns *true*. In the preceding code sample, an *if* statement was added to evaluate the return value of the *every* method and take an appropriate action. In this example, the *evenNumber-Check* function returns *false* on the sixth item in the array, because 9 is an odd number, so the test for even fails.

Using the *some* method

The *some* method works very much like the *every* method. The difference is that *some* checks only whether any item in the array meets the criteria. In this case, the *some* method returns *true* if the called function returns *true* for any single element. If all elements in the array return *false*, the *some* method returns *false*. By this definition, you can use *some* to achieve the exact opposite of the *every* method when the *some* method returns *false*. The following code is updated from the previous example so that it uses the *some* method:

```
var evenNumbers = new Array(0, 2, 4, 6, 8, 9, 10, 12);
var allEven = evenNumbers.some(evenNumberCheck, evenNumbers);
if (allEven) {
    …
} else {
    …
}
function evenNumberCheck(value, index, array) {
    return (value % 2) == 0;
}
```

With the code updated to use the *some* method, the return result isn't *true*, because some of the values in the array are even numbers. Had this result returned *false*, you would know that all the elements in the array were odd numbers.

Using the *forEach* method

The *forEach* method enables an application to process some logic against each item in the array. This method runs for every single item and doesn't produce a return value. *forEach* has the same signature as the other methods you've seen so far in this section. The following code demonstrates the *forEach* method:

```
var sportsArray = ['soccer', 'basketball', 'hockey', 'football', 'cricket', 'rugby'];
sportsArray.forEach(offerSport);
function offerSport(value, index, array) {
    var sportsList = document.getElementById("sportsList");
    var bullet = document.createElement("li");
    bullet.innerText = value;
    sportsList.appendChild(bullet);
}
```

In this sample, the code assumes that a list element on the HTML page is ready to be filled with the list of sports, each formatted as a child node. Each element in the list is passed to the function and added as an *<li>* element. The array elements aren't sorted in this case. You can chain the methods together to ensure that the elements are, for example, alphabetized:

```
sportsArray.sort().forEach(offerSport);
```

Like with all the advanced methods shown thus far, the elements are passed to the function in ascending index order. So you could call the *sort* method and chain it together with the *forEach* method to ensure that the elements are displayed to the user in order.

Using the *filter* method

The *filter* method provides a way to remove items for an array based on some processing done in the callback function. The *filter* method returns a new array containing the elements that are included based on a return value of *true* or *false* from the callback function. In the even number example, you can use the *filter* method to scrub the array and ensure that the program continues to use only an array that contains even numbers, as demonstrated here:

```
var evenNumbers = new Array(0, 2, 4, 6, 8, 9, 10, 12);
var allEven = evenNumbers.filter(evenNumberCheck, evenNumbers);

//work with the even numbers....

function evenNumberCheck(value, index, array) {
    return (value % 2) == 0;
}
```

In this example, the *evenNumberCheck* method is the same as the one used previously. However, rather than use the *every* or *any* method to determine the quality of the data with respect to containing only even numbers, the *filter* method simplifies the removal of the odd numbers. You can use any logic in the callback function to process the element and determine whether it should be included in the returned array, such as pattern matching or a database lookup.

Using the *map* method

The *map* method enables you to replace values in the array. Every element in the array is passed to a callback function. The callback function's return value replaces the value for the position in the array that was passed in. The following example demonstrates having every number in an array rounded off appropriately:

```
var money = [12.8, 15.9, 21.7, 35.2];
var roundedMoney = money.map(roundOff, money);
...
function roundOff(value, position, array) {
    return Math.round(value);
}
```

This example provides the square of a series of numbers:

```
var numbers = [1, 2, 3, 4, 5, 6, 7, 8];
var squares = numbers.map(squareNumber, numbers);
...
function squareNumber(value, position, array) {
    return value * value;
}
```

Using the *reduce* and *reduceRight* methods

The *reduce* and *reduceRight* methods are recursive. Each result of the callback function is passed back into the *callback* method as the previous return value along with the current element to be passed in. This provides some interesting scenarios. The *reduce* method processes the elements of the array in ascending order, whereas the *reduceRight* processes the elements of the array in descending order. The following example demonstrates using the *reduce* method to calculate a factorial:

```
var numbers = [1, 2, 3, 4, 5, 6, 7, 8, 9, 10];
var factorials = numbers.reduce(factorial);
function factorial(previous, current) {
    return previous * current;
}
```

In this function, the factorial for 10 is calculated. In the math world, it's denoted as 10!

EXAM TIP

Some advanced functions enable you to change the source array, whereas others don't. This is an important aspect to keep clear.

Implementing iterative control flow

You've seen how to use *if* statements to control program flow. Another concept you can use to control the flow of JavaScript programs is *iterative* flow control, which enables you to loop over a block of code many times. You've already seen some iterative operations when you reviewed the advanced methods on the array object that use callbacks. There, the iterative flow control was built into the various array methods. In this section, you'll examine the native iterative control statements, including *for* and *while* loops.

Using the *for* loop

The *for* loop is useful in cases in which a block of code should run based on a deterministic number of items. In some cases, you might want to iterate over a list of items in an array or list; in other cases, you might want to run a block of code a specific number of times to perform some type of animation or to create a specific number of objects.

The syntax of the *for* loop is as follows:

```
for(<counter>;<expression>;<counter increment>)
{
 <code to run>
}
```

The *for* loop needs three elements: a counter, an expression, and an increment.

- The *counter* variable holds the current number of times the loop has run. You need to initialize the counter appropriately, such as to 1 or 0.

- The *expression* element evaluates the counter against some other value. Its purpose is to set a limit to the number of times the *for* loop runs. For example, if you wanted the loop to run 10 times, you could initialize the counter to 0, and the expression would be counter < 10. Doing so would ensure that the loop would run only while the expression returns true, that is, while the counter variable is less than 10. As soon as the counter equals 10, loop processing would stop, and code processing would continue after the *for* loop.

- With the counter *increment*, the *for* loop must be told how to adjust the counter variable after each loop iteration. The increment can be positive or negative depending on how the loop is set up. You can set the increment so that the loop counts sequentially, or use mathematical operators to increment by a different value.

The code or body of the loop is a block of code surrounded by curly braces. This code section runs for each loop iteration. The following code samples demonstrate various ways to use a *for* loop.

First, here's a simple *for* loop that runs a block of code 10 times:

```
for (var i = 0; i < 10; i++) {
    document.write(i);
}
```

Notice that because the counter is starting at 0, the expression is to be less than 10. If the counter is to start at 1, the expression would be <= 10. This is important to keep an eye on. The counter increment uses the addition shorthand ++ to increase the counter by one on each iteration. The following code goes in the reverse order:

```
for (var i = 10; i > 0; i--) {
    document.write(i);
}
```

In addition to using the increment or decrement operators, you can multiply or divide the counter value. The following code prints out a set of numbers that increase by a factor of 2 up to 100:

```
for(var i= 1; i<100;i*=2){
    document.write(i);
    document.write("<br />");
}
```

The expression piece of the *for* loop doesn't need to be a hard-coded value, like what has been shown so far. Instead, you can derive the expression from the length of an object or another variable, as in this example:

```
var alphabet = 'abcdefghijklmnopqrstuvwxyz';
for (var i = 0; i < alphabet.length; i++) {
    document.write(alphabet[i]);
    document.write("<br />");
}
```

Because a string is just an array of characters, this code can iterate over the string and print each character to the screen. The length of the string determines how many times the loop runs.

Using the *for...in* loop

The *for...in* loop is a method for iterating over an object's properties. Take the following example:

```
var person = { firstName: "Jane", lastName: "Doe", birthDate: "Jan 5, 1925", gender:
"female" };
for (var prop in person) {
    document.write(prop);
}
```

This *for* loop prints out the name of each property on the custom *person* object. If you want the loop to print the property values instead, each property needs to be accessed via the property indexer of the object, as in this example:

```
var person = { firstName: "Jane", lastName: "Doe", birthDate: "Jan 5, 1925", gender:
"female" };
for (var prop in person) {
    document.write(person[prop]);
}
```

Using the *while* loop

The *while* loop lets you run a code block until some condition evaluates to *false*. The construct of the *while* loop is as follows:

```
while(<expression>){
    <code block>
}
```

The expression is something that evaluates to a Boolean. While the expression is *true*, the *while* loop continues to run. The code that runs is contained within the code block inside the braces. The condition must be *true* for the *while* loop to run at all. Because the *while* loop doesn't use an incrementer like the *for* loop does, the code inside the *while* loop must be able to set the expression to *false* as appropriate; otherwise, the loop will be an endless loop. You might actually want to use an endless loop, but you must ensure that the processing of the loop doesn't block the application's main thread. The following code demonstrates a *while* loop:

```
var i = 0;
while (i < 10) {
    //do some work here.
    i++;
}
```

In this code, the *while* loop runs until the variable *i* equals 10. The expression can hold just about anything as long as it evaluates to a Boolean.

The preceding example is fairly deterministic in that you know the loop will run 10 times. However, in some situations a block of code should run until something else changes that could be outside the loop's control. Suppose that an application is moving traffic through an intersection. This type of application could move traffic as long as the traffic signal is green. The following code demonstrates this:

```
var canvas = document.getElementById("canvas1");
while (canvas.styles.backgroundColor == 'green') {
    //move traffic
}
```

This *while* loop will never end until the canvas background is no longer green. The loop depends on logic elsewhere in the application to change the background color of the canvas, such as a timer that controls how long the traffic signal stays green or red.

One other form of the *while* loop is the *do...while* loop.

Using the *do...while* loop

The key difference between the *while* loop and the *do...while* loop is that *do...while* always runs at least the first time. In contrast, the *while* loop first evaluates the expression to determine whether it should run at all, and then continues to run as long as the expression evaluates to *true*. The *do...while* loop always runs once because in this form of loop, the expression logic is at the bottom. The *do...while* loop achieves this with the following structure:

```
do{
  <code block>
}while(<expression>)
```

This code processes the code block, and then while an expression is true, continues to process this code block. The following code segment demonstrates this:

```
var canvas = document.getElementById("canvas1");
do {
    //stop traffic
}while(canvas.styles.backgroundColor == 'red')
```

In this code segment, the logic to stop traffic runs one time. Then, it evaluates the expression that checks whether the background of the canvas is red. The loop continues to run as long as this expression evaluates to *true*.

Short-circuiting the loops

Two mechanisms enable you to short-circuit a loop. The *break* keyword exits the current loop completely, whereas the *continue* keyword breaks out of the code block and continues to the next iteration of the loop.

EXAM TIP

The *break* keyword breaks out of only the currently running loop. If the loop containing the *break* is nested inside another loop, the outer loop continues to iterate as controlled by its own expression.

Thought experiment
Identifying subtleties in syntax

In this thought experiment, apply what you've learned about this objective. You can find answers to these questions in the "Answers" section at the end of this chapter.

Various constructs perform the same function but with a different syntax. For example, the real difference between a *switch* statement and nested *if...else* statements is minimal. Also, the *while* and *for* loops both evaluate a condition to know whether the loop should proceed.

1. When is a *for* loop better than a *while* loop?

2. How is the readability of the code affected?

Objective summary

- The *for* and *for...in* iterate for a known length of values.
- The *while* and *do...while* loops run until a Boolean condition is set to *false*.
- Arrays provide a mechanism in which to create lists of things.

Objective review

1. Which of the following keywords provide iterative control flow?

   A. *if* statement

   B. *switch* statement

   C. *for*

   D. *break*

2. Which of the following array methods combines two arrays?

   A. *join*

   B. *combine*

   C. *split*

   D. *concat*

3. Which iterative control syntax can guarantee that the loop is processed at least once?

   A. *for...in* loop

   B. *while* loop

   C. *do...while* loop

   D. *for* loop

4. Which keyword is used to exit a loop?

   A. *continue*

   B. *break*

   C. *stop*

   D. *next*

Objective 2.2: Raise and handle an event

The browser provides dynamic behavior through events. Actions processed by the browser user can trigger an opportunity for your code to react and create an experience for the user. This opportunity is presented in the form of an event. The DOM elements natively provide events that can be handled, and you can implement custom events on custom objects.

Events typically follow a naming convention. When looking at what events are available on a particular object, you can identify those events as properties that start with the prefix *on*. For example, some common events are *onkeypress* or *onblur*. For events to function, you need to "wire them up" by assigning an event handler. The event handler is a JavaScript function that's called when an action triggers the event. Events are firing all the time in the browser;

however, it is whether or not a handler is assigned that determines whether or not you can run your own code when the event is triggered.

This objective covers how to:

- Use events, including handling an event by using an anonymous function and declaring and handling bubbled events
- Handle DOM events, including OnBlur, OnFocus, and OnClick
- Create custom events

Using events

The reason an API provides events is so that developers can inject their own processing amid all the action taking place in a program. JavaScript enables you to do exactly this throughout the DOM. This section discusses the ability to hook up to these events.

The idea of *hooking up* an event is to tell the browser that when a certain event occurs, it should call a specified function. The function assigned to an event is said to be an *event listener* listening for that event. The need, then, is to assign a function to an event to listen for when that event occurs.

You can hook up an event in three ways:

- Declare it directly in the HTML markup.
- Assign the function to the event property of the element object through JavaScript.
- Use the newer add and remove methods on the element object to associate event handlers.

When assigning event handlers through JavaScript, you have two choices: provide a named function and assign an anonymous function. The difference between these two will be examined.

To get started, you need to understand the concept of a single object common to all DOM event handlers, and that's the event object itself.

Event objects

In general, the event object is a common object available within event handlers that provides metadata about the event. For example, if keyboard events are being handled, you might want to know which key was pressed. If mouse events are being handled, you might want to know which mouse button was pressed. The event object contains all these properties.

The event object is accessed within an event handler function, using the window object as shown:

```
var evnt = window.event;
```

The event object is a property of the window object. In this example, a reference to the event object is assigned to a variable but also can be used directly. Within the context of the current event handler, the event object contains the pertinent information—that is to say, the respective properties are set. For example, in a *keydown* event, the details of the keyboard state are available, but the mouse buttons aren't because they aren't relevant to a *keydown* event.

> **NOTE** **ACCESSING THE EVENT CONTEXT**
>
> In Internet Explorer, the *window* event is the method required to access the event object. However, in some browsers, the event object is passed to the event function as a parameter.

Declarative event handling

Handling events declaratively in the HTML markup is possible by setting up an event handlers line within the HTML elements. This is effectively no different than assigning a value to any other property or attribute of the HTML element. Look at the following HTML sample:

```
<html>
   <head>
      <script>
          function onloadHandler() {
              alert("hello event.");
          }
      </script>
   </head>
   <body onload="onloadHandler();">
   ...
   </body>
</html>
```

In this HTML markup, the *onload* attribute of the body element is assigned JavaScript to run. The *onload* event fires when the document itself is fully loaded into the browser. When the document is loaded, the *onload* event fires, which calls the *onloadHandler* function and in turn shows the alert box. Any events that will be looked at through this objective can be set up this way directly in the HTML markup. Next, you see how to set up events programmatically by assigning the function to the event property in JavaScript.

Assignment event handling

Assigning the event function to the event property through JavaScript is another way to set up event handlers. This method has been around for a long time and is still widely used. For the preceding example of the *onload* event, the following changes are required to reflect assigning an event handler through JavaScript:

```
<html>
    <head>
        <script>
            window.onload = onloadHandler();

            function onloadHandler() {
                alert("hello event.");
            }

        </script>
    </head>
    <body >
        ...
    </body>
</html>
```

In this code, the HTML element for the body is cleaned up and the *onload* event is assigned in JavaScript. The window object isn't the same as the body element, but it demonstrates the concept of assigning code that needs to run as soon as the page is loaded. Notice that the assignment of the *onloadHandler* is in the script block but not inside any function. For this to succeed, the window object must exist. Since the window object is a global object it will exist. However, to access elements of the page, the page must be loaded or the script must run after the renderer processes the HTML. For example, if the page has a canvas and the functionality to enable users to draw on it with a mouse, the event handlers for the mouse activities would have to be assigned either at the bottom of the page or within the window's *onload* event. The *onload* event is triggered when the entire page is loaded, so it's possible to get a reference to the page elements and hook up the event handlers.

A more common way to do this is to assign an anonymous function to the window's *onload* event and hook up all the necessary events. The concept of an anonymous function is discussed shortly. It's used throughout the book as shown here:

```
window.onload = function () {
    //do event setup in here.
}
```

Using the *addEventListener* and *removeEventListener* methods

addEventListener and *removeEventListener* are the two preferred methods to hook up a function to an event and then to remove it later as needed. The *addEventListener* method accepts two required parameters and one optional parameter:

```
addEventListener(<event name>,<event function>,<optional cascade rule>)
```

The event name is the name of the event to be handled. The event name will be as you've seen in the previous examples except without the *on* prefix. For example, the name of the *onload* event is just *load*. The event function is the one that should run when the event occurs, the listener. The optional cascade rule provides some flexibility in how the events move through nested DOM elements. This is examined in more detail later in the discussion on event bubbling.

The *removeEventListener* takes exactly the same parameters. What this implies is that more than one event listener can be added for the same event and then removed. Thinking in the context of a complicated program such as a game, you might need to turn on and off specific event handlers for the same event. Consider the following example:

```
<script>
    window.addEventListener("load", onloadHandler, false);
    window.addEventListener("load", onloadHandler2, false);
    window.addEventListener("load", onloadHandler3, false);

    function onloadHandler() {
        alert("hello event 1.");
    }
    function onloadHandler2() {
        alert("hello event 2.");
    }
    function onloadHandler3() {
        alert("hello event 3.");
    }
</script>
```

Each event fires in the order in which it was added when the window is finished loading. To remove the *onloadHandler2* event, all that's needed is a call to the *removeEventListener*:

```
window.removeEventListener("load", onloadHandler2, false);
```

When handling DOM events, the custom events you create are not a replacement for the built-in functionality provided by the DOM element. The handling of the event allows you to do some custom logic or manipulation, but when event handling is complete, the processing returns back to the JavaScript API, which processes its own implementation for the event. If this isn't desirable, you can stop the event processing.

Using anonymous functions

In the examples so far, event handlers have been assigned via named functions. The advantage to using named functions is that you can later remove event listeners as needed. You can't identify anonymous functions after they are assigned as event listeners to manipulate them. In the example in the preceding section, three event listeners were added to the same event, and then one event was removed. This was possible only because the name of the event listener function was known.

As expected, an anonymous function has no name. It's completely anonymous and can't be called from other code segments. Look at the following example:

```
window.onload = function () {
      }
```

This example is used throughout the book to ensure that the page is fully loaded before accessing elements in the DOM; otherwise, the elements wouldn't be available. The *onload* event for the window object is being assigned an anonymous function. This function doesn't have a name and can't be called by any other code. The inner implementation of the window object runs this function when raising the *onload* event.

In JavaScript, functions are objects that can be assigned to variables. This is how the anonymous function event listener works. It assigns a function object to the *onload* property of the *window* object, which in turn handles the event when the window is completely loaded. You can use anonymous functions in most cases where a function is expected as a parameter also. Take the following code sample:

```
window.addEventListener("load",
function () {
  document.getElementById("outer").addEventListener("click", outerDivClick, false);},
false);
```

In this sample, the *addEventListener* method is used. But instead of passing in the function name to call when the event is triggered, an anonymous function is passed in. The only potential problem with this approach is the ability to later remove the event listener with the *removeEventListener* method. That the following code would work might seem logical:

```
window.removeEventListener("load",
function () {
  document.getElementById("outer").addEventListener("click", outerDivClick, false); },
false);
```

But this isn't the case. Because the event listeners that the *addEventListener* method adds are stored by their signatures, this *removeEventHandler* method can't know the signature of the previous anonymous function. Even passing in the exact same anonymous implementation doesn't work because this isn't the same anonymous function; it's a new one and therefore doesn't match the signature of the added one.

Canceling an event

The ability to cancel event processing can be useful when you want to completely override the implementation of the native functionality of a DOM element. A perfect example is if it was required to override the inherent functionality of an anchor element. An event listener would be set up for the click event. Then in the click event, via the event object, the *returnValue* property is set to false or the function itself can return false. This tells the runtime to stop any further processing of the event. The following code demonstrates this:

```
window.onload = function () {
    var a = document.getElementById("aLink");
    a.onclick = OverrideAnchorClick;
}
function OverrideAnchorClick() {
    //do custom logic for the anchor
    window.event.returnValue = false;
    //or
    //return false;
}
```

In this case, when the anchor is clicked, the custom event handler runs but no further logic is processed. Hence, the navigation typically provided by the *<a>* element is prevented from running. Another aspect to consider is the order in which events run when you are working with a nested DOM element. In this case, the concept that is dealt with is event bubbling.

Declaring and handling bubbled events

Event bubbling is the concept that applies when the HTML document has nested elements. Consider the following HTML example:

```
<style>
    #outer {
        width: 200px;
        height: 200px;
        background-color: red;
    }
    #middle {
        width: 50%;
        height: 50%;
        position: relative;
        top: 25%;
        left: 25%;
        background-color: green;
    }
    #inner {
        width: 50%;
        height: 50%;
        position: relative;
        top: 25%;
        left: 25%;
        background-color: blue;
    }
</style>
<script>
  window.onload = function () {
        document.getElementById("outer").addEventListener("click", outerDivClick, false);
        document.getElementById("middle").addEventListener("click", middleDivClick, false);
        document.getElementById("inner").addEventListener("click", innerDivClick, false);
        document.getElementById("clearButton").addEventListener("click", clearList);
      }
    function outerDivClick() {
```

```
                appendText("outer Div Clicked");
    }

    function middleDivClick() {
                appendText("middle Div Clicked");
    }
    function innerDivClick() {
                appendText("inner Div Clicked");
    }
    function appendText(s) {
                var li = document.createElement("li");
                li.innerText = s;
                document.getElementById("eventOrder").appendChild(li);
    }
    function clearList() {
                var ol = document.createElement("ol");
                ol.id = "eventOrder";
                document.getElementById("bod").replaceChild(ol,document.
                getElementById("eventOrder"));
    }
</script>
<body id="bod">
    <div id="outer">
        <div id="middle" >
            <div id="inner">
            </div>
        </div>
    </div>
    <ol id="eventOrder"> </ol>
    <button type="button" id="clearButton">Clear</button>
</body>
```

When this HTML is rendered in the browser, the result is three nested *div* elements, as shown in Figure 2-2. In this code are three *div* elements stacked on top of each other. The styling is applied to provide a visual distinction between the boxes. When a *div* box is clicked, the click event fires. The event listener code in the assigned handler outputs the name of the clicked *div* to an ordered list so that the order in which the events are clicked is identified.

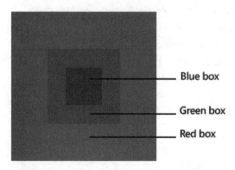

FIGURE 2-2 Three nested *<div>* elements to display the effect of event bubbling

The last parameter of the *addEventListener* method accepts an optional Boolean parameter. This parameter allows you to specify the cascading or bubbling effect of the event—that is to say, in which order the event processing occurs. The click event for each *div* has an event listener assigned. In the preceding example, the three *div* elements are nested. A user who clicks the inside or middle *div* also clicks the parent *div* because the *div* elements share the same physical space on the screen. When the blue inside box is clicked, the following output is displayed:

```
1. inner Div Clicked
2. middle Div Clicked
3. outer Div Clicked
```

One click event triggered all three events to fire. This concept is called event bubbling. Clicking directly on the middle green *div* produces the following output:

```
1. middle Div Clicked
2. outer Div Clicked
```

Finally, clicking the red outer *div* produces this output:

```
1. outer Div Clicked
```

The event has bubbled up to the top. If you prefer to have the events handled in the opposite order—that is, to have them cascade down—the last parameter specified by the *addEventListener* method is specified as true. With this change made, as follows,

```
document.getElementById("outer").addEventListener("click", outerDivClick, true);
document.getElementById("middle").addEventListener("click", middleDivClick, true);
document.getElementById("inner").addEventListener("click", innerDivClick, true);
```

the screen output is now as follows:

```
1. outer Div Clicked
2. middle Div Clicked
3. inner Div Clicked
```

The order of the event processing has reversed to be cascading instead of bubbling.

The cascading or bubbling effect of the events is convenient when you want it. However, the design of the webpage could involve nested elements, but each element's click event should run only if the element is directly clicked. In this case, you can use a property of the event object called *cancelBubble*. If this property is set to true, the event bubbling or cascading stops with the event listener that sets it. This stops only the bubbling or cascading behavior. The code to cancel the bubbling of the event is added to the inner *div* element's event listener:

```
function innerDivClick() {
    appendText("inner Div Clicked");
    window.event.cancelBubble = true;
}
```

Now, when the inner *div* is clicked, the output is as follow:

```
1. inner Div Clicked
```

The bubbling of the event up to the middle *div* and outer *div* has been prevented.

Handling DOM events

The DOM provides a large number of built-in events. The most common events used on a more day-to-day basis are covered in this section. The DOM provides these events via the JavaScript API. Functions can be specified as event listeners, and custom behavior can be implemented onto webpages based on the event occurring. These events apply to most DOM elements.

Change events

A change event occurs when the value associated with an element changes. This most commonly occurs in input elements such as text-based inputs and others such as the range element. An example of the change event in action is shown here:

```
<script>
    window.onload = function () {
        document.getElementById("aRange").addEventListener("change", rangeChangeEvent);
    }

    function rangeChangeEvent() {
        document.getElementById("rangeValue").innerText = this.value;
    }

</script>
...
<body>
    <input id="aRange" type="range" max="200" min="0" value="0"/>
    <div id="rangeValue"></div>
</body>
```

In this example, as the range slider control changes with the mouse dragging it from one side to the other, the *div* displays the value of the slider bar.

EXAM TIP

This example uses the *this* keyword. In this context, the *this* keyword provides a direct reference to the element that created the event. In this way, *this* provides shortcut access to the element rather than gets a reference via one of the document search methods.

With the text input control, the same type of code can be processed:

```
...
document.getElementById("aText").addEventListener("change", rangeChangeEvent);
...
<body>
    <input id="aRange" type="range" max="200" min="0" value="0"/>
    <input id="aText" type="text"/>
    <div id="rangeValue"></div>
</body>
```

Now when the *text* value of the text box changes, the *div* shows the value. The text box change event is raised when the cursor leaves the text box, not as each character is typed.

Focus events

Focus events occur when an element receives or loses the focus. Table 2-2 lists the available events related to focus.

TABLE 2-2 The DOM focus events

Event	Description
focus	Raised when the element receives the focus
blur	Raised when the element loses the focus
focusin	Raised just before an element receives the focus
focusout	Raised just before an element loses the focus

The number of focus events provide very good flexibility in how the focus of any particular DOM element is handled with respect to the timing. The *blur* event is commonly used to validate form fields. You can use the *focus()* method to set the focus to any element that causes the *focus* event hierarchy to occur. The following code shows how to use the *blur* event:

```
<script>
    window.onload = function () {
        document.getElementById("firstNameText").focus();
        document.getElementById("firstNameText").addEventListener("blur", function () {
            if (this.value.length < 5) {
                document.getElementById("ruleViolation").innerText =
'First Name is required to be 5 letters.';
                document.getElementById("ruleViolation").style.color = 'red';
                this.focus();
            }
        });
    }
</script>
```

Keyboard events

Keyboard events occur when keys are pressed on the keyboard. The keyboard events in Table 2-3 are available to be captured.

TABLE 2-3 Available keyboard events

Event	Description
keydown	Raised when a key is pushed down
keyup	Raised when a key is released
keypress	Raised when a key is completely pressed

The following example listens for the *keydown* event on the text box and shows the *keycode* for the pressed key:

```
document.getElementById("firstNameText").addEventListener("keydown", function () {
    document.getElementById("outputText").innerText = window.event.keyCode;
});
```

Code such as this can be used to filter out invalid characters from being entered into a text box. With keyboard events, extra properties are available on the event object to help out. For example, you might need to know whether the Shift key or Control key was also being pressed. Table 2-4 lists the event object properties for keyboard events.

TABLE 2-4 Event object properties for keyboard events

Property	Description
altKey	A Boolean value to indicate whether the Alt key was pressed
keyCode	The numeric code for the key that was pressed
ctrlKey	A Boolean value as to whether the Control key was pressed
shiftKey	A Boolean value as to whether the Shift key was pressed

EXAM TIP

In some cases, depending on the key, only the *keydown* event fires. The arrow keys are such an example: *keydown* fires but not *keyup* or *keypress*.

You can use properties such as *ctrlKey* with the *keyCode* event to give the users something similar to hotkey functionality to automatically navigate the focus to specific fields:

```
document.onkeydown = function () {
    if (window.event.ctrlKey && String.fromCharCode(window.event.keyCode) == 'F')
        document.getElementById("firstNameText").focus();
    if (window.event.ctrlKey && String.fromCharCode(window.event.keyCode) == 'L')
        document.getElementById("lastNameText").focus();
    return false;
}
```

Mouse events

The DOM provides extensive exposure to mouse activity through the mouse events. Table 2-5 describes the available mouse events.

TABLE 2-5 Available mouse events

Event	Description
click	Raised when the mouse performs a click

Event	Description
dblclick	Raised when the mouse performs a double-click
mousedown	Raised when the mouse button is pressed down
mouseup	Raised when the mouse button is released
mouseenter or *mouseover*	Raised when the mouse cursor enters the space of an HTML element
mouseleave	Raised when the mouse cursor leaves the space of an HTML element
mousemove	Raised when the mouse cursor moves over an HTML element

The mouse events provide additional information on the event object. Table 2-6 lists the applicable properties of the event object.

TABLE 2-6 Properties of the mouse event

Property	Description
clientX	The x or horizontal position of the mouse cursor relative to the viewport boundaries
clientY	The y or vertical position of the mouse cursor relative to the viewport boundaries
offsetX	The x or horizontal position of the mouse cursor relative to the target element
offsetY	The y or vertical position of the mouse cursor relative to the target element
screenX	The x or horizontal position of the mouse cursor relative to the upper-left corner of the screen
screenY	The y or vertical position of the mouse cursor relative to the upper-left corner of the screen

The following code demonstrates capturing each coordinate set:

```
window.onload = function () {
    document.getElementById("yellowBox").addEventListener("click", yellowBoxClick);
}
function yellowBoxClick() {
    document.write("Client X: " + window.event.clientX + " ClientY: "
      + window.event.clientY);
    document.write("<BR />");
    document.write("offsetX: " + window.event.offsetX + " offsetY: "
      + window.event.offsetY);
    document.write("<BR />");
    document.write("screen X: " + window.event.screenX + " screenY: "
      + window.event.screenY);
}
```

This code assumes a *div* called *yellowBox* that raises its click event when the mouse clicks it. You can easily change the event to *mousedown* or *mouseup* to achieve the same outcome.

The *mouseenter* and *mouseleave* events indicate when the mouse cursor position has entered or left the area covered by a particular element, respectively. The following code demonstrates applying a transformation to the *div* element on the *mouseenter* and removing it on the *mouseleave*:

```
<style>
    .scale {
        transform:scale(1.5);
    }
</style>
<script>
window.onload = function () {
    document.getElementById("yellowBox").addEventListener("mouseenter",
        yellowBoxEnter);
    document.getElementById("yellowBox").addEventListener("mouseleave",
        yellowBoxLeave);
}
function yellowBoxEnter() {
    this.classList.add("scale");
}
function yellowBoxLeave() {
    this.classList.remove("scale");
}
</script>
<body>
  <div id="yellowBox" style="width: 50%;height:50%;margin: 0 auto;
      background-color:yellow;"></div>
</body>
```

When the mouse moves over the yellow-filled *div*, the *div* scales up. When the mouse is moved off the *div*, it returns to the original size.

Drag-and-drop functionality

Drag-and-drop functionality enables users to pick up an element with the mouse and place it in another location. Table 2-7 lists the events related to drag-and-drop functionality.

TABLE 2-7 Events available to drag and drop

Event	Description
drag	Raised continuously while the element is being dragged
dragend	Raised on the element being dragged when the mouse is released to end the drop operation
dragenter	Raised on a target element when a dragged element is dragged into its space
dragleave	Raised on a target element when a dragged element leaves its space
dragover	Raised continuously on the target element while the dragged element is being dragged over it
dragstart	Raised on the element being dragged when the drag operation is beginning
drop	Raised on the target element when the dragged element is released

A lot happens in a drag-and-drop operation, starting with the *dragstart* event. The *drag* event continues to fire while the element is being dragged. As the element is dragged over other elements, each of those other elements' *dragenter*, *dragover*, and *dragleave* events fire. When the element finishes being dragged, its *dragend* event fires and the *drop* event of a target element fires. You can use all these events in combination to provide visual feedback to users that the drag operation is occurring and what might be a potentially valid drop location.

The following HTML demonstrates this functionality:

```
<head>
  <style>
      .dropped {
        width: 50%;
        height: 50%;
        position: relative;
        top: 25%;
        left: 25%;
        background-color:black;
      }
      .over {
        transform: scale(1.1);
      }
      .bucket {
        width: 100px;
        height: 100px;
        margin: 10px 10px 10px 10px;
        position:absolute;
      }
      .chip {
        width:20px;
        height:20px;
        position:absolute;
      }
      div:first-of-type {
        background-color: red;
      }
      div:nth-of-type(2) {
        background-color: green;
        left:25%;
      }
      div:nth-of-type(3) {
        background-color: blue;
        left:50%;
      }
      #chip {
        background-color: black;
        width:50px;
        height:50px;
      }
      .begin {
        position:absolute;
        left: 150px;
        top: 150px;
      }
```

```
        </style>
</head>
<body>
    <div id="bucket1" class="bucket"></div>
    <div id="bucket2" class="bucket"></div>
    <div id="bucket3" class="bucket"></div>
    <div id="chip" draggable="true" class="chip"></div>
</body>
```

The concept is that three buckets are defined by using *div* elements, and a chip is defined. The user can drag the chip into any one of the three buckets. For the chip to be able to be dragged, it must be draggable.

To begin the drag event, the *dragstart* must be handled:

```
var chip = document.getElementById("chip");
chip.addEventListener("dragstart", function ()
{ window.event.dataTransfer.setData("Text", this.id); });
```

In this handler, the *dataTransfer* object *setData* method is used to store what exactly is being transferred. In this case, the ID of the source object is specified.

Next, the desired target element's event listeners must be set up. The following code shows this:

```
var b1 = document.getElementById("bucket1");
b1.addEventListener("dragenter", function () {
        b1.classList.add("over");
        window.event.returnValue = false;
});
b1.addEventListener("dragleave", function () {
        b1.classList.remove("over");
});
b1.addEventListener("dragover", function () {
        window.event.returnValue = false;
});
b1.addEventListener("drop", function () {
        window.event.returnValue = false;
        var data = event.dataTransfer.getData("Text");
        var d = document.getElementById(data);
        d.classList.remove("begin");
        d.classList.add("dropped");
        this.appendChild(d);
});
```

In this code, the *dragenter* event listener is established so that the user gets a visual cue with a transform that the element can be dropped onto. In the same token, the *dragleave* event listener is set up to remove the effect. The *dragover* event is set to be ignored by canceling it. This is only because *div* elements can't be dragged and dropped by default.

The last piece is the *drop* event handler. With this event handler, the drop is received. The *dataTransfer* object's *getData* method is called to retrieve what's being dropped. The ID of the source element gets a reference to the element and places it inside the target. The same code can be repeated for the other two buckets, and then the chip can be dragged into each bucket.

Creating custom events

DOM events provide a great deal of functionality. In some cases, you might want to create a custom event to use more generically. To create a custom event, you use the *CustomEvent* object.

To use custom events, you first need to create one by using the *window.CustomEvent* object:

```
myEvent = new CustomEvent(
    "anAction",
    {
        detail: { description: "a description of the event",
                  timeofevent: new Date(),
                  eventcode: 2 },
        bubbles: true,
        cancelable: true
    }
);
```

The *CustomEvent* object constructor accepts two parameters:

- The first parameter is the name of the event. This is anything that makes sense for what the event is supposed to represent. In this example, the event is called *anAction*.

- The second parameter is a dynamic object that contains a detail property that can have properties assigned to it containing information that should be passed to the event handler. Also, the parameter provides the ability to specify if the event should bubble and whether the event can be canceled.

The next step is to assign the event to an element on the page by using the *addEventListener* method:

```
document.addEventListener("anAction", customEventHandler);
```

Finally, the event is raised by using the *dispatchEvent* method:

```
document.dispatchEvent(myEvent);
```

A function called *customEventHandler* must exist for all this to work:

```
function customEventHandler() {
    alert(window.event.detail.description);
}
```

EXAM TIP

As of this writing, Internet Explorer doesn't support this functionality. Custom events work correctly in other browsers, though. Be aware of how custom events work for the exam, however, because they are part of the official skills being measured.

Thought experiment
Creating an event-full webpage

In this thought experiment, apply what you've learned about this objective. You can find answers to these questions in the "Answers" section at the end of this chapter.

Consider an application where fields become auto-populated based on user input in other fields. Auto-population is seen sometimes on forms that require users to fill in their address. When the postal code is entered, the city, country/region, and so on are populated based on that information. How would you apply the proper event to a form that contains text boxes, check boxes, option buttons, slider bars, and so on, so that as the form is filled in, other fields are populated automatically? Perhaps when a field is filled automatically, its value triggers other fields to be populated. How can you implement the solution, considering the timing of when events are triggered?

Objective summary

- Events provide a way to interact with users when they perform actions on the webpage.
- Events cascade or bubble through the entire DOM hierarchy.
- Focus events occur when an object gets or loses focus.
- Keyboard events occur when keyboard keys are pressed on a focused object.
- Mouse events occur when the mouse clicks an object or the pointer is moved over or off an object.
- Drag-and-drop functionality provides a way to move elements from one container to another.

Objective review

1. Which of the following isn't a supported way to add an event handler to a DOM element?

   A. Declaring within the HTML element by assigning the event attribute to a JavaScript function

   B. Setting the attribute in CSS to a valid JavaScript function

   C. Dynamically through JavaScript by assigning a JavaScript function to the object's event property

   D. Dynamically through JavaScript via the assign/remove event listener methods

2. Which of the following isn't an attribute of an anonymous function?

   A. Anonymous functions can't be called by any other code.

   B. Anonymous functions have a clearly defined name.

   C. Anonymous functions can be passed as parameters.

   D. Anonymous functions can't be assigned to a DOM element declaratively.

3. Which code line would successfully cancel an event?

   A. *window.event.returnValue = false;*

   B. *return false;*

   C. *window.event.Return();*

   D. *window.Stop();*

4. Which event occurs when a DOM element receives the cursor?

   A. *focus*

   B. *change*

   C. *keydown*

   D. *mouseleave*

5. Which option provides the correct sequence of events in a drag-and-drop operation?

   A. *dragstart, drag, dragenter, drop*

   B. *dragstart, drag, dragenter, dragstop*

   C. *drag, dragstart, drop, dragenter*

   D. *drag, dragstart, dragenter, dragstop*

Objective 2.3: Implement exception handling

That a program can deal with errors and unknown conditions is critical in any software development. JavaScript is no exception and provides structured error-handling constructs to deal with these situations.

Structured error handling in JavaScript is achieved with the *try...catch...finally* construct. Good defensive programming also includes checking for null values, where appropriate, to prevent errors. In addition to handling errors, code can raise custom errors as needed to send error information back to a running program from custom objects or libraries.

This objective covers using the *try...catch...finally* construct, evaluating for the null condition, and raising custom errors.

> **This objective covers how to:**
>
> - Implement *try-catch-finally* blocks, including setting and responding to error codes and throwing exceptions
> - Check for null values

Implementing *try...catch...finally* constructs

The *try...catch...finally* construct handles exceptions that occur during program processing. It enables you to see what kind of error occurred and to do what's appropriate with it. If *try... catch...finally* isn't implemented in the program, the errors would be treated as unhandled and could cause the browser to crash or, at a minimum, display many annoying message boxes to users, such as this one shown in Figure 2-3 that is caused from this code:

```
window.dosomeunsupportedmethod();
```

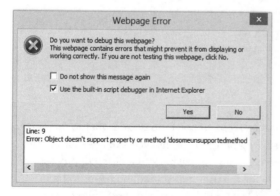

FIGURE 2-3 An unhandled exception error dialog box

With errors like this, users will likely stop coming to the website or using the application. To prevent such issues, you need to wrap the code in a try block:

```
try{
    window.dosomeunsupportedmethod();
} catch (e) {
    alert("Browser does not support the desired functionality.");
}
```

By using the *try...catch* block, you can handle the error condition gracefully. The users see a standard alert and the webpage continues to run as usual. This example code results in the message shown in Figure 2-4.

FIGURE 2-4 A clean message box to show errors

The *try...catch* block is divided into two parts. The first part, the *try* portion, says, "Try to do this work." If anything goes wrong when trying to do the work, the *catch* block receives an *exception* object with information about the error. Any code inside the try portion of the *try...catch* block is protected against encountering an unhandled error.

The *catch* block is where the error can be handled as appropriate for the application. The *catch* block receives a parameter that is an *exception* object. Table 2-8 shows the properties for the *exception* object.

TABLE 2-8 Properties available on the *exception* object

Property	Description
message	A textual description of the error that occurred
number	A numeric error code
name	The name of the *exception* object

You can use the information provided in the *exception* object to decide what to do in terms of overall program flow. For example, if the program needs access to a resource that it can't have and an exception is thrown, the program can fall back to a different process to achieve the desired functionality or simply tell the user that something needs to be changed—for example, if cookies or another HTML5 API are required for the site to work. Other ways to check for this type of thing are demonstrated shortly.

Another part to the *try...catch* block is the *finally* block. This block is added directly after the *catch* block. The significance of the *finally* block is that the code inside it runs all the time. This isn't to say that the code in the *finally* block can't have its own errors resulting in exceptions, but whether or not the code in the *try* block has an error, the code in the *finally* block still runs. Consider the following code:

```
function WorkthroughArray() {
    var canvas = document.getElementById("myCanvas");
    var context = canvas.getContext("2d");
    context.fillStyle = "blue";

    contxt.arc(50, 50, 25, 0, 360);

    context.fill();
    context.strokeStyle = "red";
    context.stroke();
}
```

This function contains an intentional spelling error, contxt, which results in an exception. Nothing after the line that causes the exception runs. However, placing a *try...catch...finally* block around this code provides more control over the flow:

```
try{

    var canvas = document.getElementById("myCanvas");
    var context = canvas.getContext("2d");
    context.fillStyle = "blue";

    contxt.arc(50, 50, 25, 0, 360);

    context.fill();
    context.strokeStyle = "red";
    context.stroke();
}
catch (e) {
    console.log(e.message);
}
finally {
    //do any final logic before exiting the method
}
```

Now, with the structured error handling in place, when the line with the typo is hit, processing jumps into the *catch* block. In this block, the error could be logged for future diagnostics. After the *catch* block completes, the *finally* block runs. If any cleanup or variable resetting needs to be done, it can be done here even though an exception occurs. The *finally* block also runs. If the typo is fixed so that no exceptions occur in the *try* block, the *catch* doesn't occur because of nothing to catch, but the *finally* block still runs. The *finally* block always runs as the last part of a *try...catch...finally* block.

Variable scope applies to each block within the *try...catch* block. If a variable is declared within the *try* portion, it won't be accessible from the catch of the *finally*. If you want to have access in those blocks, the variables need to be declared outside the *try* block. Look at this example:

```
var canvas;
var context;
try {
    document.getElementById("myCanvas");
    context = canvas.getContext("2d");
    contxt.arc(50, 50, 25, 0, 360);
    context.fillStyle = "blue";
    context.fill();
    context.strokeStyle = "red";
    context.stroke();
}
catch (e) {
    context.strokeText(e.message, 50, 50);
    console.log(e.message);
}
finally {
    //do any final logic before exiting the method
}
```

The declaration for the reference to the canvas and the canvas context is moved outside the *try* block so that it can be accessible in the *catch* block. The *catch* block can now write the error to the canvas.

> **NOTE   USING DEBUGGING TOOLS**
>
> A call to console.log was added to the *catch* block. This is a great way to add information that can be viewed in the client debugger. For example, in Internet Explorer, you can access the debugger tools by pressing F12.

Exceptions bubble up the call stack, a special stack in the processing environment that represents the functions currently being processed in sequential order. Take the following code sample:

```
window.onload = function () {
    try {
        WorkWithCanvas();
    } catch (e) {
        console.log(e.message);
    }
}

function WorkWithCanvas() {
    var canvas = document.getElementById("myCanvas");
    var context = canvas.getContext("2d");
    contxt.arc(50, 50, 25, 0, 360);
    context.fillStyle = "blue";
    context.fill();
    context.strokeStyle = "red";
    context.stroke();
}
```

Because the *WorkWithCanvas* method has no exception handling, the exception bubbles up to the calling method, the next method in the stack. This continues through the stack until either an exception handler is met or the browser receives the exception and treats it as an unhandled exception. Of course, in this case, the variables in the *WorkWithCanvas* method can't be accessed, so if anything needed to be done in a *finally* block, the *try...catch...finally* block should be either moved into the *WorkWithCanvas* method, or the *WorkWithCanvas* method can handle the error and rethrow it for further processing.

The concept of raising an error is also known as *throwing an exception*. Custom objects and libraries throw exceptions as needed to the consumers of the libraries. The objects or libraries expect you to meet certain conditions and if those conditions aren't met, they can throw an exception for the consumer to deal with. To continue with the example, the exception is handled in the *WorkWithCanvas* method and then rethrown. An exception is thrown using the throw keyword:

```
function WorkWithCanvas() {
    try {
        var canvas = document.getElementById("myCanvas");
        var context = canvas.getContext("2d");
        contxt.arc(50, 50, 25, 0, 360);
        context.fillStyle = "blue";
        context.fill();
        context.strokeStyle = "red";
        context.stroke();
    } catch (e) {
        //handle the exception as appropriate
        throw e;
    } finally {
    }
}
```

In this example, the exception can be handled in the *catch* block as needed, and then thrown back up the call stack to be handled again at another level.

More commonly when working with custom libraries, you can create custom exceptions to give users information specific to the situation that occurred:

```
var ball = {
    x: -1,
    y: -1,
    draw: function DrawBall(c) {
        if (this.x < 0)
            throw new Error(25, "Invalid X coordinate");
        }
}
window.onload = function () {
    try {
        var canvas = document.getElementById("myCanvas");
        var context = canvas.getContext("2d");
        ball.draw(context);
    } catch (e) {
        alert(e.message);
    }
}
```

In this code, a custom object to represent a ball is created. It has a draw method that expects a canvas context to draw itself on. However, if the coordinates for the ball aren't initialized, the ball object throws a custom error. The calling code has a *try...catch* block so that it can handle any unexpected errors. In this example, the consumer of the ball object would get a meaningful message that the x-coordinate needs to be set to something valid.

A new object, *Error*, is used here to create the exception. The *Error* object constructor takes two parameters, in this order: the error number followed by an error description. This information should be as specific as possible to provide as much detail as possible to the calling code.

Checking for null values

One way to prevent many errors is to check for null values before using something. A null value in a JavaScript program is what a variable equals before it's initialized. JavaScript knows about the variable's existence but doesn't yet have a value.

A common place to ensure that variables have values is in functions that accept parameters. Consider the following function:

```
window.onload = function () {
    try {
        var a, b, c;
        a = 5;
        b = 10;
        var result = multiplyNumbers(a, b, c);
        alert(result);
    } catch (e) {
        alert(e.message);
    }
}
function multiplyNumbers(first, second, third) {
    if (first == null || second == null || third == null)
    {
        throw new Error(5, "Forgot to initialize a number.");
    }
    return first * second * third;
}
```

In this code, the developer forgot to initialize the variable *c*, resulting in a null value. In the *multiplyNumbers* method, the parameters are evaluated for a null value and, if found, an error is thrown. If this method didn't check for null values and assumed that every developer calling it would never make a mistake, the results would be unexpected to the consumer of the method. In this case, the result would be NaN (not a number), a special JavaScript type. This is because of the attempt to perform a mathematical operation against a null value.

Thought experiment
Micromanaging exceptions

In this thought experiment, apply what you've learned about this objective. You can find answers to these questions in the "Answers" section at the end of this chapter.

The reason behind exception handling is, obviously, to handle exceptions. In some cases, error conditions can be predicted and if the situation occurs, it's handled and resolved. In this case, you might not want to simply wrap an entire code block into a big *try...catch* block and have the application fail to proceed.

How would you incorporate the use of *try...catch* blocks into a longer JavaScript routine with multiple points of potential error? Some errors can be corrected, and some might not be. The correctable errors should allow the script to continue successfully.

Objective summary

- Structured error handling is provided by the JavaScript language in the form of the *try...catch...finally* block.

- The *try...catch...finally* block provides a way to try some logic, catch an error and handle it appropriately, and finally do some clean up.

- The *finally* block always runs whether or not an exception is thrown.

- Checking for a null value before accessing any objects to ensure that they are initialized is good practice.

Objective review

1. Which statement correctly describes the proper error handling using *try...catch...finally* blocks?

   A. Proper error handling allows code processing to continue and to provide appropriate user feedback.

   B. Proper error handling allows users to fix problems with the webpage.

   C. Proper error handling allows you to debug the application at run time.

   D. Proper error handling allows you to suppress all the bugs in your scripts.

2. Which of the following isn't a property of the exception object?

   A. *message*

   B. *description*

   C. *number*

   D. *name*

3. Why is checking for null a good practice?

   A. Checking for null prevents the use of an object before it's initialized.

   B. Checking for null prevents errors resulting in NaN.

   C. Checking for null prevents the need to throw custom errors.

Objective 2.4: Implement a callback

Callbacks are a design pattern to implement when you are working with multiple threads or just needing to have something work asynchronously. The concept of the callback is quite straightforward and is used throughout this book quite heavily. The idea of a callback is to call a function to run but when it's done, to call back a specified function with usually some sort of result or status of the operation. The "Using advanced array methods" section earlier in this chapter demonstrates a few of the functions available on the array object that take a callback as a parameter. The general pattern is shown here:

```
<script>
    window.onload = function () {
        WillCallBackWhenDone(MyCallBack, 3, 3);
    }
    function WillCallBackWhenDone(f, a, b) {
        var r = a * b;
        f(r);
    }
    function MyCallBack(result) {
        alert(result);
    }
</script>
```

In this code example, two functions are declared: *WillCallBackWhenDone* and *MyCallBack*. One parameter to the *WillCallBackWhenDone* function is a function followed by two other variables, which in this case are numbers that will be multiplied. The product of the multiplication is passed to the callback function. This case is a bit over the top for the usage of callbacks, but it does demonstrate the pattern involved. Anytime a function is called that expects a function as a parameter, this is what it's doing. Knowing what parameters the callback function will receive is important so that they can be specified in the parameter list.

Another common use for callbacks is as events. Whenever a DOM event is fired, it's using a callback pattern. A function is provided as a parameter or property to indicate that when specific things occur, such as a *mouseover*, to call back to the specified function to run some custom logic related to the end-user action.

Many APIs that JavaScript and the browser expose as part of the HTML5 specification involve the use of callbacks. In this objective, the WebSocket API is examined. Also, the use of jQuery is introduced as it applies to making Asynchronous JavaScript and XML (AJAX) calls. The ability to wire up an event and implement a callback using anonymous functions is also discussed. Finally, this objective covers the use of the *this* pointer.

This objective covers how to:

- Implement bidirectional communication with the WebSocket API
- Make webpages dynamic with jQuery and AJAX
- Wire up an event with jQuery
- Implement a callback with an anonymous function
- Use the *this* pointer

Implementing bidirectional communication with the WebSocket API

The WebSocket API provides bidirectional communication support to your web applications. WebSocket has greatly simplified the way data can be sent and received. Traditional methods, such as long polling, have existed for a long time and are widely used all over the web today. However, traditional techniques use the heavier HTTP mechanisms, which make the application inherently less efficient. The use of the WebSocket API allows the connection directly to a server over a socket. This is a much lighter weight connection and is fully bidirectional; both binary and text-based data can be sent and received.

NOTE **ACCEPTING SOCKET CONNECTIONS**

The full implementation of a WebSocket API requires that a webserver have a proper server-side implementation that can accept socket connections. Technologies such as Node.js work well for this purpose. Implementation of such technologies is beyond the scope of this book, and these code samples assume such an implementation exists.

The use of the WebSocket API is ideal for real-time applications such as messenger/chat applications, server-based games, and more advanced scenarios, such as WebRTC (Web

Real-Time Communication) video conferencing. The data transmitted over WebSockets can be text based or binary. The code in Listing 2-1 demonstrates the WebSocket API.

LISTING 2-1 Implementation of the WebSocket API

```
<script type="text/javascript">
    window.onload = function () {
        var wsConnection;
        var chatBox = document.getElementById("chatWindow");
        var disconnectButton = document.getElementById("Disconnect");
        var connectButton = document.getElementById("Connect");
        var sendButton = document.getElementById("Send");
        var msgToSend = document.getElementById("msgSendText");
        disconnectButton.onclick = function () {
            wsConnection.close();
        }
        connectButton.onclick = function () {
            //Or the use of wss for secure WebSockets. IE: wss://studygroup.70480.com
            //Opens the WebSocket
            wsConnection= new WebSocket('ws://studygroup.70480.com', ['soap', 'xmpp']);
        }
        sendButton.onclick = function () {
            //check the state of the connection
            if (wsConnection.readyState == WebSocket.OPEN) {
                //send message to server.
                wsConnection.send(msgToSend.value);
            }
            else
                return;
            //show message in chat window.
            NewLine();
            chatBox.value = chatBox.value + "You: " + msgToSend.value;
            //clear message text box
            msgToSend.value = '';
        }
        // event handler for when the WebSocket connection is established
        wsConnection.onopen = function () {

            chatBox.textContent = chatBox.textContent +
            "System: Connection has been established";
        }
        //event handler for when the WebSocket encounters an error
        wsConnection.onerror = function (err) {
            //write an error to the screen
            NewLine();
            chatBox.value = chatBox.value + "System: Error Occurred. ";
        }
        wsConnection.onclose = function () {
            //write the connection has been closed.
            NewLine();
            chatBox.value = chatBox.value + "System: Connection has been closed.";
        }
```

```
            wsConnection.onmessage = function (msg) {
                //write message
                NewLine();
                chatBox.value = chatBox.value + "Them: " + msg.data;
            }
            //helper functions.
            function NewLine()
            {
                chatBox.textContent = chatBox.textContent + '\r\n';
            }
        }
    }
</script>
<body>
    <div align="center">
        <div>
            70-480 Study Group Chat Forum
        </div>
        <div>
            <textarea id="chatWindow" style="height: 500px; width: 300px">
            </textarea>
        </div>
        <div>
            <input type="text" id="msgSendText" style="width: 300px"/>
        </div>
        <div>
            <button id="Disconnect">Disconnect</button>
            <button id="Connect">Connect</button>
            <button id="Send">Send</button>
        </div>
    </div>
</body>
```

The primary object that you will work with is the *WebSocket* object, which connects to the socket when its constructor is invoked. In Listing 2.1, a variable is declared but not instantiated until a user invokes the connect button. When the user clicks the button, the *WebSocket* is instantiated with the appropriate connection information:

```
wsConnection=  new WebSocket('ws://studygroup.70480.com', ['soap', 'xmpp']);
```

The *WebSocket* constructor accepts two parameters:

- The URL of the server-side socket to connect to, which is always prefixed with *ws* or *wss* for secure *WebSocket* connections
- An optional list of subprotocols

When the *WebSocket* constructor is called, the WebSocket API establishes a connection to the server. One of two things can happen at this stage. The *WebSocket* will successfully connect to the server or the connection will fail, resulting in an error. Both cases should be handled so that the proper feedback is provided to the application user. The WebSocket API provides an event for each, called *onopen* and *onerror,* as shown earlier in Listing 2-1:

```
// event handler for when the WebSocket connection is established
wsConnection.onopen = function () {
    chatBox.textContent = chatBox.textContent +
        "System: Connection has been established";
}
//event handler for when the WebSocket encounters an error
wsConnection.onerror = function (err) {
    //write an error to the screen
    NewLine();
    chatBox.value = chatBox.value + "System: Error Occurred.";
}
```

In this example, both event handlers are providing feedback in the chat window to let users know of either a successful connection or the occurrence of an error. The error event could happen at any time, not just when establishing the initial connection.

When a successful connection is established, you can send and receive messages over the socket. To send messages, the WebSocket API provides the *Send* function. To receive messages, the WebSocket API provides the *onmessage* event handler. These two methods show the functions and events that handle the bidirectional communication:

```
wsConnection.onmessage = function (msg) {
    //write message
    NewLine();
    chatBox.value = chatBox.value + "Them: " + msg.data;
}
sendButton.onclick = function () {
    //check the state of the connection
    if (wsConnection.readyState == WebSocket.OPEN) {
        //send message to server.
        wsConnection.send(msgToSend.value);
    }
    else
        return;
    //show message in chat window.
    NewLine();
    chatBox.value = chatBox.value + "You: " + msgToSend.value;
    //clear message text box
    msgToSend.value = '';
}
```

The first method is an event handler for the send button provided in the HTML. Users click this button to send messages to other users of the chat application. The WebSocket API provides a mechanism to check the current status of the connection. To prevent an error, the *readyState* property is evaluated to ensure that it's now open. *readyState* provides four possible values, as described in Table 2-9.

TABLE 2-9 Possible values of the WebSocket *readyState*

Value	Description
OPEN	The connection is open.
CONNECTING	The connection is in the process of connecting and not ready for use yet. This is the default value.
CLOSING	The connection is in the process of being closed.
CLOSED	The connection is closed.

After confirming that the connection is in the appropriate state for sending a message, the send method is called with the text that the user entered into the chat application. Also, so that each user can see that his/her message is indeed part of the chat, the message is added to the chat window.

When other users of the chat application send messages into the system, the server calls the event handler specified in *onmessage*. The *onmessage* event receives a message parameter with the data property that contains the message. This message is extracted and displayed in the chat window for users to see.

When finished with a chat session, a user should be able to exit cleanly. This is accomplished by calling the close method of the *WebSocket* object. The close method can be called with no parameters. It also allows the use of two optional parameters. A numerical code and a reason can be provided but isn't mandatory. In this example, the connection is closed with no parameters. When a connection is closed, the *onclose* event handler is raised:

```
disconnectButton.onclick = function () {
    wsConnection.close();
}
wsConnection.onclose = function () {
    //write the connection has been closed.
    NewLine();
    chatBox.value = chatBox.value + "System: Connection has been closed.";
}
```

When the user clicks the close button, the close method is called. Then, the subsequent call to the *onclose* event handler is implemented so that a message can be provided to the user that the connection has indeed been closed.

Making webpages dynamic with jQuery and AJAX

So far throughout the book, you've seen some great ways to make webpages dynamic by using JavaScript. JavaScript is the language that the webpage browser understands. In some cases, using plain JavaScript or the standard JavaScript library available in the browser can be cumbersome. This is where jQuery can be helpful. jQuery is a JavaScript library that specializes in working with the DOM to make webpages dynamic.

In the preceding section, you explored how to use the WebSocket API to open a bidirectional communication channel with the server. In this section, you examine using jQuery and AJAX to make server requests to retrieve updated content for your pages. In traditional web development, when content needs to be updated on a page, a request is made to the server for the page itself where the server-side code can run to get the new content, perhaps from a database, and re-render the page with updated information. The user experience is a flicker as the entire page needs to be refreshed. The use of AJAX has solved this issue by allowing you to make server-side requests via JavaScript without having to request a full page refresh. You can implement AJAX without jQuery; however, because of the popularity and ease of use that jQuery provides, using jQuery to implement this type of functionality is much more desirable.

By requesting data from a server with JavaScript via jQuery and AJAX, you can retrieve data behind the scenes and then use the various DOM manipulation techniques that you've learned to update specific areas of the page that need to be updated. This prevents the need to send a request for the entire page back to the server and creates a much more pleasant user experience.

For this example, you will create a fictitious website for searching fruit. The page consists of a box to enter an adjective about fruit and return any fruit that match the results. The webpage is set up as shown in Listing 2-2.

LISTING 2-2 The Fruit Finder webpage

```
<html>
    <head>
        <script src="jquery-2.0.3.min.js" type="text/javascript"></script>
        <script type="text/javascript">
            window.onload = function () {
                $('#searchButton').click(function () {
                    var searchPath;
                    $('#searchResults').empty();
                    switch ($('#searchFruit').val()) {
                    case 'long':
                        searchPath = "Fruit/Long.xml";
                        break;
                    case 'round':
                        searchPath = "Fruit/Round.xml";
                        break;
                    case 'orange':
                        searchPath = "Fruit/Orange.xml";
                        break;
                    default:
                        InvalidSearchTerm();
                    }
```

```
                    $.ajax({
                        url: searchPath,
                        cache: false,
                        dataType: "xml",
                        success: function (data) {
                            $(data).find("fruit").each(
                                function () {
                                    $('#searchResults').append($(this).text());
                                    $('#searchResults').append("<BR />");
                                })
                        }
                    });
                }
                function InvalidSearchTerm() {
                    $('#searchResults').empty();
                    $('#searchResults').append('Invalid Search Term. Please try again.');
                }
        </script>
    </head>
    <body>
        <div>
            Enter search term: <input type="text" id="searchFruit"/>
                <input type="button" id="searchButton" value="Search"/>
        </div>
        <div>
            <h1>Results:</h1>
        </div>
        <div id="searchResults">
        </div>
    </body>
</html>
```

In this listing, users are presented with a very simple user interface in which they can enter a search term and retrieve a result set based on that search term. In this case, users can enter one of the supported search terms and get back the data from the server. The data request is made using AJAX and as such the entire page doesn't need to refresh, only the area that displays the results. The part of the page where the data is needed is the only part of the page that is affected by the new data being received.

The first thing that this code does is set up an event listener for the search button click event. All the magic occurs in this function. The search term is evaluated to ensure that it matches one of the supported search terms. If it doesn't, the user is presented with a message indicating this. If it does, the code proceeds to make an AJAX call to the server for the correct data set that matches the search term. In this case, it's a hard-coded XML file. However, the data source is irrelevant as long as the returned XML matches the schema that the webpage expects so that it can be parsed and displayed.

The AJAX call has a few important parameters that you can set. Look at the AJAX call from Listing 2-2:

```
$.ajax({
    url: searchPath,
    cache: false,
    dataType: "xml",
    success: function (data) {
        $(data).find("fruit").each(
            function () {
                $('#searchResults').append($(this).text());
                $('#searchResults').append("<BR/>");
            })
    }
});
```

The first parameter being set is the *url* that the AJAX call will be requesting. For security reasons, to prevent cross-site scripting, this URL must be within the same domain as the webpage itself.

The next parameter, *cache*, is optional and indicates whether the call can use a cached copy. The third parameter, *datatype*, indicates the expected data type, which could be XML or JavaScript Object Notation (JSON), for example.

The last parameter set in this example is the *success* property. This parameter takes a function that the results of the AJAX calls should be passed into for the webpage to do some work with. In this example, the results are parsed and added to the DOM so that users can see the results.

Another property that can be set on the AJAX call, as good practice, is the *error* property so that any error conditions can be handled gracefully. This is the listing updated with an error function set:

```
$.ajax({
    url: searchPath,
    cache: false,
    dataType: "xml",
    success: function (data) {
        $(data).find("fruit").each(
            function () {
                $('#searchResults').append($(this).text());
                $('#searchResults').append("<BR />");
            })
    },
    error: function (xhr, textStatus, errorThrown) {
        $('#searchResults').append(errorThrown);
    }
});
```

The error function is passed three useful parameters:

- The HTTP request itself

- The HTTP error number (such as 404)

- The error text (such as Not Found)

You can mimic a 404 error by changing one of the search words to return an invalid path.

The jQuery AJAX toolkit supports not only getting data, but also posting data to the server. The default request type is GET. To change a call to a post, you change the value of the type property to POST:

```
$.ajax({
    url: searchPath,
    cache: false,
    dataType: "xml",
    type: "POST",
    success: function (data) {
        …
    },
    error: function (xhr, textStatus, errorThrown) {
        $('#searchResults').append(errorThrown);
    }
});
```

Perhaps the site user knows of additional fruit that fit into a certain category. The page can be enhanced to allow users to enter the name of a fruit and submit it to the XML file so that subsequent searches include it. Ideally in this case, you would use the POST method to a server-side function that would accept this data and store it in the XML file.

Wiring up an event with jQuery

In Objective 2.2, "Raise and handle an event," you saw how to set up event listeners for various actions that the DOM or a user's interaction with the DOM could invoke. One of the most common issues encountered by web developers is cross-browser compatibility. Although this topic is large and this book doesn't have the space to go into great detail about cross-browser compatibility, jQuery is one of the toolkits available to help bridge the issue. In Listing 2-2, you saw an example of jQuery syntax to wire up an event:

```
$('#searchButton').click(function () {
…
}
```

In this sample, the jQuery selector syntax is used to find the search button on the page by its name. Then the click event is assigned a function that runs when the button is clicked.

This syntax is quite powerful. Aside from being cross-browser friendly, it includes much flexibility in how event handlers are assigned to objects. This jQuery selector syntax supports all the same type of searches that the document object exposes. But the part that differentiates jQuery from the document object is that jQuery can assign styles or events to everything in the result set in one line.

Assume the following HTML makes up the markup for a webpage:

```
<body>
    <table>
        <tr>
            <td id="door1">Door 1</td>
            <td id="door2">Door 2</td>
            <td id="door3">Door 3</td>
        </tr>
    </table>
</body>
```

The following script is the more traditional method to assign event handlers to the DOM elements:

```
<script type="text/javascript">
        window.onload = function () {
            document.getElementById("door1").onclick = function () { };
            document.getElementById("door2").onclick = function () { };
            document.getElementById("door3").onclick = function () { };
        }
```

This fairly simple script has only three cells to add a click event to. But if the page is to get more complex and have up to 20 or 50 doors, this code becomes tedious. This is where jQuery can simplify things. The preceding code can be replaced with this code:

```
$("document").ready(function () {
        $("td").click(function () { });
    });
```

Notice how much easier this code is. In one line, all *<td>* elements are assigned a click event. This code applies to all *<td>* elements on the page. So, if some *<td>* elements aren't part of the page, you need to ensure that the selector is unique to the required elements. This can be accomplished with cascading style sheets (CSS) or by using the DOM hierarchy, as in this example:

```
$("document").ready(function () {
        $("#GameRow td").click(function () {
            alert( $(this).text());
        });
    });
...
<table>
        <tr id="GameRow">
            <td id="door1">Door 1</td>
            <td id="door2">Door 2</td>
            <td id="door3">Door 3</td>
        </tr>
</table>
<table>
        <tr id="SomeOtherRow">
            <td id="cell1">Not a Door 1</td>
            <td id="cell2">Not a Door 2</td>
            <td id="cell3">Not a Door 3</td>
        </tr>
</table>
```

The click events are assigned only to the *<td>* elements that are children of an element named *GameRow*. jQuery provides advanced selector capabilities that allow fine control over how the DOM is manipulated.

Implementing a callback with an anonymous function

Callback functions are used everywhere. The concept of a callback is the basis for how events work. It's the mechanism by which asynchronous operations return to the caller. In traditional programming languages, a callback is achieved by passing a pointer to a function to another process so that when that process completes or is at specified stages of the process, the function is called to advise the caller of a status of some sort. This could be when the operation completes and could be passing data back to the caller. An example of this would be an asynchronous web service call that returns data. The principle is the same in JavaScript.

In JavaScript, functions are considered objects and are often noted as first-class citizens. This means that a variable can be assigned a function, or a function can be passed into another function as a parameter. Seeing functions used in this way is a common convention in JavaScript. Functions used in this way are called anonymous functions.

A function is considered anonymous when it doesn't have a name. The following function declaration has a name, so wouldn't be considered anonymous:

```
function SubmitClick() {
    //do some logic here
}
```

Here a function is declared that can be used throughout the page. This function has a name: *SubmitClick*. Because this function has a name, it's not an anonymous function. However, a named function like this can be assigned to as many button events as you want:

```
$("#Button1").click(SubmitClick);
$("#Button2").click(SubmitClick);
$("#Button3").click(SubmitClick);
```

With a named function, the convenience of reuse is there. However, in some cases this is more overhead than is necessary. This also can make the code more difficult to follow in terms of being able to easily see what's actually happening in the click event handler. In a situation that specifies distinct behavior for each button, anonymous functions simplify things greatly. The following code demonstrates using anonymous functions instead of the named function:

```
$("#Button1").click(function () { ... });
$("#Button2").click(function () { ... });
$("#Button3").click(function () { ... });
```

Each button is given its own function inline, where the implementation can be customized for each button click. In that example, the use of anonymous function is apparent because the function doesn't have a name. The syntax for an anonymous function is as follows:

```
function (n,n,…,n) { body };
```

The anonymous function declaration must begin with the *function* keyword, which must be followed by closed parentheses. The parentheses can include zero or more parameters. The parentheses are followed by closed braces in which the code block that makes up the implementation of the function is coded.

The only difference between an anonymous function and a named function is the name portion of the function signature. That the anonymous function accepts parameters is an important concept when dealing with callbacks.

When working with an API, either your own or a third party's, functionality often is provided that includes the use of callbacks. As discussed earlier, callbacks are functions that are processed when the transfer of control returns to the caller. For example, in the previous section using jQuery with AJAX, the following code sample was used:

```
$.ajax({
        url: searchPath,
        cache: false,
        dataType: "xml",
        error: function(hdr, num, txt){…}
        success: function (data) {
    …
    }});
```

In this sample, the AJAX call enables you to specify some functions to call back for different circumstances that can occur. The *error* and *success* properties allow you to specify a function that the AJAX framework calls after it either successfully completes the request or encounters an error. In each case, parameters are specified to receive the data that accompanies each callback.

Callback functions can also be used in the form of a parameter to another function. Consider the following example that accepts a user's input to evaluate if a score is a pass or a fail:

```
$("document").ready( function () {
    $("#Button1").click( function () {
        DoLongTask($("#inputValue").val(),
            function (result, data) {
                if (result == "SUCCESS")
                    alert(data + " is a Success");
                else
                    alert(data + " is a fail");
            });
    });
} );
function DoLongTask(n,f)
{
    if (n < 10)
        f("SUCCESS", n);
    else
        f("FAIL", n);
}
```

This code makes heavy use of anonymous functions and callbacks. The first instance is the document *ready* callback. In this case, you ask the renderer to call back to an anonymous function after it reaches the ready state:

```
$("document").ready( function () {…
```

Next, you want to handle a click event. In this case, you indicate to the renderer that, when it receives a click from a specific button, to call back to your anonymous function:

```
$("#Button1").click( function () {…
```

Next, in your button click is where you are coding your own logic for the page. User input is taken from the input box and passed to a function that evaluates it. The function does nothing more than evaluate the value and produce the result. Any caller that's interested in the result can provide a callback function to get the result.

```
DoLongTask($("#inputValue").val(),
        function (result, data) {
                if (result == "SUCCESS")
                    alert(data + " is a Success");
                else
                    alert(data + " is a fail");
            });
```

The call to *DoLongTask* accepts two parameters: the value to evaluate and a callback function to pass the results to when it's done. An anonymous function is passed into the *DoLongTask* function as the callback to run. In this case, the callback is known to provide two parameters, so the callback function accepts two parameters: the original value and the result of the evaluation. The callback then provides information to users about what the calculation result was.

Callback functions are very useful and widely used in JavaScript development. Callback functions can exist statically with a name or be provided inline dynamically as anonymous.

Using the *this* pointer

The *this* pointer is a special object provided by the jQuery framework. When running selections against the DOM using jQuery, *this* refers to the object that it finds or the collection of objects that it finds. It provides a shortcut to accessing the item within the current context of jQuery filter. In a simple example, the *this* keyword can be demonstrated as follows:

```
$("document").ready(
    function () {
        $('#floorDiv').click(function () {
            $(this).css("background-color", "red");
            })
        }
    );
```

In this sample, the *floorDiv* element is assigned an anonymous function to run when it's clicked. Within the function, rather than query the DOM for the element again to do something with it, the *this* keyword provides a reference to the element that initiated the event. In this case, *$(this)* provides a reference to the *floorDiv* element, and you can do whatever you want with that element. In this case, you are only changing the background color style property of the *div*. In more advanced scenarios, the result of the selector can return more than one element. The following example demonstrates this:

```
$("document").ready(
        function () {
            $('#floorDiv').click(function () {
                $("div").each(function () { $(this).css("background-color", "red");
});
            })
        }
    );
```

In this example, when *floorDiv* is clicked, *$("div")* finds all the *div* elements in the page. Then it calls the *each* operator, which calls the callback function passed into it for each element that's returned. Then, *$(this)* is used to modify the background color of each *div*. In this way, the use of the *this* keyword is extremely efficient because it provides quick direct access to each element with very little code.

Thought experiment
Creating a chat application

In this thought experiment, apply what you've learned about this objective. You can find answers to these questions in the "Answers" section at the end of this chapter.

Would you use WebSockets or would you use AJAX to create an asynchronous bidirectional communication application in JavaScript? For this though experiment, describe how you would create an HTML5 JavaScript based real-time chat application.

Objective summary

- WebSockets provide bidirectional communication with a server.
- WebSockets support both non-secure (*ws*) and secure (*wss*) connections to the server.
- The jQuery AJAX framework provides a mechanism to make asynchronous web requests.
- You can wire up events by using the jQuery selector syntax.

Objective review

1. Which of the following is a valid WebSocket instantiation?

   A. *wsConnection = new WebSocket('http://studygroup.70480.com');*

   B. *wsConnection = new WebSocket('tcp://studygroup.70480.com',['soap','xmpp']);*

   C. *wsConnection = new WebSocket('wss://studygroup.70480.com',['soap','xmpp']);*

   D. *wsConnection = new WebSocket('ftp://studygroup.70480.com',['soap','xmpp']);*

2. Which of the following statements properly handles the reception of data from a WebSocket?

   A. *wsConnection.onpost = function(msg){..};*

   B. *wsConneciton.onreceive = function(msg){...};*

   C. *wsConnection.onmessage = function(msg){...};*

   D. *wsConnection.ongetdata = function(msg){...};*

3. Which list identifies the properties that need to be set up to make an AJAX call?

   A. *cache, datatype, success*

   B. *url, cache, datatype, success*

   C. *url, datatype, onsuccess*

   D. *url, datatype, oncomplete*

4. Why is wiring up events with jQuery easier?

   A. It allows you to assign the event listener to many elements at once via the selector syntax.

   B. There is no difference wiring up events with jQuery versus *addEventListener* method.

   C. jQuery works more efficiently in a loop.

   D. jQuery allows both named and anonymous functions to be used as event listeners.

Objective 2.5: Create a web worker process

Web workers present a way of developing multithreaded JavaScript applications. JavaScript is a single-threaded environment. Everything run in JavaScript is queued up synchronously. This might not be evident in most applications because the available processing power on client computers usually far exceeds what's required by a webpage on a client computer. However, in more intense web applications, you have seen warning messages from the browser that the scripts are running and taking a long time to complete. In fact, these warnings give users the option to stop running scripts on the page immediately. This type of user experience won't have users coming back to the website. This is where the Web Worker API is useful.

> **This objective covers how to:**
> - Get started with a web worker process
> - Create a worker process with the Web Worker API
> - Use a web worker
> - Understand web worker limitations
> - Configure timeouts and intervals

Getting started with a web worker process

The Web Worker API enables you to specify that pieces of work should be processed on their own thread. Doing so has many advantages but also some pitfalls that you need to respect. In this objective, you learn how to use the Web Worker API to take advantage of the flexibility this brings to web applications. You also learn about the disadvantages and cautions that come with using web workers.

This objective uses the bouncing ball example to demonstrate the use of a web worker. Listing 2-3 shows the basic code for the bouncing ball. It will be adjusted as you work through the sections within this objective to achieve moving work to a web worker process.

LISTING 2-3 Bouncing ball

```
<html>
    <head>
        <script>
            window.requestAnimFrame = (function (callback) {
                return window.requestAnimationFrame || window.webkitRequestAnimationFrame
|| window.mozRequestAnimationFrame || window.oRequestAnimationFrame ||
window.msRequestAnimationFrame ||
                function (callback) {
                    window.setTimeout(callback, 1000 / 30);
                };
            })();
```

```javascript
        window.setTimeout(getDirection, 30000);

var x = 176, y = 176, w = 600, h = 600, r = 26;
var d,c,s;
var rColor,gColor,bColor;
var hd = "r";
var horizontal = true;

window.onload = function () {
    try{
        c = document.getElementById("c");
        w = c.width;
        h = c.height;
        s = parseInt( document.getElementById("speedy").value);

        getDirection();
        drawBall();

        document.onkeydown = function () {
            switch (window.event.keyCode) {
                case 40:
                    horizontal = false;
                    hd = "d";
                    break;
                case 37:
                    horizontal = true;
                    hd = "l";
                    break;
                case 38:
                    horizontal = false;
                    hd = "u";
                    break;
                case 39:
                    horizontal = true;
                    hd = "r";
                    break;
            }
        }
    } catch (e) {
        alert(e.message);
    }
}
function increaseSpeed() {
    s++;
    document.getElementById("speedy").value = s;
}
function decreaseSpeed() {
    s--;
    document.getElementById("speedy").value = s;
}
function changeDirection() {
    var cx = window.event.offsetX;
    var cy = window.event.offsetY;
    x = cx;
    y = cy;
```

```javascript
        document.getElementById("speedy").value = s;
}
function setNewPoint(d) {
    try{
        switch (horizontal) {
            case true:
                if (x < (w - r) && hd == "r")
                    x += s;
                else if(x > r && hd == "l")
                    x -= s;
                break;
            case false:
                if (y < (h - r) && hd == "d")
                    y += s;
                else if (y > r && hd == "u")
                    y -= s;
                break;
        }
        if (x >= (w - r))
            hd = "l";
        if (x <= r)
            hd = "r";
        if (y >= (h - r))
            hd = "u";
        if (y <= r)
            hd = "d";
    } catch (e) {
        alert(e.message);
    }
}
function getDirection() {
    horizontal = !horizontal;
    var d = Math.ceil(Math.random() * 2);
    if (horizontal) {
        if (d == 1) {
            hd = "r";
        } else {
            hd = "l";
        }
    } else {
        if (d == 1) {
            hd = "u";
        } else {
            hd = "d";
        }
    }
}
function drawBall() {
    try {
        var rgbFill = "rgb(0,0,0)";
        var rgbStroke = "rgb(128,128,128)";

        setNewPoint(d);
        var ctxt = c.getContext("2d");
```

```
                ctxt.clearRect(0, 0, c.width, c.height);
                ctxt.beginPath();

                ctxt.lineWidth = "5";
                ctxt.strokeStyle = rgbStroke;
                ctxt.arc(x, y, r, 0, 360);
                ctxt.fillStyle = rgbFill;
                ctxt.fill();
                ctxt.stroke();
                s = parseInt( document.getElementById("speedy").value);
                requestAnimFrame(function () {
                    drawBall();
                });
            } catch (e) {
                alert(e.message);
            }
        }
    }
    </script>
</head>
<body>
        <canvas id="c" width="1200" height="800" style="border: 2px solid black;
position: absolute; top: 50px; left: 50px;"></canvas>
        <input id="intensiveWork" type="button" value="Do Work" /><span
id="workResult"></span>

        <input id="speedy" type="range" min="0" max="10" value="10"
style="position:relative; visibility:hidden;" step="1"/>
    </body>
</html>
```

This code simply displays a small ball bouncing around inside a canvas. Users can use the arrow keys to change the ball's direction. Users would expect a smooth experience. Now you can introduce an intensive mathematical operation to occur at the click of a button. The button is on the form already and is called *intensiveWork*. Add the following function to the bottom of the script block to do some intense math:

```
function DoIntensiveWork() {
    var result = document.getElementById("workResult");
    result.innerText = "";
    var work = 10000000;
    var i = 0;
    var a = new Array(work);
    var sum=0;
    for (i = 0; i < work; i++) {
        a[i] = i * i
        sum += i * i;
    }
    result.innerText = sum;
}
```

This function does nothing more than calculate the sum of a series of squares and display the result to users. The amount of work to do is hard coded in this example but could be extended to get the information from users as well.

Next, add the click event handler to the button:

```
<script>
    …
    getDirection();
    drawBall();


    document.getElementById("intensiveWork").onclick = function () { DoIntensiveWork(); };
    …
</script>
```

Now, users can click a button and get the sum of the squares for a series of sequential numbers.

The problem with this code is that although the math work is occurring, the ball interaction is blocked completely. The ball stops moving and user input is seemingly ignored until the math call returns. The call to run the calculations takes too long and interferes. You can experiment with smaller numbers and see that eventually the number can be small enough so the work happens fast enough that the ball isn't stopped. This doesn't mean that the application is doing work concurrently, although visibly no interruption occurs.

Creating a worker process with the Web Worker API

The Web Worker API is based on the JavaScript messaging framework. This underlying structure enables your code to send parameters to a worker and have the worker send results back. A basic web worker is established by creating a separate file to contain the script that will be processed on the separate thread. The *Worker* object is available from the global namespace and is created like so:

```
var webWorker = new Worker("workercode.js");
```

This instantiates a new worker process and specifies what file contains the code to be run on the worker thread. The *Worker* object supports the functionality described in Table 2-10.

TABLE 2-10 *Worker* object operations

Method	Description
postMessage	Starts the worker process. This method expects a single parameter containing the data to pass to the worker thread. If nothing is required in the worker thread, an empty string can be supplied.
terminate	Stops the worker process from continuing.
onmessage	Specifies the function for the worker thread to call back to when complete. This function accepts a single parameter in the form of *EventData* with a property named *data* containing the values.

Method	Description
onerror	Specifies a function to call when an error occurs in the worker thread. The onerror method receives event data, including the following: message: textual message of the error filename: the filename the error occurred in lineno: the line number in the file that created the error

As soon as the *Worker* object is instantiated, it's available for use at any time. All that's needed to start the process is to call the *postMessage* method:

```
webWorker.postMessage("");
```

As soon as the *webWorker* is running, the main application continues as usual. If something occurs that the worker process should be canceled, a call to the terminate method would achieve this:

```
webWorker.terminate();
```

After the worker process completes and results need to be processed, the *onmessage* function is called from the worker. This should be set up before starting the worker:

```
webWorker.onmessage = function(evt) {…}
```

That's everything required on the calling side or in the web application to create and manage a worker process. Next, you need to create the worker code itself. For this, you create the workercode.js file that was used in the constructor. The first line of the file will be the *onmessage* property being assigned a function to process:

```
onmessage = function(e){…}
```

This tells the runtime the entry point to the work to be run within the worker process. Somewhere in the worker process, where a result should be sent back to the calling application, the *postMessage* method is called:

```
onmessage = function(e){
…
self.postMessage(result);
}
```

That's what's involved in creating a worker process. In the last piece, notice the user of the *self* keyword. The *self* keyword is similar to the *this* keyword. The worker process runs in its own context, meaning that it has its own global namespace. The *self keyword* gives access to the global namespace within the worker process.

Using web workers

Now that you've examined the foundation of web workers, you can go back to the bouncing ball example and move the intensive math operations over to a worker process so that it doesn't interfere with the bouncing ball activity. To do this, create a new JavaScript file called CalculateWorker.js with the following code in it:

```javascript
onmessage = function (evt) {
    var work = 10000000;
    var i = 0;
    var a = new Array(work);
    var sum = 0;
    for (i = 0; i < work; i++) {
        a[i] = i * i;
        sum += i * i;
    }
    self.postMessage(sum);
}
```

This code starts with assigning the *onmessage* handler a function to run when spawned within the context of a worker. At the end of the message, it calls *postMessage* to return a result back to the caller. Save this file, and then change the click event handler for the *intensiveWork* button in the bouncing ball code as follows:

```javascript
document.getElementById("intensiveWork").onclick = function () {
    var result = document.getElementById("workResult");
    result.innerText = "";
    var worker = new Worker("CalculateWorker.js");
    worker.onmessage = function (evt) {
        try {
            result.innerText = evt.data;
        } catch (e) {
            alert(e.message);
        }
    }
worker.onerror = function (err) {
    alert(err.message + err.filename + err.lineno);
}
    worker.postMessage("");
};
```

In this code, the pattern described in the previous section is implemented. A new *Worker* object is instantiated with CalculateWorker.js specified. Then the *onmessage* is assigned a function to handle the result of the worker thread. The *onerror* is assigned a function to handle any error conditions. Finally, the *postMessage* is called to invoke the worker.

Run this code and click the Do Work button. The ball now continues to move on the screen and is responsive to the arrow keys. To make the worker process take longer, simply increase the size of the number it needs to work with.

To provide an option to stop the worker process, you need to implement the terminate method. Add a button to the page like so:

```
<input id="stopWorker" type="button" value="Stop Work" />
```

And add the following script beneath the *postMessage* call:

```
document.getElementById("stopWorker").onclick = function () {
    worker.terminate();
}
```

Next, click the Do Work button followed by the Stop Work button to see that the work is terminated and no result is returned.

Understanding web worker limitations

Web workers are very convenient. They can solve many processing problems in intensive web applications. However, be aware of the limitations imposed on workers as well.

Passing parameters

The *postMessage* method accepts a parameter that enables it to pass data to the worker that it might need to operate on or with. The *postMessage* parameter is a string—it can take any serializable object such as native data types, JSON objects, or XML. The parameter can't be a function.

In the bouncing ball example, the input for what number to work with could come from users. An input box can be added to the HTML and the entered value can be passed to the worker. This would look like this:

```
var value = document.getElementById("inputValue").value;
worker.postMessage(value);
```

Then in the worker, the value would be accessed like this:

```
onmessage = function (evt) {
    var work = evt.data;
…
}
```

The function receives an event object with a property called *data* that contains whatever was passed into the worker.

Number of workers

Although no limit is imposed on how many workers can be processed or created concurrently, the number of workers used is something that you need to be pay attention to. Creating workers is a heavy operation. Each worker creates threads at the operating system level and their use should be managed accordingly. If you want a high volume of workers, consider creating a pool that can be used in a round-robin fashion so that not too many workers are created.

DOM access

Workers operate in their own global context, which means that they don't have access to the DOM of the page that invoked them. The DOM shouldn't be manipulated from a worker process. The worker context has no access to the window object, document object, or any parent object.

Subworkers

Following the same patterns as for a worker from the main webpage, a worker can create workers as well. All constructs must be followed for passing data and getting data returned. However, knowing how many total workers will be created becomes increasingly important.

Configuring timeouts and intervals

You can set up a web worker to run on a specified interval in the background. This is done by using any existing *setTimeout* or *setInterval* methods. The *setTimeout* method calls a specified function after the specified delay. The *setInterval* calls the specified function repeatedly after each specified time interval. For example, the following code runs the worker after 3 seconds:

```
var work = new Worker("workerFile.js");
setTimeout(function(){
work.postMessage("");
},3000);
```

However, the following code runs the worker every 3 seconds:

```
var work = new Worker("workerFile.js");
setInterval(function(){
work.postMessage("");
},3000);
```

Thought experiment

Creating a page that performs a fireworks show

In this thought experiment, apply what you've learned about this objective. You can find answers to these questions in the "Answers" section at the end of this chapter.

As an exercise to create a webpage using timeouts and intervals, think about how you would create a page that would perform a fireworks show. Different types of fireworks need to fire at different intervals and delays. They each need to travel to a different height, and different types of fireworks have different explosion effects and colors.

1. Would a larger firework show be too intensive? Why or why not?

2. Would web workers help make it more fluid? Why or why not?

Objective summary

- Web workers allow the JavaScript runtime to provide multithreading.
- Web workers can have sub-workers.
- The number of workers that you can use is limitless, but too many workers can hinder performance.
- Web workers can receive a single parameter containing any data needed for the worker.
- Web workers don't have access to the DOM of the calling page.
- Use *setTimeout* to delay before running a script function. Use *setInterval* to repeat a script function after every specified interval.

Objective review

1. Which of the following isn't a valid web worker operation?

   A. *postMessage*

   B. *onmessage*

   C. *close*

   D. *terminate*

2. Which method cancels a web worker?

   A. *close*

   B. *terminate*

   C. *suspend*

   D. *sleep*

3. Where must you place the JavaScript code to run in the context of a web worker?

   A. Between the *<head></head>* elements

   B. In any *<script>* block in the page

   C. In its own JavaScript file

   D. As a dynamic function assigned to the *self.worker*

4. How many web workers/subworkers can run concurrently?

   A. A multiple of four web workers including subworkers, per processor

   B. 16 workers by default, but you can change that number via *self.configuration*

   C. A limitless number of workers

   D. A limit of eight workers, each with a maximum of eight subworkers

5. To have a script run continually every 30 seconds, which line of code should be used?

   A. *wsConnection.repeatWork("workerFile.js",30000);*

   B. *setTimeout(function(){ worker.postMessage("");}, 30000);*

   C. *setTimeout(worker.postMessage(""), 30000);*

   D. *setInterval(function(){ worker.postMessage("");}, 30000);*

Answers

This section contains the solutions to the thought experiments and answers to the objective review questions in this chapter.

Objective 2.1: Thought experiment

Writing clean JavaScript comes with some clear advantages. Choosing the correct construct to handle a problem is imperative to achieving the goal of clean script.

A *for* loop and *while* loop can both get the same jobs done interchangeably, but some semantic differences make one more preferable over the other in various situations. When you know how many times a loop must run, the *for* loop is ideal. It has all the built-in semantics to handle a counter to iterate a known number of times. It can be replaced with a *while* loop, but the *while* loop requires extra variables and code added to the loop to take care of the counting of the number of times the loop runs.

The *while* loop is better when you don't know the number of times a loop will run; it's indeterminate. This is where the loop runs until the logic within the loop achieves a certain state; hence, why the *while* loop evaluates on a Boolean expression.

You can apply the same logic when choosing between an *if* statement and a *switch* statement. Although a *switch* statement can easily be replaced by an *if* statement, the inverse isn't true. Checking single values for equality in an *if...else* construct can become long and cumbersome. *if* statements allow for more complex evaluations, including compound evaluations using AND and OR logic. *switch* statements are more useful for evaluating a single value against a long list of possible values such as enumeration. Choosing the correct construct for the problem is imperative to readable and maintainable script.

Objective 2.1: Review

1. **Correct answer:** C

   A. **Incorrect:** The *if* statement provides branch flow control.

   B. **Incorrect:** The *switch* statement provides branch flow control.

   C. **Correct:** The *for* loop provides iterative flow control.

   D. **Incorrect:** The *break* keyword is used to exit an iterative control block such as a *for* or *while* loop.

2. **Correct answer:** D

   A. **Incorrect:** The *join* method joins all the elements of an array into a string.

   B. **Incorrect:** *combine* isn't a valid method.

   C. **Incorrect:** The *split* method is used to split a string into an array of substrings.

   D. **Correct:** The *concat* method combines the elements of two arrays into one array.

3. **Correct answer:** C

    A. **Incorrect:** The *for...in* loop runs only if the target list contains at least on element.

    B. **Incorrect:** The *while* loop runs only if the Boolean condition evaluates to true.

    C. **Correct:** The *do...while* loop runs a Boolean condition after it runs once.

    D. **Incorrect:** The *for* loop runs only if the values specified in the conditions are true.

4. **Correct answer:** B

    A. **Incorrect:** The *continue* keyword exits the current iteration but continues to the next iteration if the conditional values are still true.

    B. **Correct:** The *break* keyword exits an iterative control loop.

    C. **Incorrect:** *stop* isn't a valid statement.

    D. **Incorrect:** *next* isn't a valid statement.

Objective 2.2: Thought experiment

This interesting scenario can lead to a complex chain of event handling in which one event triggers other events. This requires deciding on the flow of the events through the page. Good practice is to do this on paper or workflow software to design the workflow of the events. This will require knowing when to cancel the event chain or allow it to continue processing further down the controls.

Objective 2.2: Review

1. **Correct answer:** B

    A. **Incorrect:** This is a valid method.

    B. **Correct:** CSS doesn't provide a way to assign events handlers.

    C. **Incorrect:** This is a valid method.

    D. **Incorrect:** This is a valid method.

2. **Correct answer:** D

    A. **Incorrect:** Anonymous functions can't be called.

    B. **Incorrect:** Anonymous functions don't have a name.

    C. **Incorrect:** Anonymous functions can be passed as parameters.

    D. **Correct:** Anonymous functions can't be assigned to a DOM element declaratively.

3. **Correct answer:** A

  A. **Correct:** *window.event.returnValue = false;* cancels the event.

  B. **Incorrect:** *return false;* doesn't cancel the event.

  C. **Incorrect:** *window.event.Return();* isn't valid.

  D. **Incorrect:** *window.stop();* isn't valid.

4. **Correct answer:** A

  A. **Correct:** The *focus* event fires when an element receives the focus.

  B. **Incorrect:** The *change* event fires when the value of an element is changed.

  C. **Incorrect:** The *keydown* event fires when a keyboard key is pressed down.

  D. **Incorrect:** The *mouseleave* event fires when the mouse pointer leaves the area of an element.

Objective 2.3: Thought experiment

Implementing a *try...catch* block in every function at the top of the call stack is an important way to catch unforeseen scenarios that result in the application getting into a bad state. However, this error handling routine might include situations from which you want to be able to recover. Nesting *try...catch* blocks allow this to happen. You can implement as many *try...catch* blocks as you want. Nesting them allows you to catch a specific scenario within the outer block, handle it, correct data and/or assumptions, and allow the script to continue running.

Objective 2.3: Review

1. **Correct answer:** A

  A. **Correct:** By using structured error handling, you can provide feedback to users and handle unknown situations properly.

  B. **Incorrect:** Proper error handling allows users to fix problems with the webpage.

  C. **Incorrect:** Proper error handling allows you to debug the application at run time.

  D. **Incorrect:** Proper error handling allows you to suppress all the bugs in your scripts.

2. **Correct answer:** B

  A. **Incorrect:** *message* is a valid property that gives the textual description of the error.

  B. **Correct:** *description* isn't a valid property.

  C. **Incorrect:** The *number* property provides the number associated with the error.

  D. **Incorrect:** The *name* property provides the name of the exception object.

3. **Correct answer:** A

    A. **Correct:** Checking for null prevents the use of an object before it initializes and prevents unexpected results.

    B. **Incorrect:** NaN is a different construct than null.

    C. **Incorrect:** Custom errors aren't related to checking for null. Throwing a custom error can be used in many different scenarios.

Objective 2.4: Thought experiment

The concept of real-time chat or real-time communications isn't new. However, HTML5 Web-Sockets make the concept easier than ever to implement in HTML5 webpages. Implementing this type of application is beyond the scope of the book but is very useful in understanding the power that WebSockets provide. The following URL provides many search results that provide examples: *http://www.bing.com/search?q=WebSocket+JavaScript+chat+application.*

AJAX provides asynchronous communication but doesn't provide a bidirectional functionality that can deliver real-time communications.

Objective 2.4: Review

1. **Correct answer:** C

    A. **Incorrect:** http isn't a valid WebSocket protocol.

    B. **Incorrect:** tcp isn't a valid WebSocket protocol.

    C. **Correct:** wss or ws is a valid protocol to create a WebSocket.

    D. **Incorrect:** ftp isn't a valid WebSocket protocol.

2. **Correct answer:** C

    A. **Incorrect:** *wsConnection.onpost* isn't a method.

    B. **Incorrect:** *wsConneciton.onreceive* isn't a method.

    C. **Correct:** *wsConnection.onmessage* receives the resulting data.

    D. **Incorrect:** *wsConnection.ongetdata* isn't a method.

3. **Correct answer:** C

    A. **Incorrect:** *cache* isn't required.

    B. **Incorrect:** *cache* isn't required.

    C. **Correct:** *url*, *datatype*, and *onsuccess* are required.

    D. **Incorrect:** *oncomplete* isn't a property.

4. **Correct answer:** A

   A. **Correct:** Wiring up events with jQuery allows you to assign the event listener to many elements at once by using the selector syntax.

   B. **Incorrect:** jQuery provides much more flexibility.

   C. **Incorrect:** jQuery doesn't work differently inside a loop.

   D. **Incorrect:** This isn't unique to jQuery.

Objective 2.5: Thought experiment

For an application such as this, you must consider the amount of work required to get it done. The larger the show, the more intense the application will be. You could use *setInterval* and *setTimeout* to control the show's flow. However, the actual delivery of the firework display and explosion would be suited nicely for a web worker. This allows the user interface thread to continue to work uninterrupted while the complex logic of animating the fireworks occurs on a worker.

Objective 2.5: Review

1. **Correct answer:** C

   A. **Incorrect:** *postMessage* initiates the script to run in the worker.

   B. **Incorrect:** *onmessage* is the event handler used to receive the messages across the worker boundaries.

   C. **Correct:** *close* isn't a method on the web worker.

   D. **Incorrect:** *terminate* is used to cancel a web worker.

2. **Correct answer:** B

   A. **Incorrect:** *close* doesn't cancel a web worker.

   B. **Correct:** *terminate* cancels a web worker.

   C. **Incorrect:** *suspend* isn't a valid method.

   D. **Incorrect:** *sleep* isn't a valid method.

3. **Correct answer:** C

   A. **Incorrect:** The code must be in its own file.

   B. **Incorrect:** The code can't be inside a *<script>* block.

   C. **Correct:** The code must be in its own JavaScript file, and the name of the file is passed to the web worker as a parameter.

   D. **Incorrect:** There is no such property as *self.worker*.

4. **Correct answer:** C

   A. **Incorrect:** There is a limit associated with processors.

   B. **Incorrect:** There is no such property as *self.configuration*.

   C. **Correct:** There is no limit on the number of workers that can be created. However, too many will result in performance issues.

   D. **Incorrect:** There is no such limitation.

5. **Correct answer:** D

   A. **Incorrect:** *wsConnection.repeatWork("workerFile.js",30000);* isn't valid code.

   B. **Incorrect:** *setTimeout(function(){ worker.postMessage("");}, 30000);* delays for 30 seconds before running the anonymous function once.

   C. **Incorrect:** In *setTimeout(worker.postMessage(""), 30000);*, setTimeout waits for the specified delay before running the passed-in function. In this case, the parameter isn't a function.

   D. **Correct:** *setInterval(function(){ worker.postMessage("");}, 30000);* calls the passed-in function every interval as specified by the second parameter in milliseconds.

CHAPTER 3

Access and secure data

Most web applications require static or dynamic data. *Static* data is written directly into the HTML markup, not altered or loaded by code such as JavaScript. It's rendered and displayed to users without any way for the data to change. *Dynamic* data can change. Dynamic data can update a ticker on a webpage from a news feed, capture user data to perform an operation and provide results, or perhaps even store just a user's registration information in a database.

Both approaches to data have benefits as well as disadvantages. Static data is quite secure because it doesn't provide much of an attack surface for a malicious user. However, as a website transitions into a more dynamic site, with live updates of data and the ability for users to enter information into various fields, an attack surface opens and the site can become less secure.

Knowing how to prevent malicious users from causing harm to your application and possibly your users is important. You can implement the same mechanisms used to prevent malicious usage to simplify the user experience and to keep your data generally clean. Certain data elements, such as phone numbers and email addresses, can be provided in different formats. Because such information can be very important, you want to make it as easy as possible for users to enter it. Having complete address information and ensuring that all the necessary fields are populated also can be very important. HTML5 supports constructs such as regular expressions and required attributes to support implementing these types of rules. Throughout the objectives in this chapter, validating user input both declaratively via HTML5 and also by using JavaScript is covered.

In other scenarios, data coming to and from the website is either consuming data feeds or providing data to another destination. Websites today commonly have a direct link to social networking updates. In these cases, the retrieving and sending of the data is invisible in that users aren't engaged with the process. These processes should be streamlined and not interfere with the website's user experience. In this chapter's objectives, consuming data from external sources, transmitting data, and serializing and deserializing data are all covered.

Objectives in this chapter:

- Objective 3.1: Validate user input by using HTML5 elements
- Objective 3.2: Validate user input by using JavaScript
- Objective 3.3: Consume data
- Objective 3.4: Serialize, deserialize, and transmit data

Objective 3.1: Validate user input by using HTML5 elements

This objective examines the user interface elements made available by HTML5 that allow users to provide input. The ability to capture information from users is a great feature. However, you must ensure that user privacy and safety are protected as best as possible. You also must ensure that the website doesn't open any holes that an attacker can exploit to disrupt the site's services. Part of protecting the site is choosing the correct user input controls for the job and setting the appropriate attributes on those controls to ensure that the data is validated. For the exam, you need to know these input controls and the attributes they use for this purpose.

> **This objective covers how to:**
> - Choose input controls and HTML 5 input types
> - Implement content attributes

Choosing input controls

HTML5 provides a wide assortment of controls to make capturing user input simple and secure. In this section, you explore the user input controls in greater detail and see examples of their usage. A simulation of a survey form will be created to demonstrate when each type of control should be used. Listing 3-1 shows the entire markup for the survey.

LISTING 3-1 HTML5 markup for a customer survey,

```
<form>
    <div>
        <hgroup>
            <h1>Customer Satisfaction is #1</h1>
            <h2>Please take the time to fill out the following survey</h2>
        </hgroup>
    </div>
    <table>
        <tr>
            <td>Your Secret Code:
            </td>
            <td>
                <input type="text" readonly="readonly" value="00XY998BB"/>
            </td>
        </tr>
        <tr>
            <td>Password:
            </td>
            <td>
                <input type="password"/>
            </td>
        </tr>
```

```
        </tr>
        <tr>
            <td>First Name:
            </td>
            <td>
                <input type="text" id="firstNameText" maxlength="50"/>
            </td>
        </tr>
        <tr>
            <td>Last Name:
            </td>
            <td>
                <input type="text" id="lastNameText"/>
            </td>
        </tr>
        <tr>
            <td>
                Your favorite website:
            </td>
            <td>
                <input type="url"/>
            </td>
        </tr>
        <tr>
            <td>
                Your age in years:
            </td>
            <td>
                <input type="number"/></td>
        </tr>
        <tr>
            <td>
                What colors have you colored your hair:
            </td>
            <td>
                <input type="checkbox" id="chkBrown" checked="checked"/>
                Brown
                <input type="checkbox" id="chkBlonde"/>
                Blonde
                <input type="checkbox" id="chkBlack"/>
                Black
                <input type="checkbox" id="chkRed"/>
                Red
                <input type="checkbox" id="chkNone"/>
                None
            </td>
        </tr>
        <tr>
            <td>Rate your experience:
            </td>
            <td>
                <input type="radio" id="chkOne" name="experience"/>
                1 - Very Poor
                <input type="radio" id="chkTwo" name="experience"/>
                2
```

```html
            <input type="radio" id="chkThree" name="experience"/>
            3
            <input type="radio" id="chkFour" name="experience"/>
            4
            <input type="radio" id="chkFive" name="experience" checked="checked"/>
            5 - Very Good
        </td>
    </tr>
    <tr>
        <td>How likely would you recommend the product:
        </td>
        <td>
            <br/>
            <br/>
            <br/>
            <br/>
            <input type="range" min="1" max="25" value="20"/>
        </td>
    </tr>
    <tr>
        <td>
            Other Comments:
        </td>
        <td>
            <textarea id="otherCommentsText" rows="5" cols="20" spellcheck="true">
            </textarea>
        </td>
    </tr>
    <tr>
        <td>
            Email address:
        </td>
        <td>
            <input type="email" placeholder="me@mydomain.com" required/>
        </td>
    </tr>
    <tr>
        <td>
            <input type="submit"/>
            <input type="reset"/>
            <input type="button" value="Cancel"/>
        </td>
    </tr>
    </table>
</form>
```

> **NOTE   INPUT CONTROLS**
>
> The HTML5 specification defines many more input controls than are explained in this book. This book focuses specifically on the controls now supported by Internet Explorer, followed by smaller examples to demonstrate some of the other controls as supported by other browsers such as Google Chrome.

The *<input>* element in HTML denotes input controls. This element contains a *type* attribute that specifies the type of input element to render. The exceptions to the *<input type="">* rule are the *<textarea>* and *<button>* elements, which have their own element support. Table 3-1 outlines the input elements supported in HTML5 and indicates whether an element is now supported in Internet Explorer. The additional attributes available to an *<input>* element are discussed in later sections.

TABLE 3-1 HTML5 input elements

Element	Description
color*	Provides a color picker
date*	Provides a date picker
datetime*	Provides a date/time picker
month*	Enables users to select a numeric month and year
week*	Enables users to select a numeric week and year
time*	Enables users to select a time of day
number*	Forces the input to be numeric
Range	Allows users to select a value within a range by using a slider bar
tel*	Formats entered data as a phone number
url	Formats entered data as a properly formatted URL
Radio†	Enables users to select a single value for a list of choices
Checkbox†	Enables users to select multiple values in a list of choices
Password†	Captures a password and glyphs the entered characters
Button†	Enables users to perform an action such as run script
Reset†	Resets all HTML elements within a form
Submit†	Posts the form data to a destination for further processing

*Not supported currently by Internet Explorer
†Not new in HTML5

Using *text* and *textarea* input types

The *text* and *textarea* input controls are the most flexible. By using these controls, you allow users to enter any text that they want into a regular text box. A *text* box provides a single-line text entry, whereas a *textarea* allows for a multiline data entry. The following HTML shows the markup for both types of controls:

```
<table>
    <tr>
        <td>
          First Name:
        </td>
```

```
        <td>
            <input type="text" id="firstNameText"/>
        </td>
    </tr>
    <tr>
        <td>
            Last Name:
        </td>
        <td>
            <input type="text" id="lastNameText"/>
        </td>
    </tr>
...
    <tr>
        <td>Other Comments:
        </td>
        <td>
            <textarea id="otherCommentsText" rows="5" cols="20"></textarea>
        </td>
    </tr>
</table>
```

Figure 3-1 shows the output of this code.

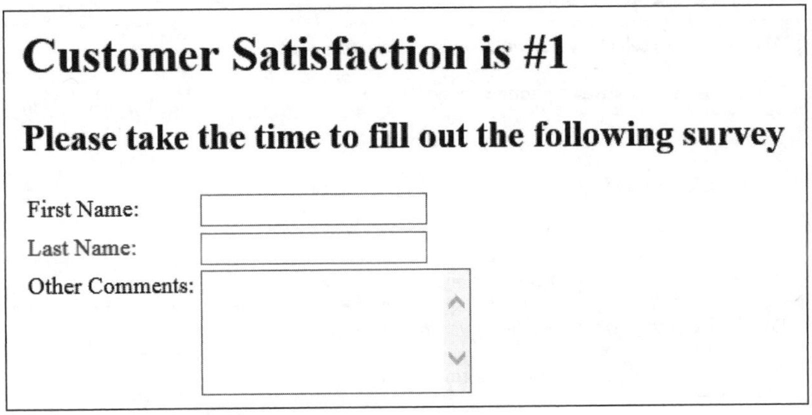

Customer Satisfaction is #1

Please take the time to fill out the following survey

First Name:
Last Name:
Other Comments:

FIGURE 3-1 HTML markup showing text box data-entry fields

This code adds text boxes to capture information such as first name, last name, and additional comments. For the first and last names, the input is a standard text box as denoted by *type="text"*. This tells the renderer to display an input field into which users can enter free-form text. However, this type of input field is limited to a single line. The Other Comments text box provides a multiline text area for users to enter text into. The *rows* and *cols* attributes define the viewable size of the text area. In this case, users can enter many lines of text into the text area.

Other attributes that help with controlling how much information is entered into the text fields is the *maxlength* attribute:

```
<input type="text" id="firstNameText" maxlength="50"/>
```

Users can't enter any more than 50 characters into the text field with the *maxlength* set to a value of 50.

In some cases, you might want to ensure that users enter only certain information in a certain format.

url input type

The *<input>* type of *url* displays a text box similar to what the *<input>* type of *text* provides. However, the renderer is instructed that the input type is *url*, so when users try to submit a form with this type of information on it, it validates that the text in the box matches the format of a valid URL.

EXAM TIP

You can validate data in many ways. Even more options become available in HTML5, such as the *url* input type. Also available are the *pattern* attribute and the use of regular expressions in JavaScript. Both of these are discussed later in this chapter.

The following code demonstrates a *url* type added to the survey:

```
<tr>
    <td>Last Name:
    </td>
    <td>
        <input type="text" id="lastNameText"/>
    </td>
</tr>
<tr>
    <td>
        Your favorite website:
    </td>
    <td>
        <input type="url"/>
    </td>
</tr>
<tr>
    <td>
        Other Comments:
    </td>
    <td>
        <textarea id="otherCommentsText" rows="5" cols="20"></textarea>
    </td>
</tr>
...
<tr>
    <td>
        <input type="submit"/>
    </td>
</tr>
```

This code produces the output shown in Figure 3-2 to the HTML page making up the survey. This HTML code also adds an input button, as discussed later in the section, "Using the *button* input type."

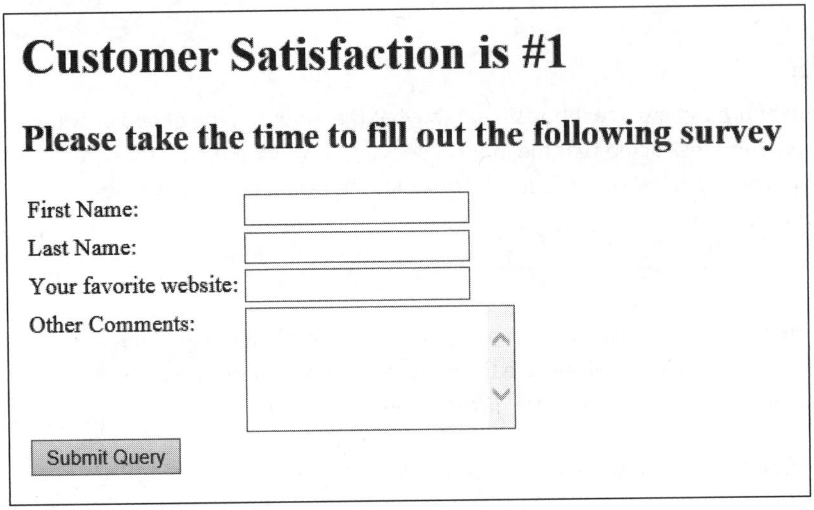

Customer Satisfaction is #1

Please take the time to fill out the following survey

First Name:

Last Name:

Your favorite website:

Other Comments:

Submit Query

FIGURE 3-2 The *url* input box added to the survey

This code demonstrates the power of the *url* input type in validating that the text a user entered is indeed a valid URL format. If a user typed something other than a URL or an incomplete URL into the Your Favorite Website box, such as *contoso.com*, and then clicked the Submit Query button, the result would be similar to the output shown in Figure 3-3.

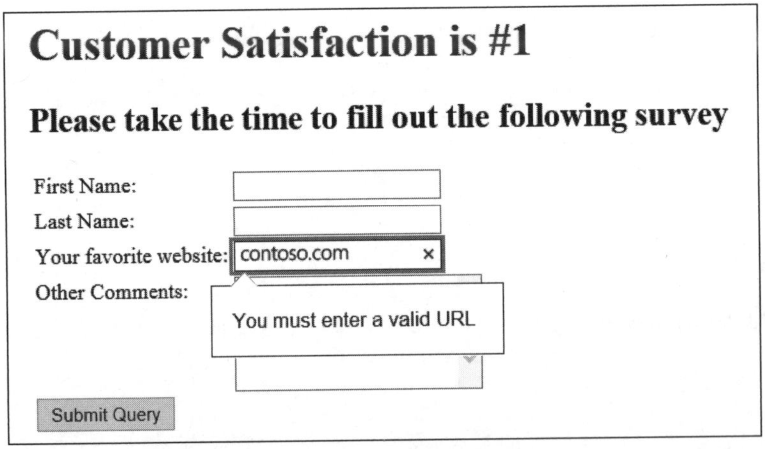

Customer Satisfaction is #1

Please take the time to fill out the following survey

First Name:

Last Name:

Your favorite website: contoso.com ×

Other Comments:

You must enter a valid URL

Submit Query

FIGURE 3-3 Demonstrating the validation of the *url* input type

Click the button to invoke the validation. The *url* box is outlined in red, and a tooltip pops up to explain the validation error. In this case, it has detected that a valid URL hasn't been entered. If the user corrects the data by specifying the URL as *http://www.contoso.com*, the validation error doesn't occur and the input can be submitted successfully.

If you require more flexibility and want to accept partially entered URL information, such as *contoso.com*, don't use the *url* input box. A regular *text* input with a *pattern* specified would be more appropriate.

Using the *password* input control

The *password* input control is the standard method of prompting users for sensitive information. As you type your password, each character is replaced with a glyph so that any onlookers can't see your password.

EXAM TIP

You can't specify default text in a *password* box or write to it via JavaScript. This is a security safeguard to help ensure the safety of passwords. However, the browsers provide a mechanism to store a password should a user choose to have the password remembered by the browser.

You can add a password text box to the survey to provide a way to retrieve a survey if a user wants to complete it later. The password could be stored in a server for later retrieval. The following markup is added to the HTML:

```
<tr>
    <td>
        Password:
    </td>
    <td>
        <input type="password"/>
    </td>
</tr>
```

With this HTML added, the survey now appears as shown in Figure 3-4.

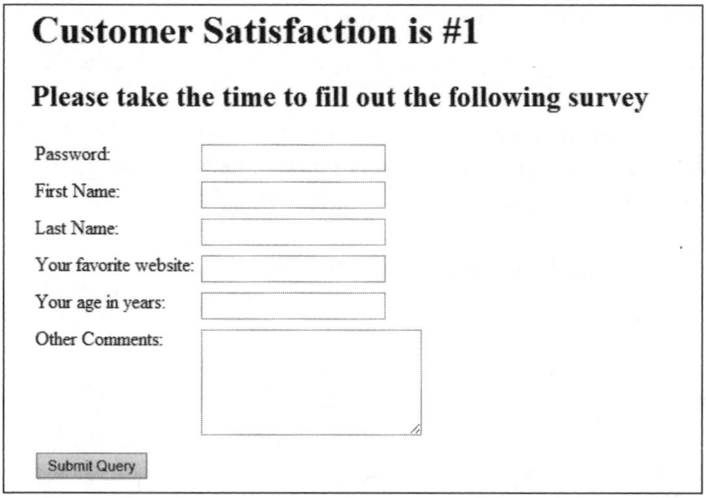

Customer Satisfaction is #1

Please take the time to fill out the following survey

Password:

First Name:

Last Name:

Your favorite website:

Your age in years:

Other Comments:

Submit Query

FIGURE 3-4 A password input field added to the form

Again, the password text box doesn't look any different than any other text box. However, typing into the box provides a different experience, as shown in Figure 3-5.

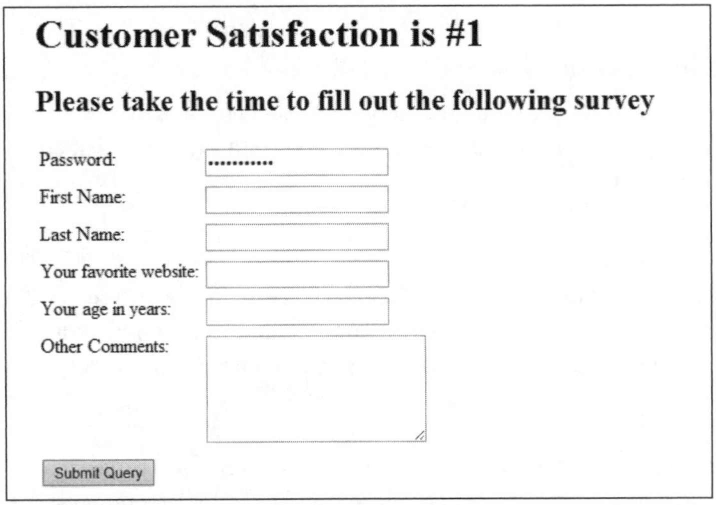

Customer Satisfaction is #1

Please take the time to fill out the following survey

Password: `••••••••••`

First Name:

Last Name:

Your favorite website:

Your age in years:

Other Comments:

Submit Query

FIGURE 3-5 Replacing password input with the glyph character

The *password* input type captures information securely. Users typing this information don't want others who are nearby to be able to see what they've been typing and hence compromise their data.

Using the *email* input type

You can use the *email* input type to ensure that the format of the text entered into the text box matches that of a valid email address. Being able to capture an email address is often important to enable further follow up with a user. This control helps ensure that the information entered matches what's expected in the form of an email address.

EXAM TIP

Validation of the *email* input type confirms only that the information entered matches the expected format of a valid email address. It in no way verifies that the email address itself is a valid mailbox that can receive messages.

The following HTML adds an email address input type to the survey:

```
<tr>
    <td>
        Email address:
    </td>
    <td>
        <input type="email"/>
    </td>
</tr>
<tr>
```

```
    <td>
        <input type="submit"/>
    </td>
</tr>
```

Figure 3-6 shows the output of this HTML.

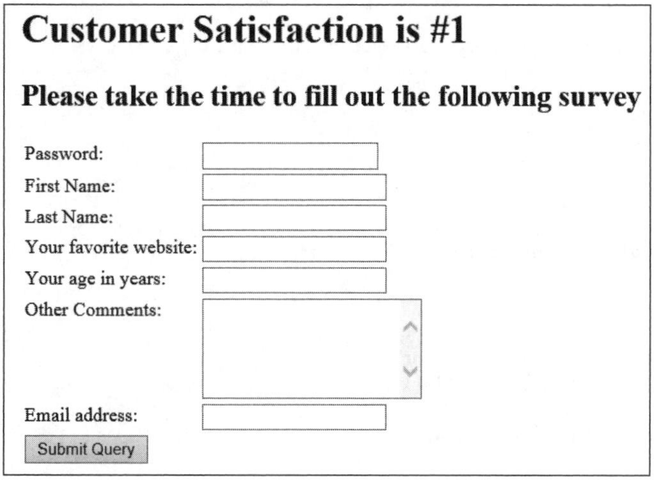

Customer Satisfaction is #1

Please take the time to fill out the following survey

Password:
First Name:
Last Name:
Your favorite website:
Your age in years:
Other Comments:

Email address:

Submit Query

FIGURE 3-6 Output of the *email* address input type

Just as with the *url* input type, if you type text that doesn't match the format of an email address, you receive a warning message (see Figure 3-7).

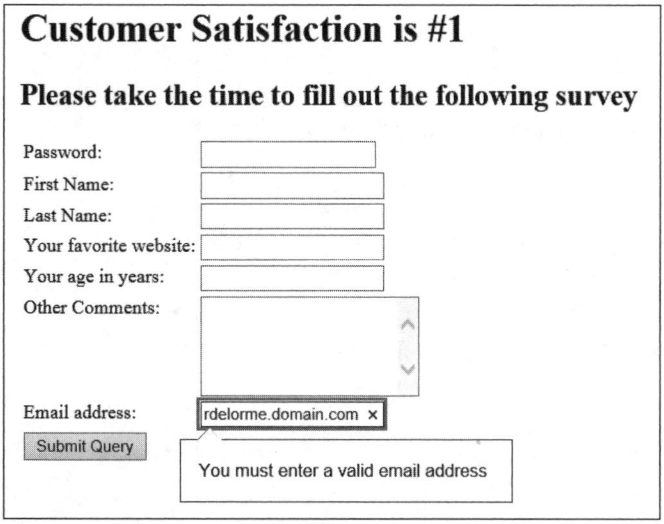

Customer Satisfaction is #1

Please take the time to fill out the following survey

Password:
First Name:
Last Name:
Your favorite website:
Your age in years:
Other Comments:

Email address: rdelorme.domain.com ×

Submit Query

You must enter a valid email address

FIGURE 3-7 Validation for the email address input type

This validation helps ensure that you don't mistype your email address. Of course, it doesn't prevent you from entering an invalid email address, only one where the format doesn't match correctly to what would be expected such as having the @ symbol and ending with a .com or other domain suffix.

Using the *checkbox* input type

In some cases when capturing information from users, you need to be able to capture more than one choice as it relates to a specific question. In this case, the *checkbox* input control is the best choice. You can provide a series of check boxes and allow users to select all that apply.

The survey will now add a question where users can select multiple items, as follows:

```
<tr>
    <td>Your age in years:</td>
    <td><input type="number" /></td>
</tr>
<tr>
    <td>
        What colors have you colored your hair:
    </td>
    <td>
        <input type="checkbox" id="chkBrown"/> Brown
        <input type="checkbox" id="chkBlonde"/> Blonde
        <input type="checkbox" id="chkBlack"/> Black
        <input type="checkbox" id="chkRed"/> Red
        <input type="checkbox" id="chkNone"/> None
    </td>
</tr>
```

In this HTML example, users see a list of hair colors that they might have used. Because a user possibly might have used more than one, she has the option to choose more than one. Figure 3-8 shows the output of this HTML.

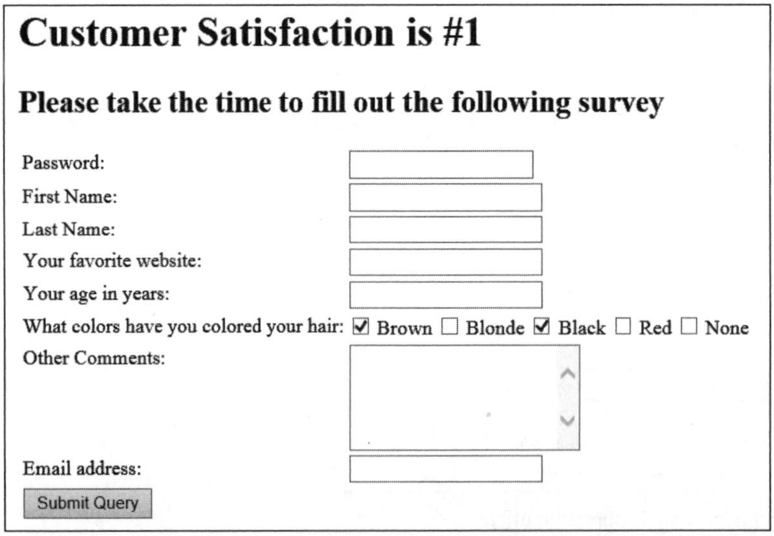

FIGURE 3-8 The input check box added to the HTML form

An additional attribute available on the check box is the *checked* attribute. This attribute provides a way to default a check box to the "checked" (or selected) state. By default, check boxes aren't selected. However, by adding the attribute as follows, the check box defaults to the "checked" state when the page is loaded:

```
<input type="checkbox" id="chkBrown" checked="checked"/> Brown
```

In other cases, when presented with a list of items, users might be able to choose only a single item from the list.

Using the *radio* input type

The radio button is similar to the check box in that it provides a list of options for users to select from. The difference from the check box is that users can select only a single item from the list. An example would be asking users to rate something on a scale from 1 to 5. To add this type of question to the survey, incorporate the following HTML beneath the check boxes:

```
<tr>
    <td>
        Rate your experience:
    </td>
    <td>
        <input type="radio" id="chkOne" name="experience"/> 1 - Very Poor
        <input type="radio" id="chkTwo" name="experience"/> 2
        <input type="radio" id="chkThree" name="experience"/> 3
        <input type="radio" id="chkFour" name="experience"/> 4
        <input type="radio" id="chkFive" name="experience"/> 5 - Very Good
    </td>
</tr>
```

Notice that as with all HTML elements, each *radio* input type needs a unique *id*. However, the *name* attribute ties all the radio buttons together. With the same name specified for each *radio* type, the browser knows that they are part of a group and that only one radio button of the group can be selected. Figure 3-9 shows the output of the radio buttons added to the survey.

In this output, the radio buttons are shown from left to right and enable users to select only one option. When a user changes the selection to a different option, the previously selected option is automatically cleared.

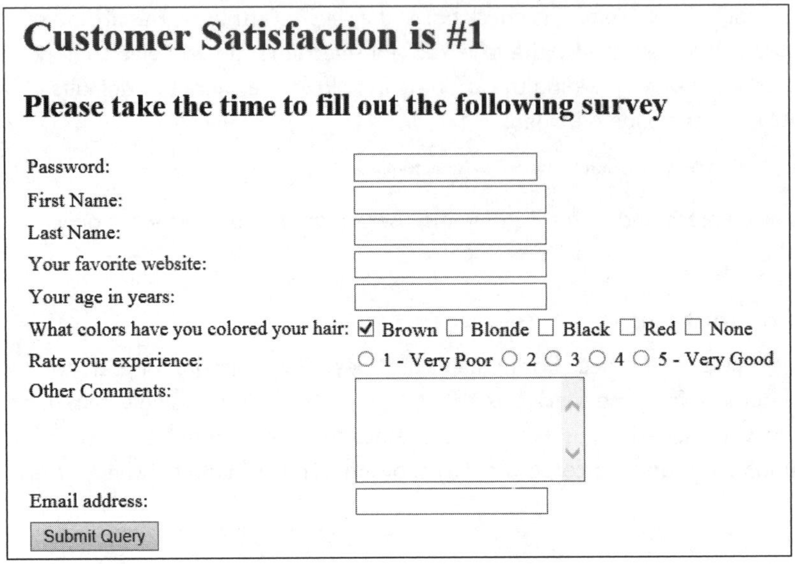

Customer Satisfaction is #1

Please take the time to fill out the following survey

Password:

First Name:

Last Name:

Your favorite website:

Your age in years:

What colors have you colored your hair: ☑ Brown ☐ Blonde ☐ Black ☐ Red ☐ None

Rate your experience: ○ 1 - Very Poor ○ 2 ○ 3 ○ 4 ○ 5 - Very Good

Other Comments:

Email address:

Submit Query

FIGURE 3-9 Adding some *radio* input types to the form

Like with the *checkbox* input types, defaulting the state of the *radio* input to selected is possible. This is done in exactly the same way, by specifying the *checked* attribute:

```
<input type="radio" id="chkFive" name="experience" checked="checked"/> 5 - Very Good
```

In this case, the rating of 5 - Very Good defaults to selected for the group of radio buttons.

You can have multiple groups of radio buttons on the same page by specifying a different name for each group of buttons. Another way to provide users with the ability to specify a single value within a group of values is with the use of the range control.

Using the *range* input type

Using the *range* input type enables users to specify a value within a predefined range by using a slider bar. This type can be used in cases where a wider range of values is required to choose from but using radio buttons would be too unwieldy. Add another rating question to the survey, as shown in the following HTML after the radio buttons:

```
<tr>
    <td>How likely would you recommend the product:
    </td>
    <td>
        <input type="range" min="1" max="25" value="20"/>
    </td>
</tr>
```

This HTML markup provides users with a slider bar that they can use to specify a value between 1 and 25. The *min* attribute specifies the minimum value of the range; the *max* attribute specifies the maximum value. The *value* attribute specifies a default value. If you omit the *value* attribute, the range defaults to the minimum value. This HTML displays the output shown in Figure 3-10.

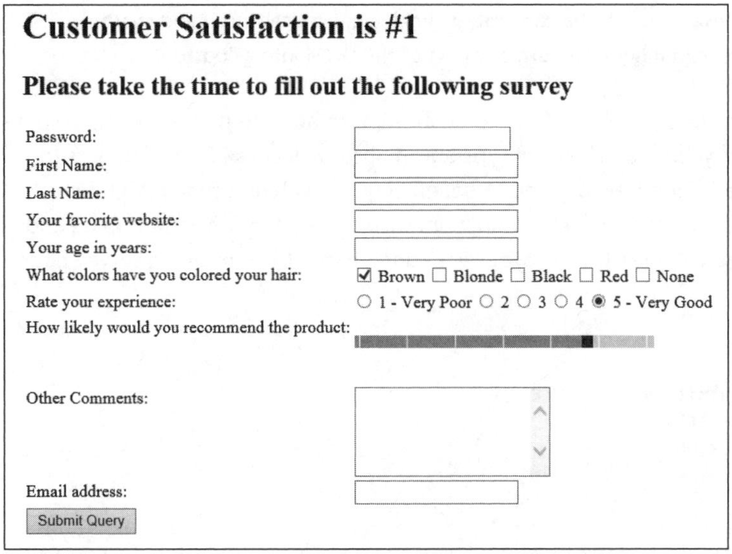

Customer Satisfaction is #1

Please take the time to fill out the following survey

Password:

First Name:

Last Name:

Your favorite website:

Your age in years:

What colors have you colored your hair: ☑ Brown ☐ Blonde ☐ Black ☐ Red ☐ None

Rate your experience: ○ 1 - Very Poor ○ 2 ○ 3 ○ 4 ● 5 - Very Good

How likely would you recommend the product:

Other Comments:

Email address:

Submit Query

FIGURE 3-10 A range input element added to the HTML form

In this output, the range control is displayed as a slider bar. The bar defaults to the value of 20 as specified in the markup. Users can grab the black endpoint of the slider and change the value lower or higher by dragging it left or right. As a user changes the value, a tooltip shows the current value where the slider resides. In this case, the user is now at the value 17 (see Figure 3-11).

FIGURE 3-11 The tooltip displaying the current value of the range as the user changes it.

After users enter all the needed information, they need a way to submit or save the information. The submit button has already been previewed.

Using the *button* input type

The input type that allows users to submit the form or clear it is *button*. The *button* input isn't new to HTML5 but is an essential piece to the data-capture puzzle. Buttons are what tell the website when a user finishes doing something and that they want to perform an action. The *<input>* element supports three types of button controls: *submit*, *reset*, and *button*.

EXAM TIP

Anything can be a "button." Because most DOM elements have a *click* event or at least a *mousedown* and *mouseup* event, the concept of clicking can be captured and custom actions processed. This can inherently turn any part of the DOM into a "button."

The *submit* input type tells the HTML form to post its information to the server (or, in some cases, to another site or webpage). The *reset* type automatically clears all form elements to their default values. The *button* type provides a generic button with no predefined functionality. It can be used to provide a custom function, such as cancel out from this page and return to the home page. All three button types are added to the bottom of the survey page as follows:

```
<tr>
    <td>
        <input type="submit"/>
        <input type="reset"/>
        <input type="button"/>
    </td>
</tr>
```

That's all that's required to add the functionality to the page for each button. Of course, *type="button"* requires some JavaScript to be wired up to actually do something. However, the submit and reset buttons come with the described functionality built in. The HTML provides the output on the form as shown in Figure 3-12.

Customer Satisfaction is #1

Please take the time to fill out the following survey

Password:
First Name:
Last Name:
Your favorite website:
Your age in years:
What colors have you colored your hair: ☑ Brown ☐ Blonde ☐ Black ☐ Red ☐ None
Rate your experience: ○ 1 - Very Poor ○ 2 ○ 3 ○ 4 ● 5 - Very Good
How likely would you recommend the product:

Other Comments:

Email address:

Submit Query   Reset

FIGURE 3-12 Buttons added to the HTML form

The text on the buttons is the default text. The submit button comes with the text Submit Query, and the reset button comes with the text Reset. This can't be changed. However, the *button* type doesn't have any text on it because none was specified and the button doesn't come with any predetermined behavior. To specify text for this button, add the *value* attribute:

```
<input type="button" value="Cancel"/>
```

This produces a button as shown in Figure 3-13.

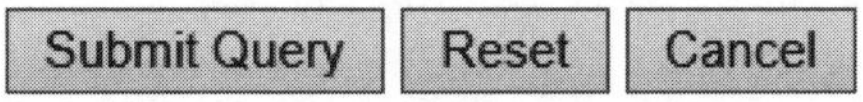

| Submit Query | Reset | Cancel |

FIGURE 3-13 The button type with text specified

That's what you get with the input type of *button*. However, in some cases, more flexibility in the button's content is desired. This is where the *button* element comes in handy.

Using the *button* element

The *button* element provides a button on the user interface, just as the name implies. However, from a graphical perspective, this element behaves very differently.

The *button* element also supports a *type* attribute, like as the ones seen previously: *submit*, *reset*, and *button*. This example steps away from the survey and demonstrates these buttons on a stand-alone page. The following HTML is added to a page, and the subsequent output is shown in Figure 3-14:

```
<button type="button"/>
<button type="reset"/>
<button type="submit"/>
```

FIGURE 3-14 All three types of *button* elements

This output displays three buttons, as expected. However, it doesn't provide any text on the buttons. The *button* element provides only the desired click behavior, such as submitting, resetting, or providing a custom behavior like with *type="button"*. Everything else must be specified in the HTML, including the label or text that goes on the button. In this way, you have much more control over what's put on the button. Instead of Submit Query as with the *<input>* element, the text can be set as Submit Survey or Save Data. The following HTML shows the text on the buttons, and Figure 3-15 shows the output:

```
<button type="button">Go Home</button>
<button type="reset" >Reset</button>
<button type="submit">Submit Survey</button>
```

FIGURE 3-15 The button elements with text specified

You can take the *button* element even further. The element's contents don't have to be just plain text. You can embed images within the element by using the *<img>* element in addition to text, or embed an entire clickable paragraph. You also can apply cascading style sheets (CSS) to the button to change its appearance, as shown in Figure 3-16. The HTML is as follows:

```
<button type="button" style="border-radius: 15px;">
    <p>Something exciting lies behind this button</p>
    <img src=".\myimage.jpg"/>
</button>
```

FIGURE 3-16 A customized *button* element

Within the *button* element lies the capability to create a highly customized button and get default behavior from the browser.

In addition to what's provided by the various input types, such as *range*, *email*, and *url*, other attributes are available and common across most of the input controls and provide additional flexibility in how the fields are validated. This is covered next.

Implementing content attributes

Input controls provide content attributes that allow you to control their behavior in the browser declaratively rather than have to write JavaScript code.

Making controls read-only

Part of the specification for the HTML input controls includes a *readonly* attribute. If you want to present information to users in elements such as text boxes but don't want them to be able to alter this data, use the *readonly* attribute. When *readonly* is specified, the renderer won't allow users to change any of the data in the text box. The following HTML demonstrates the *readonly* property:

```
<tr>
    <td>
        Your Secret Code:
    </td>
    <td>
        <input type="text" readonly value="00XY998BB"/>
    </td>
</tr>
```

In this code, at the top of the survey form, users are provided a secret code to correspond with their survey. They can't change this because the *readonly* attribute is specified.

Where fields aren't read-only and users can type whatever they want into the text box, providing them with the capability to check spelling is a good idea.

Providing a spelling checker

Checking spelling is another method available to validate user input. The *spellcheck* attribute helps provide feedback to users that a word they've entered is misspelled. Again, this attribute is applied to the input element:

```
<textarea id="otherCommentsText" rows="5" cols="20" spellcheck="true"></textarea>
```

In this HTML, the *spellcheck* option has been turned on for the Other Comments text area because users can type whatever they want and might make spelling errors.

The output of a text box with *spellcheck* isn't any different until a user starts typing and enters a spelling error. Figure 3-17 shows the red underlining for the words that are detected as spelled incorrectly.

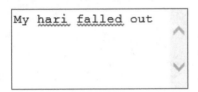

FIGURE 3-17 A *textarea* with *spellcheck* enabled

In some cases, the built-in validation provided by the input controls isn't sufficient, and providing a custom pattern to validate is better, as explored in the next section.

Specifying a pattern

As you saw with the *email* and *url* input types, built-in validation is fairly thorough in ensuring that the information entered is accurate and as expected. However, in some cases you might require looser or stricter validation. Suppose that you don't want users to have to specify the HTTP protocol in a *url* type, but you want to allow only .com or .ca websites. This can be achieved by using the *pattern* attribute, which allows the use of a regular expression to define the pattern that should be accepted.

EXAM TIP

The *pattern* attribute applies only to text boxes. It can't be used to override the validation built into the *email* or *url* types.

The following code shows the *pattern* attribute used to achieve the desired validation:

```
<input type="text" title="Only .com and .ca are permitted."
 pattern="^[a-zA-Z0-9\-\.]+\.(com|ca)$"/>
```

Plenty of regular expressions are available to validate a URL; this one is fairly simple. When specifying the *pattern* attribute, you should specify the *title* attribute as well. The *title* attribute specifies the error message to users in the tooltip when validation fails.

To ensure that users enter the data in the correct format, you should show them a sample of what the data should look like. This is achieved with the *placeholder* attribute.

Using the *placeholder* attribute

The *placeholder* attribute enables you to prompt users with what's expected in a certain text box. For example, an email text box might show placeholder text such as me@mydomain.com. More importantly, this placeholder text doesn't interfere with users when they start typing their information into the text box. The *placeholder* attribute achieves this, as shown in the following HTML and subsequent output in Figure 3-18.

```
<input type="email" placeholder="me@mydomain.com" /></td>
```

me@mydomain.com

FIGURE 3-18 The *placeholder* attribute demonstrating to users what is expected

The placeholder text is slightly lighter in color. As soon as a user puts the mouse cursor into the box to type, the placeholder text disappears and the user's typing takes over.

HTML fields can be validated in many ways. In some cases, it's not so much what is put into the field, but that the field is indeed filled in. The *required* attribute controls this for the HTML elements.

Making controls required

To ensure that a user fills in a field, use the *required* attribute with the *<input>* element. Doing so ensures that users will be told that the field is required. In this example, the email address will be made a required text box:

```
<input type="email" placeholder="me@mydomain.com" required/>
```

With the required control specified, if users try to submit the form without specifying an email address, they get an error message (see Figure 3-19). Now users can't submit until they specify a valid email address.

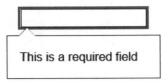

This is a required field

FIGURE 3-19 The required field validation invoked

The capabilities of the input controls can provide quite a robust validation framework. However, more needs to be done to ensure that the website is safe and secure.

Thought experiment
Creating dynamic forms

In this thought experiment, apply what you've learned about this objective. You can find answers to these questions in the "Answers" section at the end of this chapter.

Building on the thought experiment from Objective 1.3, consider what you need to do to add custom validation to a control based on what a user has entered in the previous field. Having a dynamically created form where you can change the validation rules as a user progresses through the form can be quite powerful. Consider different cultural variations to rules on phone numbers, postal codes, and email address suffixes. Describe how you would implement the validation so that you could provide context rich validation for the user.

Objective summary

- Input controls such as *text* and *textarea* allow users to type information into a webpage.
- Some input controls provide built-in validation, such as for URLs and email addresses.
- Radio buttons and check boxes provide controls for users to select items in a list.
- Reset and submit buttons control behavior of the HTML form.
- Users can't modify the content of a control that has the *readonly* attribute assigned.
- You can add a spelling checker to a text box to help users avoid spelling errors.
- The *pattern* attribute helps define a regular expression for custom validation of formatted data.
- The *required* attribute ensures that a field is populated before users can submit the form.

Objective review

1. Which input control is better suited for allowing users to make multiple selections?

   A. *radio button*

   B. *textarea*

   C. *checkbox*

   D. *radio or checkbox*

2. Which input control is designed to allow users to enter secure information in a way that keeps others from seeing what's typed?

   A. *text*

   B. *textarea*

   C. *url*

   D. *password*

3. Which input control posts form data to a server?

   A. *button*

   B. *Submit*

   C. *Reset*

   D. *radio*

4. Which of the following declarations are valid ways to make a text control non-editable?

   A. *<input type="text" edit="false"/>*

   B. *<input type="text" editable="false"/>*

   C. *<input type="text" readonly="yes"/>*

   D. *<input type="text" readonly/>*

5. How can you ensure that all necessary fields are populated before a form can be submitted?

   A. Write a JavaScript function to evaluate all the controls on the form for content.

   B. On the server, evaluate all the controls for data and return an error page for missing content.

   C. Add the *required* attribute on each control so that users get a message that the field is required.

   D. Add a label to the page to let users know which controls they must fill in.

Objective 3.2: Validate user input by using JavaScript

The new HTML controls discussed in Objective 3.1 provide some great functionality to validate user data. However, this functionality has some limitations. This is where further validation performed in JavaScript comes in handy. JavaScript provides additional functionality that's not readily available in the core HTML controls. Although some controls aren't yet available in all browsers, you might need to validate user input such as dates, telephone numbers, or alphanumeric postal codes. This objective demonstrates how to use regular expressions to validate the input format and how to use the JavaScript built-in functions to ensure that data is the correct data type. This objective also adds a layer of security by demonstrating how to prevent malicious code injection.

> **This objective covers how to:**
> - Evaluate regular expressions
> - Validate data with built-in functions
> - Prevent code injection

Evaluating regular expressions

You saw the use of regular expressions in Objective 3.1. In fact, the core HTML input controls support a *pattern* attribute that allows you to apply a regular expression to validate user input. In some cases, though, validating user input in JavaScript can be more effective than inline with attributes. This section introduces regular expressions. The basic syntax of a regular expression is explained, as is how to use the expression in JavaScript.

Regular expressions have a unique syntax of their own. They can be daunting to use but can also be very powerful. Although a full instruction on regular expressions is beyond the scope of this book, a brief introduction is provided to support the later examples.

EXAM TIP

Regular expressions tend to make their way onto the exams. You should prepare by studying them in more detail. An Internet search should yield many resources freely available on the topic. Be familiar with how to read an expression for such things as email addresses, URLs, and phone numbers, among other things.

Regular expressions are a mix of special characters and literal characters that make up the pattern that someone would want to match. Table 3-1 lists the special characters and their meaning.

TABLE 3-1 Regular expression special characters

Symbol	Description
^	The caret character denotes the beginning of a string.
$	The dollar sign denotes the end of a string.
.	The period indicates to match on any character.
[A-Z]	Alphabet letters indicate to match any alphabetic character. This is case-sensitive. To match lowercase letters, use [a-z].
\d	This combination indicates to match any numeric character.
+	The plus sign denotes that the preceding character or character set must match at least once.
*	The asterisk denotes that the preceding character or character set might or might not match. This generates zero or more matches.
[^]	When included in a character set, the caret denotes a negation. [^a] would match a string that doesn't have an 'a' in it.
?	The question mark denotes that the preceding character is optional.
\w	This combination indicates to match a word character consisting of any alphanumeric character, including an underscore.
\	The backslash is an escape character. If any special character should be included in the character set to match on literally, it needs to be escaped with a \. For example, to find a backslash in a string, the pattern would include \\.
\s	This combination indicates to match on a space. When it's combined with + or *, it can match on one or more spaces.

This list encompasses the main functions available when string matching with regular expressions. Building regular expressions requires taking the definition of those characters and essentially creating a mask out of them to be used by the regular expression engine to interpret and decide whether there is a match. For example, a Canadian postal code is comprised of the format A1A 1A1—that is, alternating alphabetic characters and numeric characters with a space in the middle. Some characters aren't used in postal codes because the machines confuse them with other characters (for example, Z and 2). Also, the space isn't mandatory. When you need to enforce the data format of the user input, deciding how you want the data to be captured and how flexible you want it to be is important. Then build your regular expression to match this.

Now, build the regular expression for a postal code. You first need to denote the beginning of the string, because it helps eliminate unnecessary white space at the lead of the string:

^

The first part of the expression is the caret. The next character must be alphabetic:

^[A-Z,a-z]

Because postal codes aren't case sensitive, the expression allows the first character to be either uppercase or lowercase. The next character in the postal code must be a digit:

```
^[A-Z,a-z]\d
```

Because the postal code accepts all digits 0–9, \d is used to specify any digit. However, [0-9] could have been used as well. And now the pattern continues, letter-number-letter number-letter-number:

```
^[A-Z,a-z]\d[A-Z,a-z]\d[A-Z,a-z]\d
```

As was indicated earlier, the space in the middle of the postal code, while common convention, is optional. This is where deciding how flexible the data validation should be is required. The expression as it is won't allow for any space in the middle because the expression is set to match on consecutive alternating letter-number-letter. Perhaps, for formatting purposes, a space should be required. In this case, \s would require that a space is included:

```
^[A-Z,a-z]\d[A-Z,a-z]\s\d[A-Z,a-z]\d
```

Now, users would be required to enter the postal code with a space in the middle of the two sets of three characters. But maybe the website doesn't care about the space in the middle, because it doesn't really affect anything. In this case, the \s can be denoted with the *:

```
^[A-Z,a-z]\d[A-Z,a-z]\s*\d[A-Z,a-z]\d
```

Now, the expression allows for alternating letter-number-letter and one or more spaces can occur in the middle. The space is now optional, but a problem has been introduced. The user can now enter any number of spaces and still pass the validation, such as:

A1A   1A1

That would pass the validation because one or more spaces is required by the \s*. The desired outcome here is to allow only one space or no spaces. For this, a new element is added to limit the number of occurrences to just one. This is accomplished by specifying the maximum length allowed for the character set being matched:

```
^[A-Z,a-z]\d[A-Z,a-z]\s{1}\d[A-Z,a-z]\d
```

The {1} says to match the previous character only the specified number of times—in this case, one time. Now the expression is back to functionality that's no different than just specifying the \s. What is needed next is something to make the single space optional, as denoted with the ?. To achieve this effect, the space segment is wrapped in square brackets to make it a set and followed by the ? to make it optional:

```
^[A-Z,a-z]\d[A-Z,a-z][\s{1}]?\d[A-Z,a-z]\d
```

Now you have a regular expression that requires the correct alphanumeric pattern for a Canadian postal code with an optional space in the middle.

This simple example demonstrates the key elements to a regular expression. Although this regular expression can be placed into the *pattern* attribute of the *<input>* element, this next section discusses how to use the JavaScript framework to perform pattern matching with regular expressions.

Evaluating regular expressions in JavaScript

Just like with strings and integers, regular expressions are objects in JavaScript. As such, they can be created and can provide methods to evaluate strings. Regular expression objects are created in a similar fashion as strings; however, rather than use " to encapsulate the expression, use the forward slash /<expression>/ instead. JavaScript knows that text surrounded by forward slashes in this way is a regular expression object. Going back to the postal code example, the following HTML is provided:

```
<script type="text/javascript">
    function CheckString() {
        try{
            var s = $('#regExString').val();
            var regExpression = /^[A-Z,a-z]\d[A-Z,a-z][\s{1}]?\d[A-Z,a-z]\d/;
            if (regExpression.test(s))
                alert("Valid postal code.");
            else
                alert("Invalid postal code.");
        } catch (e) {
            alert(e.message);
        }
    }
</script>
<body>
    <form>
        <input type="text" id="regExString" />
        <button onclick="CheckString();" >Evaluate</button>
    </form>
</body>
```

This HTML provides a very basic page with a text box and a button. The button does nothing more than call a function to validate whether the entered text matches the format desired for a postal code. This page shouldn't contain anything that you haven't seen already, except the line in which the regular expression object is created:

```
var regExpression = /^[A-Z,a-z]\d[A-Z,a-z][\s{1}]?\d[A-Z,a-z]\d/;
```

With this line, a regular expression object is created and, as a result, methods are available. The string is extracted from the text box and passed to the *test* method of the regular expression. The *test* method returns a Boolean to indicate whether the input string matches the regular expression that was created.

The regular expression object also provides a method called *exec*. This method returns the portion of the input string that matches the expression. The following code example illustrates this by adding another button and function to use the *exec* method instead of *test*:

```
function CheckStringExec() {
    var s = $('#regExString').val();
    var regExpression = /^[A-Z,a-z]\d[A-Z,a-z][\s{1}]?\d[A-Z,a-z]\d/;
    var results = regExpression.exec(s);
    if(results != null)
        alert("Valid postal code." + results[0]);
    else
        alert("Invalid postal code.");
...
<button onclick="CheckStringExec();" >Evaluate with Exec</button>
```

With this button, the expression is evaluated just like it was with the *test* method, except the match is returned as a string array. That the return result is a string array is important to note because using regular expressions can result in multiple matches. If a match isn't made, the return result will be null. In this example, the results are evaluated by checking whether the array isn't null; if it's not, the postal code is valid and shown back to the user. If the match isn't made, the return value will be null.

The string object also provides regular expression methods. The string could be used directly to evaluate the expression. The string provides the *search* and *match* methods. The *search* method returns the index of the character in the string where the first match occurred. The *match* method returns the part of the string that matches the pattern, much like the *exec* method. In addition to these two methods, many of the other string methods accept a regular expression object, such as *indexOf*, *split*, and *replace*. This provides some advanced functionality for manipulating strings in JavaScript.

EXAM TIP

The example uses a regular expression to validate user input of data entered into the webpage. Keep in mind that data can come from anywhere, such as an RSS feed or back-end server providing JavaScript Object Notation (JSON). In this context, where a website is expecting specifically formatted data, you can use regular expressions to validate the incoming data and prevent the possible crashing of the website or at least errors being presented to users.

Although regular expressions provide a great deal of power in evaluating strings for patterns and ensuring that the data is in the desired format, JavaScript also provides built-in functions to evaluate the type of data received.

Validating data with built-in functions

JavaScript provides built-in functions to evaluate data type. Some functions are provided directly within JavaScript; others are provided by the jQuery library.

The *isNaN* function provides a way to evaluate whether the value passed into it isn't a number. If the value isn't a number, the function returns true; if it is a number, it returns false. If the expected form of data being evaluated is numeric, this function provides a defensive way to determine this and handle it appropriately:

```
if (isNan(value)) {
    //handle the non number value
}
else {
    //proceed with the number value
}
```

The opposite of the *isNaN* function is the *isFinite* function. The *isFinite* function is used in the same way but returns true if the value is a finite number and false if it's not.

Being able to validate data is very important as previously outlined. Equally important to validating the data explicitly is ensuring that data-entry fields prevent users from injecting script. *Code injection* is a widely discussed topic in website security. The next section discusses preventing code injection.

Preventing code injection

Code injection is a technique that attackers use to inject JavaScript code into your webpage. These attacks usually take advantage of dynamically created content to have additional script run so that malicious users can try to gain some sort of control over the website. Their intentions can be many, but among those intentions might be to trick other site users into providing sensitive information. Depending on the content of the page, different measures need to be considered.

Protecting against user input

A web application accepting user input opens up a potential attack surface for malicious users. The size of the attack surface depends on what's done with the entered data. If the website takes data and doesn't do anything with it outside the scope of the current webpage, such as send it to another server or store it in a database, the effects are limited to the current page and browser session. Little can be accomplished except to disrupt the design of the website for this particular user. However, if the captured data includes an account creation form or survey, for example, a malicious user has much more potential to do harm—especially when that information is later rendered to the webpage dynamically. This inherently allows anyone to add script to the site, which can open up the site to behavior such as phishing. As a webpage developer, you need to ensure that all user input is scrubbed of script elements. For example, don't allow < > text to be entered into the form. Without those characters, a script block can't be added.

Using the *eval* function

The *eval* function is used to run JavaScript dynamically. It takes a string as a parameter and runs it as a JavaScript function. Never use the *eval* function against any data provided by an external source over which you don't have 100 percent control.

Using iFrames

iFrames open up a new opportunity to attackers. Search engines provide a plethora of results dealing with exploits regarding the use of iFrames. The *sandbox* attribute should always be used to restrict what data can be placed into an iFrame. The *sandbox* attribute has four possible values, as listed in Table 3-2.

TABLE 3-2 Available sandbox attribute values

Value	Description
""	An empty string applies all restrictions. This is the most secure.
allow-same-origin	iFrame content is treated as being from the same origin as the containing HTML document.
allow-top-navigation	iFrame content can load content from the containing HTML document.
allow-forms	iFrame can submit forms.
allow-scripts	iFrame can run script.

Thought experiment
Encoding input data

In this thought experiment, apply what you've learned about this objective. You can find answers to these questions in the "Answers" section at the end of this chapter.

The primary way in which malicious users seek out vulnerabilities in your webpages is through the use of code injections. These are used to find weaknesses in the code where malicious users could trick legitimate users into redirecting to a malicious site or—worse—steal private data. What additional strategies can you design into your webpages to help prevent these types of attacks?

Objective summary

- Regular expressions are strings of special characters that an interpreter understands and uses to validate text format.
- Regular expressions are objects in JavaScript that provide methods for testing input data.

- *isNaN* is a built-in function to determine whether a value isn't a number, whereas *isFinite* validates whether the value is a finite number.
- Code injection is a technique that attackers use to inject malicious code into your application.
- iFrames and dynamic JavaScript are dangerous if not used properly in a webpage.

Objective review

1. Which of the following regular expression characters denote the end of the string?

   A. $

   B. %

   C. ^

   D. &

2. Which of the following *sandbox* attributes allows the iFrame to load content from the containing HTML document?

   A. *allow-script-execution*

   B. *allow-same-origin*

   C. *allow-forms*

   D. *allow-top-navigation*

   E. *allow-top-document*

3. Which function should never be used to run JavaScript?

   A. *execute*

   B. *JSDynamic*

   C. *eval*

   D. *evaluate*

Objective 3.3: Consume data

This objective covers how to consume data in an HTML5 web application. The ability to consume data from external sources is more popular than ever. Website mash-ups and social integration are major catalysts for this.

> **This objective covers how to:**
> - Consume JSON and XML data by using web services
> - Use the *XMLHTTPRequest* object

Consuming JSON and XML data by using web services

The two data formats commonly used in data transmission are JSON and XML. JSON is unstructured data, whereas XML is structured. JSON uses a special syntax that allows the definition of name value pairs in a lightweight string format. XML, as a relative of HTML, is more structured than JSON with named tags and opening and closing tags. Tags can have attributes. The following are examples of what a person object might look like in both formats where the person object has a first name, last name, hair color, and eye color:

- JSON:

  ```
  {firstName: "Rick", lastName: "Delorme", hairColor: "brown", eyeColor: "brown" }
  ```

- XML (Elements):

  ```
  <Person>
          <firstName>Rick</firstName>
          <lastName>Delorme</lastName>
          <hairColor>Brown</hairColor>
          <eyeColor>Brown</eyeColor>
  </Person>
  ```

- XML (attributes):

  ```
  <Person firstname="Rick" lastName="Delorme" hairColor="Brown" eyeColor="Brown"/>
  ```

When publishing data services such as Web Services or a REST API, you can control how you publish the data. When consuming third-party resources, you won't have control over how they've published the data.

Using the *XMLHttpRequest* object

JavaScript provides built-in support for receiving HTML data via the *XMLHttpRequest* object. The object makes a call to a web service, REST API, or other data provider services. The advantage of doing this via JavaScript on the client side is to be able to reload portions of the page from an external source without having to post the entire page back to the server.

XMLHttpRequest makes an HTTP request and expects to receive back data in XML format. Both synchronous and asynchronous calls are supported. Table 3-3, Table 3-4, and Table 3-5 list the available events, methods, and properties of the *XMLHttpRequest* object.

TABLE 3-3 Available events of the *XMLHttpRequest* object

Events	Description
Onreadystatechange	Sets an event handler for when the state of the request has changed. Used for asynchronous calls.
Ontimeout	Sets an event handler for when the request can't be completed.

TABLE 3-4 Available methods of the *XMLHttpRequest* object

Method	Description
Abort	Cancels the current request
getAllResponseHeaders	Gives a complete list of response headers
getResponseHeader	Returns the specific response header
Send	Makes the HTTP request and receives the response
setRequestHeader	Adds a custom HTTP header to the request
Open	Sets properties for the request such as the URL, a user name, and a password

TABLE 3-5 Available properties of the *XMLHttpRequest* object

Property	Description
readyState	Gets the current state of the object
Response	Gets the response returned from the server
responseBody	Gets the response body as an array of bytes
responseText	Gets the response body as a string
responseType	Gets the data type associated with the response, such as *blob*, *text*, *array-buffer*, or *document*
responseXML	Gets the response body as an XML DOM object
Status	Gets the HTTP status code of the request
statusText	Gets the friendly HTTP text that corresponds with the status
Timeout	Sets the timeout threshold on the request
withCredentials	Specifies whether the request should include user credentials

In its simplest form, a request to the server using the *XMLHttpRequest* object looks like this:

```
<script>
    $("document").ready(function () {
        $("#btnGetXMLData").click(function () {
            var xReq = new XMLHttpRequest();
            xReq.open("GET", "myXMLData.xml", false);
            xReq.send(null);
            $("#results").text(xReq.response);
        });
    });
</script>
```

This script assumes a button on the HTML form and a div to show the results. A new *XMLHttpRequest* object is created. The *open* method is called to specify the request type, URI, and whether to make the call asynchronous. Table 3-6 lists all the parameters to the *open* method.

TABLE 3-6 Parameters for the *XMLHttpRequest open* method

Parameter	Description
Method	The HTTP method being used for the request: GET, POST, etc.
URL	The URL to make the request to.
async	A Boolean value to indicate whether the call should be made asynchronously. If true, an event handler needs to be set for the *onreadystatechanged*.
User name	A user name if the destination requires credentials.
Password	A password if the destination requires credentials.

EXAM TIP

The *open* method doesn't make any server requests. If the user name and password is specified, it doesn't send this information to the server in the *open* method. When the *send* method is called, the user name and password aren't passed to the server either. The credentials are passed to the server only in response to a 401 security response from the server.

The *XMLHttpRequest* object provides some mechanisms for handling errors. The most common error to account for is a timeout error. By default, the value of the timeout is zero, which is infinite. A timeout value should always be specified. The code is updated as follows:

```
var xReq = new XMLHttpRequest();
xReq.open("GET", "myXMLData.xml", false);
xReq.timeout = 2000;
xReq.ontimeout = function () {
    $("#results").text("Request Timed out");
}
xReq.send(null);
$("#results").text(xReq.response);
```

This results in not allowing the call to take any more than two seconds. The timeout is expressed in milliseconds. After the timeout period, the *ontimeout* event handler is called to allow for this condition to be handled appropriately in the webpage.

An additional consideration for this code is whether to make the call synchronously or asynchronously. Ideally, you should ensure that the call to the service to get the data won't interfere with users and won't block them, unless of course they need to wait on the reply before taking any further action. Synchronous calls, as the examples so far have shown, block the user interface while the request is being made. To prevent this, the call should be asynchronous, as shown here:

```
var XMLHTTPReadyState_COMPLETE = 4;

var xReq = new XMLHttpRequest();
xReq.open("GET", "myXMLData.xml", true);
xReq.timeout = 2000;
xReq.ontimeout = function () {
    $("#results").text("Request Timed out");
}
xReq.onreadystatechange = function (e) {
    if (xReq.readyState == XMLHTTPReadyState_COMPLETE) {
        if (xReq.status = "200") {
            $("#results").text(xReq.response);
        } else {
            $("#results").text(xReq.statusText);
        }
    }
}
xReq.send(null);
```

The *onreadystate* event is assigned a function to run when the state of the *XMLHttpRequest* object is changed. When the request is complete, the *readyState* changes to complete (*readyState* == 4). At this point, the HTTP return status can be evaluated for a success value such as 200, and then the processing of the XML data can occur.

The same code that has been used so far to retrieve XML data can also be used to make a request for JSON data. The following update to the code shows this:

```
var XMLHTTPReadyState_COMPLETE = 4;

var xReq = new XMLHttpRequest();
xReq.open("GET", "myJSONData.json", true);
xReq.timeout = 2000;
xReq.ontimeout = function () {
    $("#results").text("Request Timed out");
}
xReq.onreadystatechange = function (e) {
    if (xReq.readyState == XMLHTTPReadyState_COMPLETE) {
        if (xReq.status = "200") {
            $("#results").text(xReq.response);
        } else {
            $("#results").text(xReq.statusText);
        }
    }
}
xReq.send(null);
```

The only difference to this code is the name of the URL being passed. In this case, the endpoint is a data source that returns JSON-formatted data instead of XML. The JSON is displayed to the screen in the same way that the XML is displayed.

When the data is received via the *XMLHttpRequest* object, the data will need to be deserialized into a more user-friendly format. You also might want to submit data to the server in response to user actions. The next objective examines these concepts.

Thought experiment
Creating a webpage with a stock ticker

In this thought experiment, apply what you've learned about this objective. You can find answers to these questions in the "Answers" section at the end of this chapter.

You are tasked with building a webpage for your client that involves a stock ticker. You need to provide real-time stock quotes to your page users in a scroll across the top of the page. Explain how you would build a web application that will do this dynamically without posting back the whole webpage.

Objective summary

- JSON and XML are the most common formats used for data exchange.
- JSON consists of name/value pairs.
- XML is a structured element-based document.
- JavaScript provides built-in support for receiving data via the *XMLHttpRequest* object.

Objective review

1. Which of the following is a valid JSON string?

    A. *{firstName, Rick, lastname, Delorme, hairColor, brown, eyeColor, brown}*

    B. *{firstName: Rick; lastname: Delorme; hairColor: brown; eyeColor: brown}*

    C. *{firstName: "Rick"; lastname: "Delorme"; hairColor: "brown"; eyeColor: "brown"}*

    D. *{firstName: "Rick", lastname: "Delorme", hairColor: "brown", eyeColor: "brown"}*

2. With the *XMLHttpRequest* object, which of the following properties provides the response in a human readable format?

    A. *Response*

    B. *responseBody*

    C. *responseText*

    D. *responseXML*

3. At which stage during an *XMLHttpRequest* are user credentials sent to the server?

   A. When the connection is opened

   B. When the request is sent

   C. When the ready state is complete

   D. When the server sends a security response requesting the credentials

Objective 3.4: Serialize, deserialize, and transmit data

Data can be received and sent in many forms. In the preceding objective, JSON and XML were examined specifically. The notion of presenting JSON or XML data directly to users isn't ideal. Users would appreciate receiving the data in a more usable or readable and meaningful way. For this, you need to have the data converted from an XML string or JSON string into something else. The concept of converting the data from one form to another is called serialization or deserialization.

With *serialization*, the data is put into a format for transmission. With *deserialization*, the transmitted data is converted into something that can be worked with, such as a custom object. In addition to working with string data, applications can work with binary data. An application might capture drawings or pictures on a canvas and send that data back to the server. The data needs to be serialized into a binary stream to achieve this.

This objective reviews the serialization, deserialization, and transmission of binary and text data. The ability to submit data via the HTML Form and sending data with the *XMLHttpRequest* object is also reviewed.

> **This objective covers how to:**
> - Send data by using *XMLHttpRequest*
> - Serialize and deserialize JSON data
> - Serialize and deserialize binary data

Sending data by using *XMLHttpRequest*

Sending data to the server is similar to receiving data. The code examples in the preceding objective used the *XMLHttpRequest* object to receive data. The *XMLHttpRequest* object itself is agnostic to sending or receiving. It can accomplish both tasks based on how the object is set up. To send data, the *send* method must have data passed into it, and that data can be transmitted to the endpoint specified in the URL of the *open* method. The following code sends the XML data to the server:

```
var xmlData = "<Person firstname='Rick' lastName='Delorme' hairColor='Brown'
eyeColor='Brown' /> ";
var xReq = new XMLHttpRequest();
xReq.open("POST", "/ReceiveXMLData.aspx", false);
xReq.responseType
xReq.send(xmlData);
```

When data is transmitted to the server, it needs to be serialized into a format that the URL endpoint can understand. If the endpoint is expecting XML, the data must be XML; if it's expecting binary data, the data must be in a binary format.

Serializing and deserializing JSON data

The browser provides native support for working with JSON and XML. The JSON object is available for converting a JSON string to and from an object (serialize/deserialize). The following code shows how this is accomplished:

```
var person = {
    FirstName: "Rick",
    HairColor: "Brown"
};
var jsonPerson = JSON.stringify(person);
```

The person object has been serialized into a JSON string that can be sent to an endpoint URL for processing. To return the person back to a person object from a JSON string, the object can be deserialized by using the *parse* method:

```
var req = new XMLHttpRequest();

req.open("GET", "MyJsonData.json", false);
req.send(null);
var jsonPerson = JSON.parse(req.responseText);
```

When this code runs, the person object is reconstructed from the JSON string.

Serializing and deserializing binary data

Capturing dynamic image data follows a similar pattern as with the other techniques reviewed. The key difference is now the *responsetype* property must be set to *blob*. The following code demonstrates retrieving a binary image object and deserializing it into the webpage:

```
var xReq = new XMLHttpRequest();
xReq.open("GET", "orange.jpg", false);
xReq.responseType = 'blob';
xReq.send(null);
var blob = xReq.response;
document.getElementById("result").src = URL.createObjectURL(blob);
```

The *XMLHttpRequest* object's *responseType* property has been set to *blob*. Then by using the response property to extract the binary data, the BLOB is passed to the *URL.createObjectURL* method. The *createObjectURL* method gives the *img* element a URL linking to the BLOB, and the image is displayed in the browser. For the inverse, the data can also be submitted to the server as soon as it's serialized into a BLOB:

```
var xReq = new XMLHttpRequest();
xReq.open("POST", "saveImage.aspx", false);
xReq.responseType = 'blob';
xReq.send(data);
```

Using the *Form.Submit* method

The *form* element of an HTML page is the area of the form that contains elements that are typically input controls to gather information from users. The *form* element contains an *action* attribute that tells the form where to submit its data. Submitting the data in this way submits the entire HTML page back to the server for processing. However, another available mechanism is to hook up to the form's *submit* event and handle the submission through JavaScript. This is useful for submitting the form's data through an AJAX request so that users don't have to leave the current page while the request is being processed. The *form* element at its simplest is as follows:

```
<form id="signupForm" action="processSignUp.aspx">
</form>
```

The form in this case will post its data to the *processSignUp* server page for processing, which in turn should redirect users back to a confirmation page of some sort. The other option for handling the form's submission is to wire up the event in JavaScript:

```
$("document").ready(function () {
    $("form").submit(function () {
    });
});
```

Iterating over all the form elements, capturing the data out of them, and constructing a query string for use with an AJAX call would be possible inside the click event. The following code reviews this concept:

```
$("form").submit(function () {

    var fName = $("#firstName").val();
    var lName = $("#lastName").val();
    var qString = "Last Name=" + lName + "&First Name=" + fName;

    $.ajax({
        url: 'processSignUp.aspx',
        type: "POST",
        data: qString,
        success: function (r) {
        }
    });
    return false;
});
```

The data from each field in the form is extracted and concatenated into a query string to submit to the server from the AJAX call. Although this method is functional, it has some drawbacks. First, a form with many elements will cause this code to get long. As new elements are added, the code will need to be updated. There is another option in the form of a jQuery method called *serialize()*.

Using the *jQuery.serialize* method

jQuery provides a seamless way to encode data from an HTML form by traversing the form that's passed into it and looking for input boxes to construct and return a query string. Then the query string can be posted to the server for processing. The preceding code is rewritten like this:

```
$("form").submit(function () {
    var qString = $(this).serialize();
    alert(qString);
    $.ajax({
        url: 'processSignUp.aspx',
        type: "POST",
        data: qString,
        success: function (r) {
        }
    });
    return false;
});
```

In this case, the *jQuery.serialize* method handles the extraction of the data from all the input elements and creates the query string. The advantage of using this method— beyond saving a lot of code—is that the query string is also encoded.

EXAM TIP

The *serialize* method requires that all elements have the *name* attribute specified. The preceding code works with the HTML modified as such:

```
<form id="signupForm">
    First Name:
    <input type="text" id="firstName" name="firstName"/><br/>
    Last Name:
    <input type="text" id="lastName" name="lastName"/><br/>
    <button type="submit">Submit</button>
</form>
```

The *serialize* method acts on any results from the selector that's passed into the $() segment of the jQuery. However, the serialize method has some limitations that you should know about. Only successful controls are serialized—meaning, only controls that are in a valid state. For input controls such as check boxes and radio buttons, only the ones that are in a selected state are considered. For radio buttons, because the *name* attribute must be the same for them all to be considered in a radio button group, you would specify the *value* attribute to differentiate them in the query string:

```
<input type="radio" name="gender" value="m"/>Male
<input type="radio" name="gender" value="f"/>Female
```

The *jQuery.serialize* method makes the code involved to generate a query string of the parameters from a form much simpler to create and less error prone.

Thought experiment
Saving a form

In this thought experiment, apply what you've learned about this objective. You can find answers to these questions in the "Answers" section at the end of this chapter.

In Objective 3.1, a customer survey was built. Extending this concept, how can you use the *XMLHttpRequest* object to post the data captured in the form to the server? Before submitting the form, how can you process server-side validation in real time? Add validation to the form so that you can compare an email address entered against a database of email addresses to ensure that it hasn't been used before.

Objective summary

- Browsers provide native support via the JSON object to work with serializing and deserializing JSON strings.

- The *JSON.parse* method deserializes a JSON string into an object, and the *JSON.stringify* method serializes an object into a JSON string.

- By setting the *XMLHttpRequest responseType* property to the value *'blob'*, you can retrieve binary data.

- By default, the form submit action sends the entire page to the server (based on the *action* attribute) for processing.

- Handling the *submit* event allows you to customize how the form data is posted to the server.

- The *jQuery.serialize* method provides a convenient shortcut to convert specified input controls into a query string.

Objective review

1. Which of the following code lines is the correct way create an object from a JSON string stored in a variable called *jsonString*?

    A. *var o = JSON.split(jsonString);*

    B. *var o = JSON.stringify(jsonString);*

    C. *var o = JSON.parse(jsonString);*

    D. *var 0 = JSON.join(jsonString);*

2. Which of the following code lines allows an *XMLHttpRequest* to return binary data?

    A. request.responseType = 'binary';

    B. request.responseType = 'image/jpg';

    C. response.type = 'blob';

    D. request.responseType = 'blob';

3. How do you control what's sent to the server when submitting a form?

    A. Add a *submit* button to the form.

    B. Handle the *submit* event of the form.

    C. Specify the *action* attribute of the form element.

    D. Ensure that all elements on the form have a name.

Answers

This section contains the solutions to the thought experiments and answers to the objective review questions in this chapter.

Objective 3.1: Thought experiment

You've already seen how to get access to the DOM and modify elements through JavaScript. By using these techniques, you can get a reference to the input controls on the form and, based on user input in certain elements, this can trigger modification to the validation rules (for example, change the regular expression validation dynamically). You can get regional context about a user from the Geolocation API. From this you can derive what part of the world the user is in and apply the exact validation on the input controls.

Objective 3.1: Review

1. **Correct answer:** C

   A. **Incorrect:** A radio button is suited for allowing a single selection.

   B. **Incorrect:** A text area is suited for a multi-line text box.

   C. **Correct:** Check boxes allow multiple selections.

   D. **Incorrect:** A radio button doesn't allow more than one selection.

2. **Correct answer:** D

   A. **Incorrect:** A text box allows data entry but is plainly visible.

   B. **Incorrect:** A text area allows data entry but is plainly visible.

   C. **Incorrect:** *url* is a type of text box with special validation rules.

   D. **Correct:** A *password* input type hides the characters being entered.

3. **Correct answer:** B

   A. **Incorrect:** A button is generic and must have an event handler to perform custom logic.

   B. **Correct:** The submit button invokes the forms submit action.

   C. **Incorrect:** The reset button clears all input fields on the form.

   D. **Incorrect:** A radio button is used for a selection list.

4.   **Correct answer:** C

   A.   **Incorrect:** You can do this with a custom event, but that's more work than necessary.

   B.   **Incorrect:** The goal is to validate the data before submitting the form.

   C.   **Correct:** The *required* attribute ensures that a field contains a value before being submitted.

   D.   **Incorrect:** A label would be informative but doesn't guarantee that all the required fields are populated before submitting.

Objective 3.2: Thought experiment

The safest approach to restricting input data is to restrict the characters that a user can enter into a specific field. If a field is designed to accept only numeric data, ensure that the validation on that input control will allow only numeric data. The same is true for dates, text, and any other input that a user can freely type into. Regular expressions simplify this type of validation by verifying that only the expected characters are entered. If a text box is expecting a person's name, don't allow HTML characters such as the < or > symbols to be input into the field. Also, restrict the field length so that it matches the type of the data expected. A field expecting the age of a person doesn't need to be 500 characters; you can probably get away with allowing only 3 characters.

Objective 3.2: Review

1.   **Correct answer:** A

   A.   **Correct:** The $ sign denotes the end of the string.

   B.   **Incorrect:** The % sign doesn't denote the end of the string.

   C.   **Incorrect:** The ^ character denotes the start of the string.

   D.   **Incorrect:** The & character doesn't denote the end of the string.

2.   **Correct answer:** D

   A.   **Incorrect:** Allows scripts to run

   B.   **Incorrect:** Only allows content from the same origin

   C.   **Incorrect:** Allows forms

   D.   **Correct:** Allows content from the containing HTML document

   E.   **Incorrect:** Not a valid option

3. **Correct answer:** D

   A. **Incorrect:** Credentials aren't passed with the *open* method.

   B. **Incorrect:** Credentials aren't passed with the *request* method.

   C. **Incorrect:** Ready state is a property that indicates the current state of the connection.

   D. **Correct:** Credentials are passed only if the server requests them with a return code 401.

Objective 3.3: Thought experiment

The task assigned here to build a scroll across the top of the page is seen in many websites today. A stock price ticker is a typical application of this. This solution would potentially incorporate different technologies. At its core, you can implement the *XMLHttpRequest* object to make a call to an API that provides stock data. When the data is retrieved, you can display in the browser. Because the solution calls for not posting the entire page, you would need to use dynamic DOM manipulation to display the results and have them scroll across the top of the page. Because the quotes must be updated regularly, you would likely include the use of a timer to poll for the results at a regular interval.

Objective 3.3: Review

1. **Correct answer:** D

   A. **Incorrect:** A JSON string isn't just a comma-separated list.

   B. **Incorrect:** A JSON string isn't a list delimited by semi-colons.

   C. **Incorrect:** A JSON string isn't a list delimited by semi-colons.

   D. **Correct:** A JSON string is a series of name/value pairs where the name of the property is followed by a colon and a quoted string. Multiple name value pairs are comma separated.

2. **Correct answer:** C

   A. **Incorrect:** *Response* doesn't provide any direct information.

   B. **Incorrect:** *responseBody* provides the result in binary format.

   C. **Correct:** *responseText* provides the result as text that's human readable.

   D. **Incorrect:** *responseXML* isn't a valid property.

3. **Correct answer:** D

    A.   **Incorrect:** Credentials aren't passed with the *open* method.

    B.   **Incorrect:** Credentials aren't passed with the *request* method.

    C.   **Incorrect:** Ready state is a property that indicates the current state of the connection.

    D.   **Correct:** Credentials are passed only if the server requests them with a return code 401.

Objective 3.4: Thought experiment

In this application, you now need to know when users finish entering information into a field. You can use the *onblur* event for this. By hooking up *onblur* to the email field, you can use the *XMLHttpRequest* object to send a request to the server to validate that the address is unique and hasn't been used before. The results of the data evaluation on the server are passed back in the response and can be used to highlight to users that the data isn't unique. This provides a much better user experience in that users don't need to wait until they fill out the entire form to have all the fields validated. Did you remember to encode the data before submitting it to the server to prevent an injection attack?

Objective 3.4: Review

1. **Correct answer:** C

    A.   **Incorrect:** This isn't a valid method on the JSON object.

    B.   **Incorrect:** This method is used to serialize an object into a JSON string.

    C.   **Correct:** This method is used to deserialize a JSON string into an object.

    D.   **Incorrect:** This isn't a valid method on the JSON object.

2. **Correct answer:** D

    A.   **Incorrect:** *'binary'* isn't a valid option for the *responseType*.

    B.   **Incorrect:** *'image/jpg'* isn't a valid option for the *responseType*.

    C.   **Incorrect:** *type* isn't a valid property name on the *response* object.

    D.   **Correct:** The response object's *responseType* property must be set to *'blob'*.

3. **Correct answer:** B

    A. **Incorrect:** A submit button submits the entire form to the server by default.

    B. **Correct:** Handling the *submit* event on the form allows you to intercept the form before submitting and perform custom actions with it.

    C. **Incorrect:** The *action* attribute indicates what server-side page the form should submit.

    D. **Incorrect:** All elements on the form should have a name to use jQuery to serialize them. However, this has no effect on form submission.

CHAPTER 4

Use CSS3 in applications

The use of cascading style sheets (CSS) is not a new concept. However, the functional capabilities of CSS3 have advanced tremendously. In this chapter, you review the capabilities of CSS3 and how they can be leveraged into your HTML5 web applications to provide end users with the desired experience.

> **NOTE VARYING RESULTS**
>
> You might see slightly different results in some of the code samples. Not all features work in all browsers. Internet Explorer 11 and Chrome v35+ were used to validate the examples throughout this chapter.

Objectives in this chapter:

- Objective 4.1: Style HTML text properties
- Objective 4.2: Style HTML box properties
- Objective 4.3: Create a flexible content layout
- Objective 4.4: Create an animated and adaptive UI
- Objective 4.5: Find elements by using CSS selectors and jQuery
- Objective 4.6: Structure a CSS file by using CSS selectors

Objective 4.1: Style HTML text properties

Text is the basis for all web applications. Some web applications have more text than others. Ultimately, the viewer of the website will read the content of the website that is in text. CSS provides many capabilities to customize the appearance of the text in order to provide your own unique look and feel to your web application. Throughout this objective, you will explore the various ways to style text.

Apply styles to text appearance

Applying styles such as color, bold, or italic makes certain text stand out on a webpage. Any of these styling techniques can be applied in combination or individually.

Applying color to text

The color of text can be changed by specifying the color property to the CSS element. CSS3 accepts the color value in any of the following three methods.

- Hexadecimal value: Specify the color as a hexadecimal value, for example as #00FF00 to display the text in green. The first two digits (base 16) are the value for Red, the second two digits are the value for Green, and the last two digits are the value for Blue. This is commonly referred to as the RGB code.

- Color name: Use a word to specify the color value, such as *green* to display the text in green.

- RGB function: Specify the color value using the RGB function, which takes three parameters, each representing a color spectrum bit value from 0 to 255. For example, rgb(0,255,0) specifies green as the text color.

The following code demonstrates each method in use.

```
<style>
    h1{
        color:#00FF00;
    }
    h2 {
        color: green;
    }
    h3{
        color: rgb(0,255,0);
    }
</style>
```

The output in Figure 4-1 shows the result of applying these styles to a page.

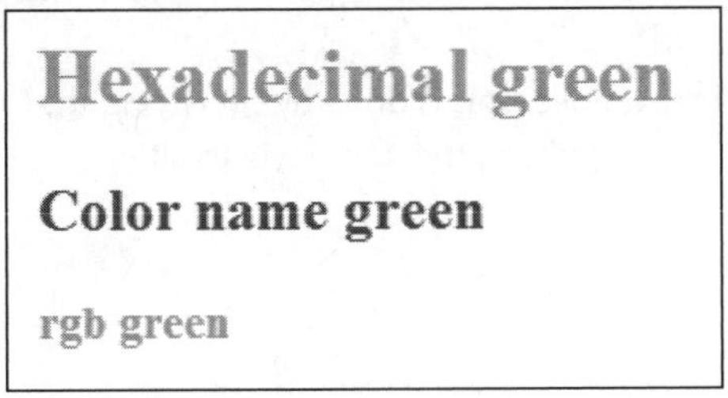

Hexadecimal green

Color name green

rgb green

FIGURE 4-1 Specifying the color of text using CSS

With this code, each of the *h1* through *h3* headers have a CSS style applied to change the color to green, each using a different method. Using the hexadecimal or RGB method gives you more granular control over the color then using the color name as was done on the *<h2>* element. There are just far more colors that exist then could be named. The hexadecimal and RGB methods allow you to access the full range of colors.

> **NOTE   DEFAULT STYLES**
>
> In Figure 4-1, you see that even though all three text items are set to pure green, one is darker than the others. It is important to know that some elements, such as the various header elements, have default styles already applied to them. In this case, the style for the element defaults to a bolder type.

Applying bold to text

CSS also provides access to other properties of the text display via the font object. The font object provides the ability to make text bold or italic . The following code demonstrates changing the text to bold for all *<p>* elements:

```
p {
    font-weight: bold;
}
```

The above styles produce the output shown in Figure 4-2.

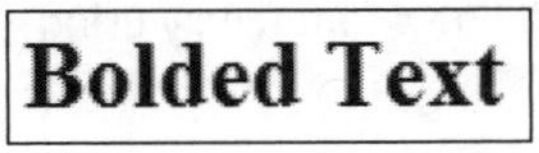

Bolded Text

FIGURE 4-2 Displaying the bold style applied to the text

The *font-weight* CSS property accepts the following values to specify how bold you would like the text to be: *lighter, normal, bold,* and *bolder.* In addition, the numeric values 100 (lighter) to 900 (darker) are supported. The values increase by 100, providing nine values in total to control the weight of the text.

Applying italic style to text

Through the font object, you can also make specific text italic. This is done by specifying the *font-style* for the text. The following code demonstrates applying the italic style to all *<p>* elements on the webpage:

```
p{
    font-style:italic;
}
```

Applying the italic style to a text element produces the output shown in Figure 4-3.

FIGURE 4-3 The italic style applied to a text element.

Apply styles to text font

The font CSS object contains other properties to allow you to control how text is rendered on your pages. You can change the font typeface and control the size of the text. You can control the font typeface in a few different ways. The first method is to simply rely on the fonts that are installed on the system rendering the webpage. This is achieved using the *font-family* as shown in the following code:

```
p{
        font-family:Arial,'Times New Roman',Webdings;
}
```

This CSS code renders the fonts in order from left to right until it finds one that is available on the client computer. If the font name contains spaces, it must be contained within quotes. If none of the specified fonts are available, the text falls back to the browser's default font. In the previous example, the client looks first for the Arial font. If that is not installed, it then looks for the Times New Roman font, and so on. This is a simple approach, but many people prefer to use fonts that are not available on the system. There are many custom fonts available on the Internet for inclusion in your web applications. These fonts are known as WOFF (Web Open Font Format). To use these fonts in your webpage, you define a font family using the special keyword *@font-face*.

EXAM TIP

Be aware that certain font types will work in some browsers but not others. It is important to declare each font type by using *@font-face* so that the browser has access to the one it needs.

The following code defines a *@font-face* for a webpage and implements it for the *<p>* elements of the page:

```
@font-face {
    font-family: "My Nicer Font";
    src: url('fonts/my_woff_font.eot');
    src: url('fonts/my_woff_font.woff');
}
p {
    font-family: 'My Nicer Font';
}
```

First, you add the *@font-face* keyword to the page, then you give it a name by specifying the *font-family* property. Next, you specify where the font can be loaded from. This could be from the local web server if you downloaded the fonts to it or from an Internet source. In the previous declaration, both *eot* and *woff* types are specified.

After you have decided on a font for your web application, you might decide to resize the text for different scenarios as you see fit. Of course, the *<h1>* through *<h6>* elements provide some default formatting, but you would not want to use those elements throughout a website to control the size of the text. Instead you can use the *font-size* property. The *font-size* property accepts relative values that when rendered are relative to the default text size in the browser. The available values are: *xx-small, x-small, small, smaller, medium, larger, large, x-large, xx-large*. The following code demonstrates setting the *font-size* for the *<p>* elements:

```
p{
    font-size: x-large;
}
```

The application of the *size* attribute to the font results in the text rendering as shown in Figure 4-4.The first line of text shows the default size while the bigger text shows the *x-large* size.

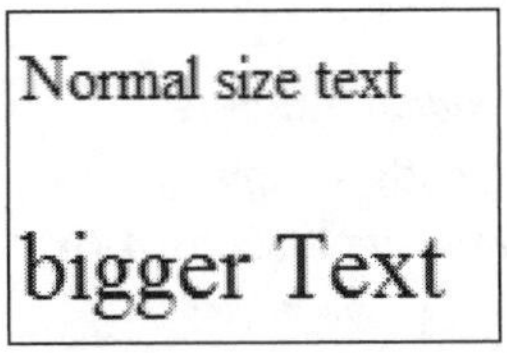

Normal size text

bigger Text

FIGURE 4-4 The size of the text increases through the use of the *font-size* attribute

Applying styles to text alignment, spacing, and indentation

CSS3 can also be used to alter text alignment, spacing, and indentation. This provides great control over positioning text within parent containers.

Text alignment

To control the alignment of text within a container, you specify the *text-align* attribute. The *text-align* attribute supports the values outlined in Table 4-1.

TABLE 4-1 Supported values for *text-align*

Value	Description
right	Aligns text to the right side of the parent container
left	Aligns text to the left side of the parent container
center	Aligns text to the horizontal center of the parent container
justify	Stretches text horizontally to fill the full width of the parent container

The following code sample demonstrates the use of the *text-align* attribute, and Figure 4-5 displays the results within the boundaries of a defined *div* element.

```
p {
    text-align: center;
}
```

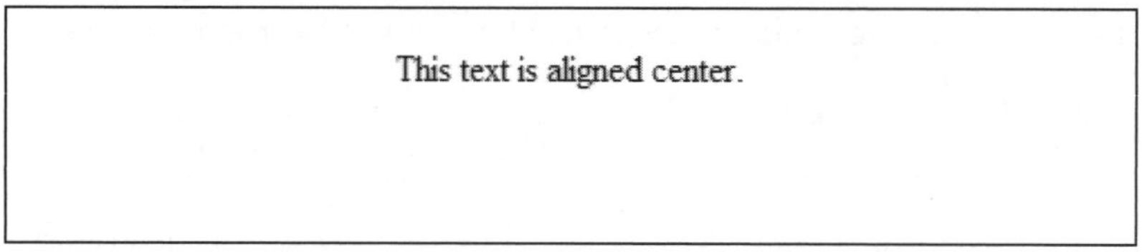

This text is aligned center.

FIGURE 4-5 The *text-align* attribute used to position text in the center of a *div* element

Text indentation

Text indentation is configured using the *text-indent* attribute. The *text-indent* attribute accepts an integer value to indicate how much to indent. The following code sample illustrates how to indent the text from the left border of the parent *div* element. Figure 4-6 shows the results of this code.

```
p {
    text-indent: 50px;
}
```

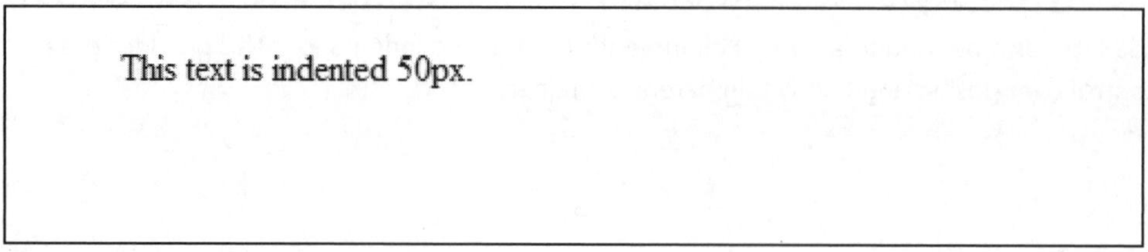

This text is indented 50px.

FIGURE 4-6 Text indented using the *text-indent* attribute

Text spacing

There are two ways to control the spacing of text. This can be done by specifying the spacing between each character in the text or by specifying the spacing between each word in the text. The following CSS code demonstrates both examples. Figure 4-7 shows the output of this code.

```
p {
    letter-spacing: 8px;
}
p {
    word-spacing: 8px;
}
```

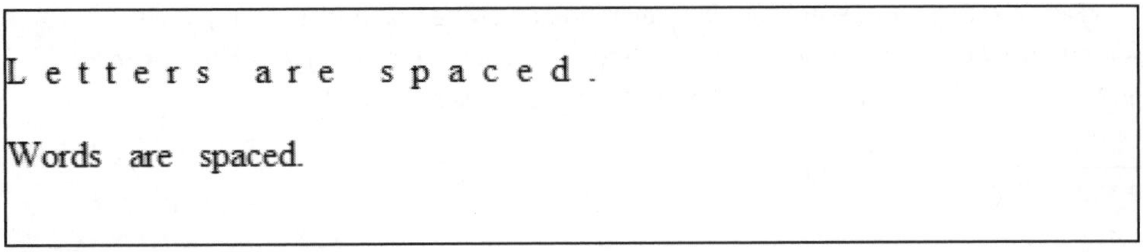

L e t t e r s   a r e   s p a c e d .

Words are spaced.

FIGURE 4-7 Letter and word spacing using CSS3

Applying styles to text hyphenation

Applying styles to text hyphenation allows you to control how a sentence or word wraps or breaks at the end of the line. The *hyphen* attribute can be specified to control this behavior. The values available for the *hyphen* attribute are defined in Table 4-2.

TABLE 4-2 Values available for the hyphen attribute

Value	Description
none	Words will not break with a hyphen and the sentence will only break on whitespace.
Auto	Words will break based on a predefined algorithm.
Manual	Words will break based on specified hints in the words indicating an appropriate space for the break. This is done using the *­* notation within the text.

The following code demonstrates using the *none* value, and the results are shown in Figure 4-8.

```
div {
    hyphens: none;
}
```

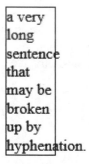

FIGURE 4-8 The results of specifying *none* for the *hyphen* attribute

In Figure 4-8, the browser is not hyphenating any of the text and is letting it overflow beyond the boundaries of the container. To force hyphenation, specify *auto* for the value of the *hyphen* attribute. The output of this change is shown in Figure 4-9.

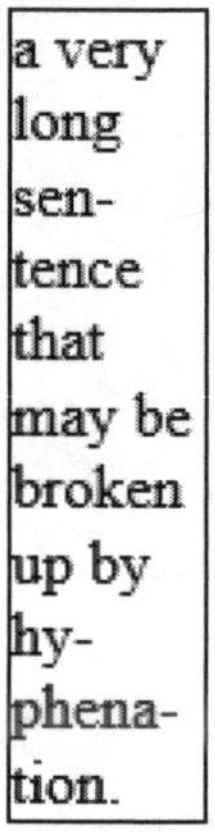

FIGURE 4-9 The results of specifying *auto* for the *hyphen* attribute

When *auto is specified*, the browser calculates where to hyphenate the words based on its own rules so that the text does not go outside the bounds of the container. The *manual* option behaves much the same way except that you can specify an external rule set to use and also supply hints by using the *­* (soft hyphen) notation.

Applying styles for a text drop shadow

You'll find information about applying styles for a text drop shadow in the next section. Microsoft uses the phrase "text drop shadow" but you'll note that it has been shortened to "text shadow" in this book.

Thought experiment
Altering styles

In this thought experiment, apply what you've learned about this objective. You can find an answer to this question in the "Answers" section at the end of this chapter.

CSS provides the ability to make websites look great. In some cases, you may want to alter the styles based on user input or actions. How would you alter the styles of your page in this fashion?

Objective summary

- CSS3 provides the ability to style the appearance of text in the following ways:
    - Changing the color with the *color* property
    - Changing the text to bold with the *font-weight* property
    - Changing the text to italics with the *font-style* property
    - Changing the font type with the *font-family* property
    - Changing the size of the text with the *font-size* property
- CSS3 provides the ability to style the alignment of text with the *text-align* property.
- CSS3 provides the ability to alter text indentation with the *text-indent* property.
- CSS3 provides the ability to alter the spacing between letters and the spacing between words with the *letter-spacing* and *word-spacing* properties.
- CSS3 allows you to control how text hyphenates when the text needs to wrap within the boundaries of its container.

Objective review

Answer the following questions to test your knowledge of the information in this objective. You can find the answers to these questions and explanations of why each answer choice is correct or incorrect in the "Answers" section at the end of this chapter.

1. Which of the following CSS would not change the appearance of text?

    A. font-style: italic;

    B. font-weight: heavy;

    C. font: bolder 12px arial;

    D. color: green;

2. Which of the following aligns text to the full width of the available box?

   A. *right*

   B. *full*

   C. *center*

   D. *justify*

3. Which of the following is a way to configure the amount of space between words?

   A. *word-margin*

   B. *letter-margin*

   C. *word-spacing*

   D. *word-padding*

Objective 4.2: Style HTML box properties

Every HTML element has box properties. These are the properties that control how the element is spaced on the page and control the position of the box contents. In addition, the graphic effects can be applied to the box of an element.

This objective covers how to:

- Apply styles to alter appearance attributes
- Apply styles to alter graphic effects
- Apply styles to establish and change an element's position

Applying styles to alter appearance attributes

There are a variety of ways to alter the appearance of a box as it applies to an HTML element. This section demonstrates how to alter the appearance by changing the attributes related to size, bordering, outlining, padding, and margin.

Altering the size

The size of any element is controlled by its *height* and *width* properties. These can be set on any object or class in CSS. By default, an object will size itself to be able to display its contents. So, a *div* element with some text inside it will have a width and height that is sufficient to display the text. The size can be changed by setting a value for the *width* and/or *height*. The width and height can be specified as a measurement in pixels (px) or centimeters (cm) or can be specified as a percentage of its parent element. For example, the following code will set the width of a table to be 50 percent of its parent container, which in this case is just the window object.

```
table {
    height: 50%;
    width: 50%;
}
```

In another example, the size of a *<div>* element can be set to a specific value as in this case:

```
div {
    width: 200px;
    height: 100px;
}
```

Bordering

CSS provides very granular control over the styles of the borders of any HTML element. The name of the root CSS property to do this is the *border* property. With the use of the *border* property, you can control the style, spacing, color, and width of the border.

The first thing that you need to set on the border is the style. This will essentially bring the border into existence. There are a variety of border styles that exists. These include, solid border, dashed border, dotted line border, grooved line border, and so on. The border is set by specifying the *border-style* property:

```
p {
    border-style: solid;
}
```

The color of the border can be changed by specifying the *border-color* property. This is demonstrated with the following code:

```
p {
    border-style: solid;
    border-color: black;
}
```

All the *<p>* elements will now be displayed with a solid black border. This is demonstrated in Figure 4-10.

| Some text with a border |

FIGURE 4-10 A *<p>* element with *border* properties set

> **NOTE** **SETTING *BORDER-STYLE***
>
> Note that the border needs to exist before it can have any visible changes done to it. This is why in the above example, the *border-style* is set first.

Border-spacing is used to set the amount of space desired between adjacent elements. The following CSS will provide 250 px border spacing to all paragraph elements on the page:

```
p {
    border-style: solid ;
    border-color: black;
    border-spacing: 250px;
}
```

Another border property that can be controlled with CSS is the border's width. The *border-width* is a property that is set using a fixed measurement, in pixels for example. The following code sets the width of the border to 5 px:

```
p {
    border-style: solid ;
    border-color: black;
    border-spacing: 250px;
    border-width: 5px;
}
```

Figure 4-11 demonstrates the new width set on the paragraph element.

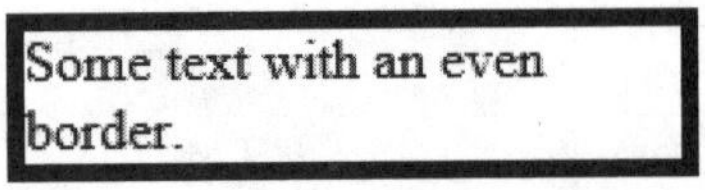

Some text with an even border.

FIGURE 4-11 A thicker width on the border of the paragraph element set by the *border-width* property

So far, you have been setting each of the properties of the border as individual lines in the style sheet. The *border* CSS property supports a shorthand technique where you can specify the key properties in a single line. The following code demonstrates this concept:

```
p {

    border: 5px solid black;
}
```

In this case, the border is set to a 5-px width with a solid line and the color black.

EXAM TIP

The *border* element supports many variants in its ability to set properties in a single line. Take some time to experiment with all the possible combinations so you will be able to read them and identify them easily on the exam.

In addition to being able to set all the properties discussed so far in a single line, the *border* element allows even more granular control. The properties discussed can also be set to different values specific to each side of the box. For example, the following code produces the output shown in Figure 4-12:

```
p {
    border-top: 15px solid black;
    border-left: 10px solid black;
    border-right: 10px solid black;
    border-bottom: 5px solid black;
}
```

FIGURE 4-12 Different border properties for each side of the box

Padding and margin

Padding and margin are additional methods to create space around an HTML element. In essence, there are three layers around an HTML element. As you look from the inside to the outside of the element there is the padding, the border, and the margin. If you take a look again at the sample in Figure 4-12, the text is squished quite close to the border. The border width has been set, but the padding (the space between the text and the border) has its default value of 0 px. In order to create space between the text and the border, you must increase the padding as shown in the following code sample. The results are shown in Figure 4-13.

```
p {
    border-top: 15px solid black;
    border-left: 10px solid black;
    border-right: 10px solid black;
    border-bottom: 5px solid black;
    padding: 25px;
}
```

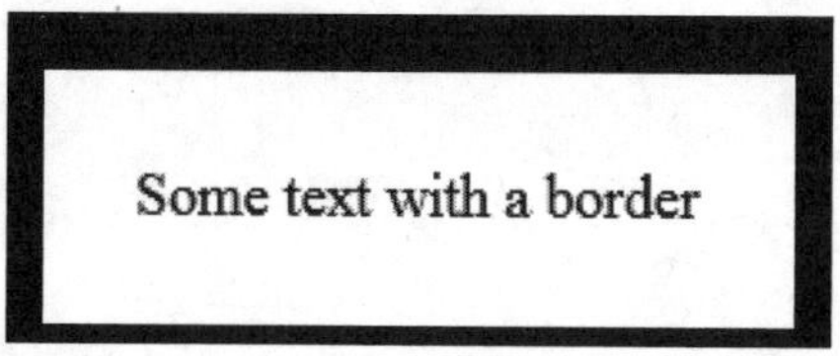

FIGURE 4-13 The use of padding to create space between text and a border

In this code, the padding is set to 25 px. With only a single value specified, it is assumed that this value is applied to all four sides of the box. However, the padding can be specified as different values for all four sides. The above code is in effect the same as saying:

```
padding: 25px 25px 25px 25px;
```

or

```
padding-top: 25px;
padding-bottom: 25px;
padding-left: 25px;
padding-right: 25px;
```

The next area where you can create spacing for your HTML elements is in the margin. The margin is the space between the border of your element and the surrounding elements. The browser provides a default margin based on the HTML element that is used. Figure 4-14 shows the default margin for the paragraph element. Figure 4-15 shows the effect of increasing the size of the margin. The margin can be controlled in exactly the same ways as the padding. You can specify a single value to be applied equally to all four sides, specify individual values in a single line, or specify each side of the box individually. The following code demonstrates increasing the margin of the paragraph element and the results are shown in Figure 4-15:

```
p {
    border-top: 15px solid black;
    border-left: 10px solid black;
    border-right: 10px solid black;
    border-bottom: 5px solid black;
    padding-top: 25px;
    padding-bottom: 25px;
    padding-left: 25px;
    padding-right: 25px;
    margin: 40px;
}
```

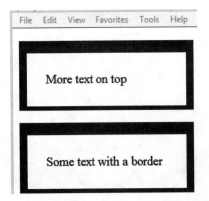

FIGURE 4-14 The layout of two paragraphs with their default margins

FIGURE 4-15 The layout of two paragraphs with margins enlarged

You can see in Figure 4-15 that not only did the margin create space between the two paragraph elements, but it also created space between the top of the window and the top of the first paragraph element.

Applying styles to alter graphic effects

There are a variety of options in applying graphic effects to a box to provide a unique display to end users. This section demonstrates setting transparency, opacity, a background image, gradients, shadows, and clipping.

Applying transparency/opacity

Setting the opacity (also known as transparency) of an element in CSS provides the ability to make the element effectively see through. The value used in setting the opacity is a ratio from 0 to 1.0. A setting of 0 indicates that the element is fully transparent, essentially invisible. A value of 1.0 indicates that the element is fully opaque, the default when no opacity value is specified. The following code sets an opacity level of 0.4 to a text element:

```
p {
    opacity: 0.4;
}
```

Figure 4-16 demonstrates the output of applying this effect to the text element. The output without the opacity specified is also provided for a comparison.

Before setting an opacity value.

After setting an opacity value.

FIGURE 4-16 The use of the *opacity* property

Applying a background image

Any HTML element can also contain a background image. This is achieved by specifying the *background-image* property. The *background* property itself has many other options to control its size and repeating pattern. However, to simply set a background image, you need only specify the image to the *backround-image* property. The following code demonstrates the use of this property to assign a background image:

```
p {
    background-image: url('orange.jpg');
    color: white;
}
```

Figure 4-17 shows the output of this code. The text color is changed to white to make it more visible over the image. Table 4-3 explains more of the options available for formatting the background image.

FIGURE 4-17 A background image on a text element

TABLE 4-3 Configuration options for the background image

Property	Description
size	Changes the dimensions of the image
repeat	Specifies whether the image should be repeated/tiled through the available space of the box
clip	Specifies whether the image should be clipped at a border
position-x/position-y	Specifies the origin position of the image within the box

All the properties are prefixed with the token *background-*. The following example demonstrates using the *repeat* property and the *size* property. It specifies that the image should be smaller and repeat. This example specifies to *repeat* continuously, both horizontally and vertically. However, you can specify *repeat-x* or *repeat-y* to repeat only in the specified direction.

```
p {
    background-image: url('orange.jpg');
    background-size: 20px;
    background-repeat: repeat;
    width: 200px;
    height: 200px;
    text-align: center;
    color: white;
}
```

This previous code produces the output in Figure 4-18.

FIGURE 4-18 The use of the *size* and *repeat* properties for a background image

Applying gradients

A gradient effect changes the color of an object gradually from one spectrum to another. There are two types of gradient effects supported. The first is a linear gradient where the color changes in a line across the object in any direction. The other gradient is a radial gradient where the color starts in the center and changes toward the outer edges. The gradient can be applied to the background of the element in the following way:

```
background:linear-gradient(black,gray);
```

The *linear-gradient* function takes a few parameters. The parameters are outlined in Table 4-4.

TABLE 4-4 Parameters for the *linear-gradient* function

Parameter	description
Direction	Specify the direction of the gradient as *to right* or *to left*. This parameter is optional and the default when blank is an up/down gradient effect. A diagonal effect can also be applied by specifying *to bottom right* or *to bottom left*. You may also specify an angle, as in *100deg*.
Color stop...n	The second and subsequent parameters is the color to start with followed by the transitional colors known as the color stops. This tells the browser what color to start with and transition into with the gradient effect.

Applying a shadow effect

Shadow effects allow you to apply a shadow to your HTML element's box or to the text. There are two CSS3 properties to control the shadow effect: *box-shadow* and *text-shadow*. The *box-shadow* controls the shadow effect surrounding the box of the HTML element. The *text-shadow* property controls the shadow of text.

The *box-shadow* property supports the parameters outlined in Table 4-5. The first two parameters are required to create the shadow effect. The *blur* and *spread* parameters are optional effects that can be applied to the *box-shadow*.

TABLE 4-5 Parameters for the *box-shadow* property

Parameter	Description
h-shadow	Specifies the position of the horizontal shadow. The value can also be a negative number.
v-shadow	Specifies the position of the vertical shadow. The value can also be a negative number.
blur	Specifies the distance of the blur effect. This parameter is optional and defaults to 0.
spread	Specifies the size of the shadow.
color	Specifies the color of the shadow.
inset	Specifies that the shadow should be inside the box instead of outside the box.

In its simplest form, the *box-shadow* property requires only that *h-shadow* and *v-shadow* are specified. The following code shows a basic shadow applied to a *div* element:

```
div{
        position: absolute;
        left: 50px;top: 50px;
        width: 100px;
        height: 100px;
        border: solid 1px black;
        box-shadow: 10px 10px;
    }
```

The *div* element is rendered with a shadow as shown in Figure 4-19.

FIGURE 4-19 A simple *box-shadow* effect

The shadow effect in Figure 4-19 is a solid box shadow. To provide an effect where the shadow fades out gradually, you will need to specify the *blur* parameter. By adding the *blur* parameter, you can create the effect shown in Figure 4-20. The following code adds the *blur* parameter:

```
div{
        position: absolute;
        left: 50px;top: 50px;
        width: 100px;
        height: 100px;
        border: solid 1px black;
        box-shadow: 10px 10px 10px;
    }
```

FIGURE 4-20 A *box-shadow* effect with the addition of a blur

The next parameter that adds a special effect to the shadow is the *spread* parameter. This parameter specifies the size of the shadow. The following code specifies a spread value to increase the size of the shadow:

```
div{
        position: absolute;
        left: 50px;top: 50px;
        width: 100px;
        height: 100px;
        border: solid 1px black;
        box-shadow: 10px 10px 10px 20px;
    }
```

This code produces the output in Figure 4-21.

FIGURE 4-21 A *box-shadow* effect with addition of the *spread* parameter to increase the shadow's size.

Figure 4-21 shows the output of the previous code with the addition of the *spread* parameter. The *spread* parameter specifies the size of the shadow. In the context of real-world objects and their shadows, the spread is like indicating how close a light source is to an object. The closer the light source, the larger the shadow it produces. The *spread* parameter can be used to elicit this type of effect on the HTML element. In Figure 4-21, the shadow was intentionally created to be larger than the HTML box itself. This was done to demonstrate an additional concept of the shadow effects. The shadow itself is a full-size box. In this case, the shadow was made to be larger than the original box so it is visible around all four sides of the box. Normally, for a box where the spread is not specified to be larger, the shadow is only visible on the two axes specified by the first two parameters. This is because the shadow box is offset from center of the HTML element it is shadowing. The rest of the shadow is still behind the HTML element being shadowed. You can demonstrate this by setting the position of the shadow to be completely away from the HTML element. This is achieved by specifying the position to be a greater number value then the size of the HTML element. The following code demonstrates this:

```
div{
        position: absolute;
        left: 50px;top: 50px;
        width: 100px;
        height: 100px;
        border: solid 1px black;
        box-shadow: 100px 100px 10px;
    }
```

In this code, the position of the box shadow is set to be 100 px along the horizontal axis and 100 px along the vertical axis, which will place the shadow to the bottom right corner of the *div* element, as shown in Figure 4-22.

FIGURE 4-22 The entire shadow of an element displayed by specifying the position to be greater then the size of the HTML element

Another parameter for the *box-shadow* is the *inset* parameter. If omitted, this parameter creates the shadow on the outside of the box. If *inset* is specified, the shadow is then created on the inside of the box. This is demonstrated in the following code:

```
div{
        position: absolute;
        left: 50px;top: 50px;
        width: 100px;
        height: 100px;
        border: solid 1px black;
        box-shadow: 10px 10px inset;
    }
```

This code produces the output shown in Figure 4-23. The shadow is now displayed on the inside of the box instead of the outside of the box.

FIGURE 4-23 The use of the *inset* parameter to place the shadow on the inside of the box

The *color* property accepts values as a hex code, rgb(), or literal color. This property changes the color of the shadow. Since the book is printed in black and white, demonstrating the use of this parameter will not present well. So, in your own code, change the color of the shadow to see what effect it has—the color should change.

> **NOTE UNDERSTANDING *H-SHADOW* AND *V-SHADOW* PARAMETERS**
>
> *h-shadow* and *v-shadow* parameters can accept negative values. To place the shadow on the left side of the box instead of the right, specify a negative value for the *h-shadow*. To place the shadow on top of the box instead of the bottom, specify a negative value for the *v-shadow* parameter.

Text shadows can be created in the same way as box shadows. The CSS property to apply a shadow to text is called *text-shadow*. The *text-shadow* property has parameters similar to those of the *box-shadow* property. The parameters are described in Table 4-6.

TABLE 4-6 *Text-shadow* parameters

Parameter	Description
h-shadow	Specifies the position of the shadow along the horizontal axis. This value accepts negative numbers.
v-shadow	Specifies the position of the shadow along the vertical axis. This value accepts negative numbers.
blur	Specifies the distance of the blur effect. This parameter is optional and defaults to 0.
color	Specifies the color of the shadow.

All of the *text-shadow* parameters are familiar. They all have the same effect as their counterparts in the *box-shadow* element. The following code demonstrates applying a shadow effect to text on an HTML page:

```
p {
    position: absolute;
    left: 250px;
    top: 250px;
    text-shadow: -10px -10px;
}
```

In this example, negative numbers are supplied to the *h-shadow* and *v-shadow* parameters in order to place the shadow to the top left of the text. The output of this code is shown in Figure 4-24.

FIGURE 4-24 *A text-shado*w on a paragraph HTML element

Applying clipping

The *clip* property allows you to specify what portion of an element is visible. The *clip* property takes only one parameter, the shape to clip to. Currently, the only shape supported is a rectangle, so the only parameter value that will yield any results is the *rect()* function. For example, the following code is the valid syntax to specify a *clip* property:

```
img{
    position: absolute;
    clip: rect(25px, 50px, 50px, 25px);
}
```

In the above code sample, the clip region is set to be a rectangle. The first two parameters of the *rect* function build the coordinates for what part of the image will be clipped. The parameters run in clockwise order as top, right, bottom, and left sides of the rectangle. In addition, all measurements are taken from the left of the top edge of the source box being clipped. So, in the above code sample, a region of the image is defined as 25 px from the top to form the top edge of the clipped region, 50 px from the left to form the right edge of the clipped region, 50 px from the top to form the bottom edge of the clipped region, and 25 px from the left to form the right edge of the clipped region. This essentially creates a rectangle starting from the point (25px, 25px) and with a height and width of 25px. Figure 4-25 shows an image before and after being clipped with these values.

FIGURE 4-25 The image on the left is the full image of a floral arrangement. The image on the right is a clipped version of the same image.

In Figure 2-25, you can see the full image on the left. On the right, the image is clipped. Only the section of the source image as specified in the *rect* function assigned to the clip property is visible. The following is the full code:

```html
<html>
<head>
 <style>
        .clipper{
            position: fixed;
            left: 325px;
            clip: rect(25px, 100px, 100px, 25px);
        }
    </style>
</head>
<body>
    <img src="flowers.jpg" style="height: 200px;width: 300px;"/>
    <img class="clipper" src="flowers.jpg" style="height: 200px;width:300px;"/>
</body>
</html>
```

> **NOTE** **UNDERSTANDING THE *CLIP* PROPERTY**
>
> The *clip* property works only on elements whose position is set as fixed or absolute.

Apply styles to establish and change an element's position

The browser provides a coordinate system for how to lay out elements on a page. The default behavior is essentially a layout where the elements, without any other position attributes specified, will simply lay out on the page in a default flow. In this context, the base coordinate is the top left corner of the window which can be understood as (x,y) coordinate (0,0). This is called static layout. CSS provides some mechanisms where you can override the default layout of the page. This is achieved by specifying the desired position behavior with the *position* property. Once the *position* property is set, other CSS properties such as *top*, *left*, *bottom*, or *right* are set. In a static layout, the elements will not respond to the *top*, *left*, *bottom*, or *right* properties. The positioning type must be specified.

> **EXAM TIP**
>
> For the exam, be sure you understand that each HTML element is a box and each box be-gins its own new coordinate system. If you place a *div* element on the page at (50px,50px), any elements placed inside it are not placed at a coordinate starting at (50px, 50px) just because that is where the *div* element is. The child elements inside the *div* start at coor-dinate (0,0), which is the top left corner of the *div* itself. All child elements are positioned relative to the container in which they are placed.

The position property allows you to specify one of three different options: *fixed*, *relative*, or *absolute*. With fixed positioning, elements are placed relative to the browser window. With relative positioning, elements are positioned relative to their position in normal flow. With absolute positioning, the element is positioned relative to its first parent element. You will start with an image placed on a page inside a *div* element. Figure 4-26 shows this element in static flow.

FIGURE 4-26 An image at its default position inside a *div* element

 EXAM TIP

The *left* and *right* properties start their measurements from the outer-most edge of the box. For the exam, keep in mind that if there are margins or padding specified, this will influence the position of the object as well.

By applying the following style to the image, you are able to reposition the image inside the *div* element. The output of this is shown in Figure 4-27.

```
img {
    position: fixed;
    left: 25px;
    top: 25px;
}
```

FIGURE 4-27 An image repositioned by setting the *top* and *left* CSS properties

Using relative positioning, you can adjust the layout of elements relative to where they would be in the normal static flow. To demonstrate this, you will copy the image element many times to show the flower picture many times inside the *div*. This is shown in static flow in Figure 4-28.

FIGURE 4-28 An image duplicated in static flow

Now, you will move all the images to the left by 25 px. This will be done by specifying relative positioning and -25 px for the *left* property. As this demonstrates, you can specify negative numbers for the *left* or *top* properties. Figure 4-29 shows the output of the following code:

```
img:nth-child(1n+0) {
    position: relative;
    left: -25px;
    top: 25px;
}
```

FIGURE 4-29 The use of the *left* property with relative positioning

As shown in Figure 4-29, all image elements have moved to the left by 25 px. Using relative positioning, you can actually make your HTML elements overlap. While the above code moves all the images over by 25 px, if you were to modify the code such that each element was moved proportionately more to make them overlap, you can create some nice effects. Recall that the elements are moved based on where they would have been in normal flow. Since the images at center are 100 px from each other, you will need to move the second image, third, and further image by the same amount as its neighbor moved, plus the amount of the desired overlap. The following code shows this:

```
img:nth-child(2) {
    position: relative;
    left: -25px;
}
img:nth-child(3) {
    position: relative;
    left: -50px;
}
img:nth-child(4) {
    position: relative;
    left: -75px;
}
```

This code produces the output in Figure 4-30. Each element after the first is moved over enough so that it overlaps its left-side neighbor by 25 px. Notice that the *left* property value is incrementally larger to account for the fact that its neighbor has moved as well.

FIGURE 4-30 The use of relative positioning to overlap images

Using absolute positioning allows you to specify the location of an element such that it is removed from the normal flow of the page. That is to say that the rest of the page flows as if this element does not exist. The element can be considered to be hovering over or under the content that is in the normal flow of the page. With this approach, it is also possible to overlap elements.

EXAM TIP

When overlapping elements using absolute positioning, CSS provides a *z-index* property. This allows you to specify in what order the elements should stack on the page along the z-axis (the third dimension!).

The following code demonstrates using absolute positioning of an image over a block of text. The text underneath the image renders in its normal flow. The image does not impact anything in the normal flow of the document. The output of this code is shown in Figure 4-31.

```
img {
    position: absolute;
    left: 215px;
    top: 100px;
    height: 50px;
    width:50px;
}
```

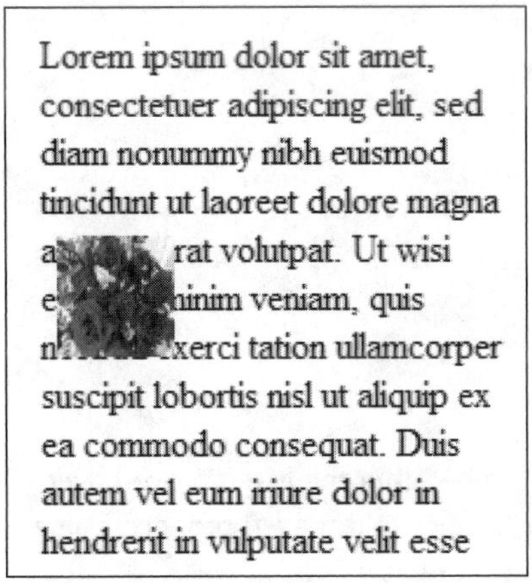

Lorem ipsum dolor sit amet, consectetuer adipiscing elit, sed diam nonummy nibh euismod tincidunt ut laoreet dolore magna a███ rat volutpat. Ut wisi e███ ███inim veniam, quis n███ ███xerci tation ullamcorper suscipit lobortis nisl ut aliquip ex ea commodo consequat. Duis autem vel eum iriure dolor in hendrerit in vulputate velit esse

FIGURE 4-31 The use of absolute positioning to overlap an image over the normal flow

The final property available to use for positioning elements is the *float* property. The *float* property automatically moves an element to the left or right of surrounding content. This is most commonly used to place images in line with text to force the text to wrap around the image. Building on the sample above, you will move the *img* element in line with the text as shown here:

```
<p style="width: 200px;margin-left: 200px;">
Lorem ipsum dolor sit amet,<img src="flowers.jpg"/> consectetuer adipiscing elit, sed
diam nonummy nibh euismod tincidunt ut laoreet dolore magna aliquam erat volutpat. Ut
wisi enim<img src="orange.jpg"/> ad minim veniam, quis nostrud exerci tation ullamcorper
suscipit lobortis nisl ut aliquip ex ea commodo consequat. Duis autem vel eum iriure
dolor in hendrerit in vulputate velit esse molestie consequat, vel illum dolore eu
feugiat nulla facilisis at vero eros et accumsan et iusto odio...</p>
```

In this paragraph element, there are two images in line with the text. An image put in this way will push the text out of the way to make room for itself. This is shown in Figure 4-32.

FIGURE 4-32 Images embedded in line with the text in normal flow

The *float* property allows you to specify how you want the element to lay out amongst the other elements around it. You can specify to *float: left* or to *float: right*. This will move the image element to the left or the right, respectively, and allow the text to flow around it smoothly. The following code demonstrates how to specify this:

```
img.flower {
    float: left;
    left: 215px;
    top: 100px;
    height: 50px;
    width: 50px;
}
img.orange {
    float: right;
    left: 215px;
    top: 100px;
    height: 50px;
    width: 50px;
}
```

The output of the above code is shown in Figure 4-33.

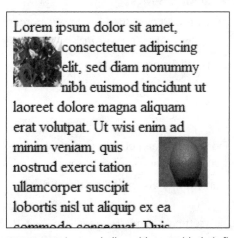

FIGURE 4-33 Images in line with text with their *float* properties specified

Now, with the *float* property specified, the text is flowing smoothly around the images.

Thought experiment

Creating a moving HTML element

In this thought experiment, apply what you've learned about this objective. You can find an answer to this question in the "Answers" section at the end of this chapter.

Create the styles and scripts to make an HTML object move across the page. This is seen in many webpages today with banner or ticker controls that display information moving across the screen. Using what you know about setting and changing the position of an object with CSS, create a moving HTML element.

Objective summary

- Every HTML element is a box and has the properties of a box such as height and width.
- CSS3 allows you to change the size of a box by specifying a new height and width.
- CSS3 allows you to style box properties in the following ways:
  - The *border-style* property allows you to specify a solid or dashed line for the border.
  - The *border-color* property allows you to specify the color of the border.
  - The *border-spacing* property allows you to specify the amount of space between adjacent elements.
  - The *border-width* property allows you to specify a thickness for the border.
  - Each side of the box can by styled differently.
- CSS3 provides a way to define the padding and margin that a box should have relative to adjacent elements. This can be configured differently for each side of the box.
- An element can be made transparent or partially transparent by setting the *opacity* property.
- An element can contain a background image by setting its *background-image* property.
- CSS3 provides the ability to create shadow effects by specifying the *box-shadow* property.
- CSS3 provides the ability to clip images using the *clip* property to show only a portion of an image.
- CSS3 can be used to establish an element's position as either fixed, absolute, or relative.
- The *left* and *top* CSS properties can be used to alter an element's position.

Objective review

Answer the following questions to test your knowledge of the information in this objective. You can find the answers to these questions and explanations of why each answer choice is correct or incorrect in the "Answers" section at the end of this chapter.

1. Which of the following is not a valid way to alter the size of an element?

   A. div{height: 50px; width: 50%;}

   B. div{height: 50px; width: 50px;}

   C. div{height: 50cm; width: 50px;

   D. div{height: 50ft; width: 50ft;}

2. Which of the following will successfully style the border of a *div* element?

   A. border-top: 5px dotted blue;
   border-right: 5px solid green;
   border-left: 3px dashed red;
   border-bottom: 10px double black;

   B. border-sides: 5px solid green;

   C. border-all: 1px solid black;

   D. border: full red;

3. When looking from the outside edge of an HTML element and moving to the inside edge, what order does the padding, margin, and border occur in?

   A. padding, border, margin

   B. margin, border, padding

   C. border, padding, margin

   D. margin, padding, border

4. Which of the following statements will apply a box shadow to the right and bottom edge of a *div* element?

   A. box-shadow: gray 5px 5px;

   B. box-shadow: gray -5px 5px;

   C. box-shadow: gray 5px -5px;

   D. box-shadow: gray -5px -5px;

5. Which of the following will place an element relative to the browser window?

   A. absolute

   B. fixed

   C. relative

Objective 4.3: Create a flexible content layout

Organizing content on the page has always been a challenge in webpage design. The concept of design patterns to separate layout from content/logic has existed for a long time in other development spaces. However, it has been less readily and easily available in the HTML space. CSS3 introduces new concepts such as the grid layout and flexbox layout that provide mechanisms to achieve this proper separation.

> **This objective covers how to:**
> - Implement a layout using a flexible box model
> - Implement a layout using multi-column
> - Implement a layout using position, floating, and exclusions
> - Implement a layout using grid alignment
> - Implement a layout using regions, grouping, and nesting

Implement a layout using a flexible box model

The flexbox is a CSS3 construct that provides a way to lay out elements that flow. *Flow* means that the elements will flow from either left to right, also known as horizontal, or up and down, also known as vertical. In order to begin with a flexbox, you need to create a container element and give it a name. Use a *<div>* element and name it as shown in this code:

```
<div id="flexbox1">
</div>
```

With this code block, you have the beginnings of a flexbox. All that is left to do is to create the CSS to indicate that the container is indeed a flexbox. The following CSS achieves this:

```
#flexbox1 {
        display: flexbox;
        border: 1px solid black;
        margin-top: 100px;
        min-height: 15px;
    }
```

With that HTML and CSS in place, you can run the page and see a container specified to have a flexbox layout. The output is shown in Figure 4-34.

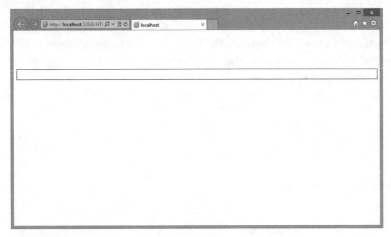

FIGURE 4-34 A *div* element set up as a flexbox

All the elements within a flexbox are called *flexbox items*. You can specify that the flexbox layout runs horizontally or vertically. You will need to be familiar with some of the key styles that can be applied to a flexbox and how the browser will interpret them. Table 4-7 outlines the important styles related to the flow of the child elements.

TABLE 4-7 CSS styles available for a flexible box

Style	Option	Description
flex-direction	*Column*	Flows the child elements of the flexbox across the vertical axis top to bottom.
	row (default)	Flows the child elements of the flexbox along the horizontal axis left to right.
	column-reverse	Renders the child elements along the vertical axis from the reverse end bottom to top.
	row-reverse	Renders the child elements along the horizontal axis from the reverse end right to left.
flex-pack	*End*	Renders the child elements from the end in relation to the layout axis set direction.
	Start	Renders the child elements from the start in relation to the layout axis set direction.
	center	Renders the child elements centered on the layout axis.
	distribute	Evenly spaces the child elements along the layout axis.

EXAM TIP

The flexbox is oriented based on the flex direction. The flex direction is based on the layout axis. If the layout of the flexbox is column, the layout axis is vertical. If the flexbox layout is row, the layout axis is horizontal. For the exam, this is important to understand in order to know how other properties on the flex grid will be rendered.

Now add some child elements to your flexbox layout:

```
<div id="flexbox1">
        <div></div>
        <div></div>
        <div></div>
 </div>
```

Just adding empty *<div>* elements will not be enough to show content. You also need to add some styles so that the flexbox layout will show your child elements. Here are the styles to add:

```
 #flexbox1 > div {
              min-width: 80px;
              min-height: 80px;
              border: 1px solid black;
              margin: 5px;
         }
#flexbox1 > div:nth-child(1) {
            background-color: green;
            }
#flexbox1 > div:nth-child(2) {
            background-color: yellow;
            }
#flexbox1 > div:nth-child(3) {
            background-color: red;
            }
```

This code produces the output in Figure 4-35.

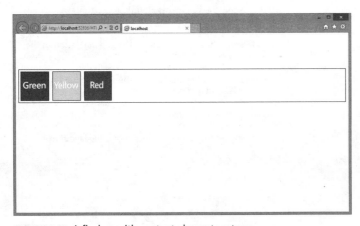

FIGURE 4-35 A flexbox with content elements set up

The default flow inside the flexbox is to display the elements left to right starting from the left edge. You can experiment with manipulating the properties to display the colored boxes in a different order. For example, what if you wanted to display the boxes in the same spot on the layout axis, but in reverse order? You could do something like this:

```
#flexbox1 {
        display: flexbox;
        flex-direction:row-reverse;
        border: 1px solid black;
        margin-top: 100px;
        min-height: 15px;
    }
```

The output from this code is shown in Figure 4-36.

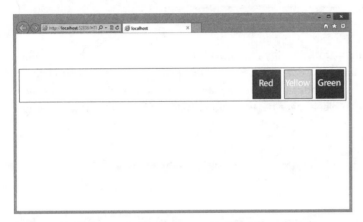

FIGURE 4-36 Flexbox content in reverse order along the same axis

Here you have changed the direction to *row-reverse*. This changes the order of the boxes. When you run this, you see that it has not only reversed the order of the boxes, but also moved them to the right end. This is because the flex direction controls what is considered the origin points on the layout axis. By reversing the direction, you have indicated that the layout start is now at the right end and the layout end is at the left end. In order to prevent reversing the order, you will need to specify the *flex-pack* property to indicate the end of the layout axis:

```
#flexbox1 {
    display: flexbox;
    flex-flow:row-reverse;
    flex-pack:end;
    border: 1px solid black;
    margin-top: 100px;
    min-height: 15px;
 }
```

With this update, the boxes are now showing in the same order (red, yellow, green) but aligned left as intended. The output is demonstrated in Figure 4-37.

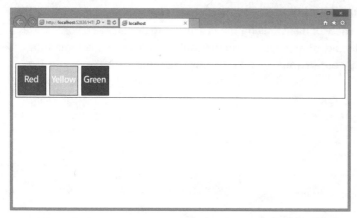

FIGURE 4-37 Flexbox content in the same order but aligned to the left end

There is also some additional functionality that provides the ability for each child element to flex itself to take up the amount of space that is specified. If you wanted one box to take up 15 percent of the space, another to take up 25 percent and the last one to take up whatever space is left without leaving in blank space between, you would implement the *flex* property. The *flex* property is specified on each of the children elements to designate the amount of space each should occupy.

You will first need to change the properties of the layout container to look as follows:

```
#flexbox1 {
        display: flexbox;
        border: 1px solid black;
        margin-top: 100px;
        min-height: 15px;
    }
#flexbox1 > div {
        min-width: 80px;
        min-height: 80px;
        border: 1px solid black;
        margin: 5px;
    }
#flexbox1 > div:nth-child(1) {
        background-color: green;
        flex: 2;
    }
#flexbox1 > div:nth-child(2) {
        background-color: yellow;
        flex: 15;
        }
#flexbox1 > div:nth-child(3){
            background-color: red;
            flex:3;
        }
```

In the updated CSS code, the *flex* property is added to each of the children elements. The *flex* property takes a parameter that is a relative value. This is not a hardcoded measurement in pixels or inches. It is relative to the value as specified among all the children elements. In this case, the first element will hold 10 percent of the space, the last element will hold 15 percent of the space, and the middle element will hold whatever space is left. To do this, you need to calculate the relative values that would be necessary to generate those proportions. The rest of the calculations to render the output will be handled by the browser.

Because we are talking about percentages, it stands to reason that the entire width of the space is 100 percent. The easy way to show this is to put into each element its respective percentage since the relative size would be what you are looking for. To illustrate the point, you can factor the units into something smaller by dividing by 20. This would make 10 percent equal 2 parts of 100 percent and 15 percent equal 3 parts of 100 percent. The remaining section will use 15 parts, or 75 percent of 100 percent. Figure 4-38 shows the output with these values.

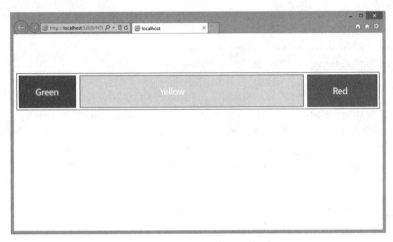

FIGURE 4-38 Distributing the flexbox content using the *flex* property

The order of the flexbox items can also be explicitly specified by using the *order* property on the flexbox items. An example of this is listed here:

```
#flexbox1 > div:nth-child(1) {
            background-color: green;
            flex-order: 2;
          }
#flexbox1 > div:nth-child(2) {
            background-color: yellow;
            flex-order: 1;
            }
#flexbox1 > div:nth-child(3) {
            background-color: red;
            flex-order: 3;
            }
```

Figure 3-39 demonstrates that the flexbox items are displayed in the order you specified instead of the default order, which would have just been in the order the items are listed in the HTML.

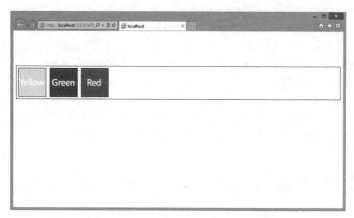

FIGURE 4-39 Explicitly setting the sequence of the flexbox items with the *order* property

Another property that is important to understand is the wrapping option. Just as with text wrapping, *flex-wrap* provides the ability to specify what the browser should do in the event that the content within the flexbox exceeds the available space of the flexbox itself. In this case, you can specify that the flexbox should wrap or not wrap. An example of wrapping is shown next. First update your flexbox to have a fixed width and then add the flexbox wrap property:

```
#flexbox1 {
        display: flexbox;
        flex-flow: row;
        flex-wrap: wrap;
        border: 1px solid black;
        margin-top: 100px;
        min-height: 15px;
        width: 200px;
    }
```

To demonstrate the wrapping functionality, you need to add a couple more flexbox items so that they will overflow the flexbox:

```
<div id="flexbox1">
        <div></div>
        <div></div>
        <div></div>
        <div></div>
        <div></div>
</div>
```

Add these additional styles to set background colors for the extra flexbox items:

```
#flexbox1 > div:nth-child(1) {
        background-color: green;
    }
#flexbox1 > div:nth-child(2) {
        background-color: yellow;
    }
#flexbox1 > div:nth-child(3) {
        background-color: red;
    }
#flexbox1 > div:nth-child(4) {
        background-color: purple;
    }
#flexbox1 > div:nth-child(5) {
        background-color: blue;
    }
```

Figure 4-40 demonstrates the wrapping functionality of the flexbox.

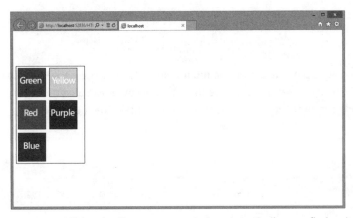

FIGURE 4-40 Using the *flex-wrap* property to automatically wrap flexbox items

EXAM TIP

On the exam, you might see the shorthand version of what you have just done with the wrapping. The *flex-flow* property supports specifying the wrap style as the second parameter: *flex-flow: row wrap*.

Implementing a layout using multi-column

CSS3 provides the ability to create a layout using columns. This provides a look and feel to the content like what you might see in a newspaper article where the content wraps up to the next column. As with the other layout techniques, the multi-column technique starts with specifying a container to hold the columns. In this case, an *article* element will be used. The following markup is added to the page:

```
<html>
<head>
    <style>
        #c_lo {
            width:80%;
            height: 400px;
            border: 1px solid black;
            column-count: 5;
            column-rule-color: black;
            column-rule-style: dashed;
            column-rule-width: 2px;
            column-gap: 5px;
        }
    </style>
</head>
<body>
    <article id="c_lo">
    </article>
</body>
</html>
```

This HTML page contains a style block to set up the multi-column layout. The body contains an *article* element that will be set up to handle the multiple columns. Some multi-column properties are already set on the *article* element. Table 4-8 details the multi-column properties.

TABLE 4-8 Multi-column properties

Property	Description
column-count	Specifies the number of columns
column-gap	Specifies the amount of space to place between columns
column-rule-color	Specifies the color of the vertical rule drawn between columns
column-rule-style	Specifies the type of vertical rule to draw between columns, for example, solid or dashed line
column-rule-width	Specifies the width of the vertical rule drawn between the columns
column-rule	A shorthand way to specify the color, style, and width of the vertical rule between the columns
column-span	Specifies how many columns the element should span across; possible values are a number of columns or all; the default value is 1
column-width	Specifies how wide the columns should be
Columns	A shorthand method to specify the number of columns and their width

After reviewing Table 4-8, you now know that the *article* element in the previous code block is set up to have five columns, each 5 px apart. The vertical rule between columns will use a dashed line that is black and 2-px wide. It is common for articles to have a title. Usually the title will span across all the columns of the article. To achieve this effect, you need to use the *column-span* property on an element to indicate that it should render across multiple columns. To achieve this, add the following code to the CSS:

```
<html>
<head>
    <style>
        #c_lo {
            width: 80%;
            height: 400px;
            border: 1px solid black;
            column-count: 5;
            column-rule-color: black;
            column-rule-style: dashed;
            column-rule-width: 2px;
            column-gap: 5px;
        }
        hgroup {
            column-span: all;
            text-align:center;
        }
    }
</style>
</head>
<body>
    <article id="c_lo">
        <hgroup>
            <h1>My Blog Article</h1>
        </hgroup>
        <p>
            ...
        </p>
    </article>
</body>
</html>
```

You have added an *hgroup* element, added *style* elements to specify that the *hgroup* text should be centered, and specified the *all* value for the *column-span* property.

This markup produces the output shown in Figure 4-41.

My Blog Article

Lorem ipsum dolor sit amet, consectetuer adipiscing elit, sed diam nonummy nibh euismod tincidunt ut laoreet dolore magna aliquam erat volutpat. Ut wisi enim ad minim veniam, quis nostrud exerci tation ullamcorper suscipit lobortis nisl ut aliquip ex ea commodo consequat. Lorem ipsum dolor sit amet, consectetuer adipiscing elit, sed diam nonummy nibh euismod tincidunt ut laoreet dolore magna aliquam erat volutpat. Ut wisi enim ad minim veniam, quis nostrud exerci tation ullamcorper suscipit lobortis nisl ut aliquip ex ea commodo consequat. Lorem ipsum dolor sit amet, consectetuer adipiscing elit, sed diam nonummy nibh euismod tincidunt ut laoreet dolore magna aliquam erat volutpat. Ut wisi enim ad minim veniam, quis nostrud exerci tation ullamcorper suscipit lobortis nisl ut aliquip ex ea commodo consequat. Lorem ipsum dolor sit amet, consectetuer adipiscing elit, sed diam nonummy nibh euismod tincidunt ut laoreet dolore magna aliquam erat volutpat. Ut wisi enim ad minim veniam, quis nostrud exerci tation ullamcorper suscipit lobortis nisl ut aliquip ex ea commodo consequat. Lorem ipsum dolor sit amet, consectetuer adipiscing elit, sed diam nonummy nibh euismod tincidunt ut laoreet dolore magna aliquam erat volutpat. Ut wisi enim ad minim veniam, quis nostrud exerci tation ullamcorper suscipit lobortis nisl ut aliquip ex ea commodo consequat.

FIGURE 4-41 Using the multi-column layout technique to display text in an article format

Implementing a layout using position, floating, and exclusions

Using position and float to position elements was discussed in the Objective 4.3 section titled, "Apply styles to establish and change an element's position." In this section, you will examine how these can be used in overall layout. *Float* is a mechanism by which the surrounding content will flow smoothly around the element with its *float* property specified to either *float: left* or *float: right*. *Left* and *right* are the only two options available for the *float* property. Exclusions provide a way to overcome this limitation with *float*. Exclusions are achieved by specifying the CSS3 property *wrap-flow*.

> **IMPORTANT** INTERNET EXPLORER VERSION REQUIREMENTS
>
> At this time, the *wrap-flow* property is only implemented in Internet Explorer 10+. Therefore, this element requires the *–ms* prefix be applied to it.

The *wrap-flow* property supports a variety of options. These options are outlined in Table 4-9. You will use most of these options in the following examples.

TABLE 4-9 Values available for the *wrap-flow* property

Value	Description
auto	This is the default value. The exclusion item will be over top of the inline element.
both	The exclusion will force the inline element to wrap smoothly on both sides.
start	The exclusion will force the inline elements to wrap only on the starting edge, and the ending edge will be empty.
end	The exclusion will force the inline element to wrap only on the ending edge, and the starting edge will be empty.
maximum	The exclusion will force the inline element to wrap only on the side with the largest available space.
clear	The exclusion will force the inline content to wrap only on the top and bottom and leave the start and end edges empty.

With the understanding of the values provided by the previous table, you can now apply these concepts to your pages. The code below will demonstrate the effect of setting the *wrap-flow* property to *both*:

```
<html>
<head>
    <style>
        p {
            width: 80%;
            padding-left: 50px;
        }
        img {
            position: absolute;
            height: 100px;
            width: 150px;
            -ms-wrap-flow: both;
        }
    </style>
</head>
<body>
    <p>
        Lorem ipsum dolor sit …
  debitis.<img src="flowers.jpg"/> Modus elaboraret temporibus no sit. At invidunt
splendide qui, ut pro choro iisque democritum. Partem timeam graecis ea vis, utamur
feugiat …
    </p>
</body>
</html>
```

This code produces the output in Figure 4-42.

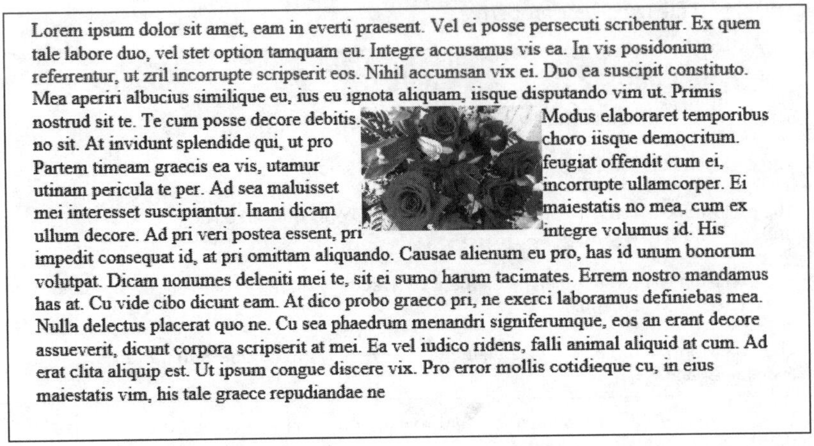

Lorem ipsum dolor sit amet, eam in everti praesent. Vel ei posse persecuti scribentur. Ex quem tale labore duo, vel stet option tamquam eu. Integre accusamus vis ea. In vis posidonium referrentur, ut zril incorrupte scripserit eos. Nihil accumsan vix ei. Duo ea suscipit constituto. Mea aperiri albucius similique eu, ius eu ignota aliquam, iisque disputando vim ut. Primis nostrud sit te. Te cum posse decore debitis. Modus elaboraret temporibus no sit. At invidunt splendide qui, ut pro choro iisque democritum. Partem timeam graecis ea vis, utamur feugiat offendit cum ei, utinam pericula te per. Ad sea maluisset incorrupte ullamcorper. Ei mei interesset suscipiantur. Inani dicam maiestatis no mea, cum ex ullum decore. Ad pri veri postea essent, pri integre volumus id. His impedit consequat id, at pri omittam aliquando. Causae alienum eu pro, has id unum bonorum volutpat. Dicam nonumes deleniti mei te, sit ei sumo harum tacimates. Errem nostro mandamus has at. Cu vide cibo dicunt eam. At dico probo graeco pri, ne exerci laboramus definiebas mea. Nulla delectus placerat quo ne. Cu sea phaedrum menandri signiferumque, eos an erant decore assueverit, dicunt corpora scripserit at mei. Ea vel iudico ridens, falli animal aliquid at cum. Ad erat clita aliquip est. Ut ipsum congue discere vix. Pro error mollis cotidieque cu, in eius maiestatis vim, his tale graece repudiandae ne

FIGURE 4-42 Setting the *wrap-flow* property to the value of *both* to make the inline text wrap on both sides of the image

The inline text wraps nicely around both the start (left edge of the image) and the end (right edge of the image). The text is quite close to the image. The *wrap-margin* property can be specified to provide a margin around the image. Add this property to your CSS code as follows:

```
img {
    position: absolute;
    height: 100px;
    width: 150px;
    -ms-wrap-flow: both;
    -ms-wrap-margin: 15px;
}
```

The output of this code is shown in Figure 4-43.

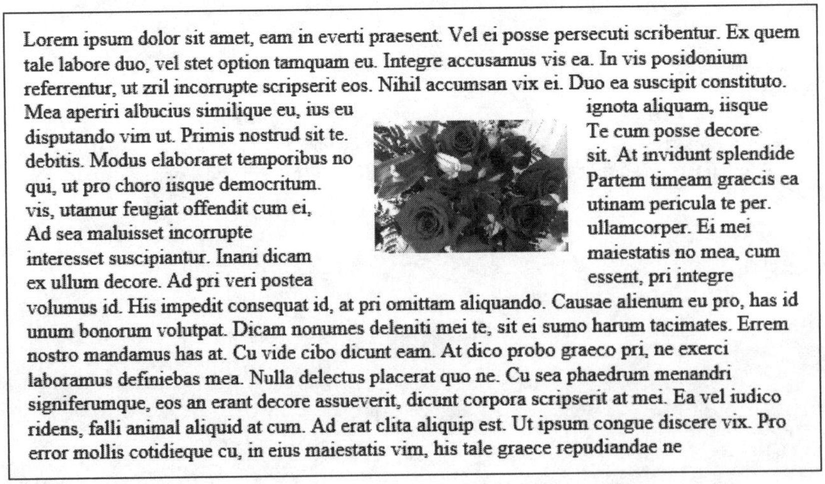

Lorem ipsum dolor sit amet, eam in everti praesent. Vel ei posse persecuti scribentur. Ex quem tale labore duo, vel stet option tamquam eu. Integre accusamus vis ea. In vis posidonium referrentur, ut zril incorrupte scripserit eos. Nihil accumsan vix ei. Duo ea suscipit constituto. Mea aperiri albucius similique eu, ius eu  ignota aliquam, iisque disputando vim ut. Primis nostrud sit te. Te cum posse decore debitis. Modus elaboraret temporibus no sit. At invidunt splendide qui, ut pro choro iisque democritum. Partem timeam graecis ea vis, utamur feugiat offendit cum ei, utinam pericula te per. Ad sea maluisset incorrupte ullamcorper. Ei mei interesset suscipiantur. Inani dicam maiestatis no mea, cum ex ullum decore. Ad pri veri postea essent, pri integre volumus id. His impedit consequat id, at pri omittam aliquando. Causae alienum eu pro, has id unum bonorum volutpat. Dicam nonumes deleniti mei te, sit ei sumo harum tacimates. Errem nostro mandamus has at. Cu vide cibo dicunt eam. At dico probo graeco pri, ne exerci laboramus definiebas mea. Nulla delectus placerat quo ne. Cu sea phaedrum menandri signiferumque, eos an erant decore assueverit, dicunt corpora scripserit at mei. Ea vel iudico ridens, falli animal aliquid at cum. Ad erat clita aliquip est. Ut ipsum congue discere vix. Pro error mollis cotidieque cu, in eius maiestatis vim, his tale graece repudiandae ne

FIGURE 4-43 Setting the *wrap-margin* property to create a margin around the exclusion

In the case where you want to have the inline content wrap only on the left or the right, you will specify either *start* or *end* respectively as the value for the *wrap-flow* property. Figure 4-44 demonstrates the output if you change the value to *start*. Setting the value to *end* will have the opposite effect.

Lorem ipsum dolor sit amet, eam in everti praesent. Vel ei posse persecuti scribentur. Ex quem tale labore duo, vel stet option tamquam eu. Integre accusamus vis ea. In vis posidonium referrentur, ut zril incorrupte scripserit eos. Nihil accumsan vix ei. Duo ea suscipit constituto. Mea aperiri albucius similique eu, ius eu ignota aliquam, iisque disputando vim ut. Primis nostrud sit te. Te cum posse decore debitis. Modus elaboraret temporibus no sit. At invidunt splendide qui, ut pro choro iisque democritum. Partem timeam graecis ea vis, utamur feugiat offendit cum ei, utinam pericula  te per. Ad sea maluisset incorrupte ullamcorper. Ei mei interesset suscipiantur. Inani dicam maiestatis no mea, cum ex ullum decore. Ad pri veri postea essent, pri integre volumus id. His impedit consequat id, at pri omittam aliquando. Causae alienum eu pro, has id unum bonorum volutpat. Dicam nonumes deleniti mei te, sit ei sumo harum tacimates. Errem nostro mandamus has at. Cu vide cibo dicunt eam. At dico probo graeco pri, ne exerci laboramus definiebas mea. Nulla delectus placerat quo ne. Cu sea phaedrum menandri signiferumque, eos an erant decore assueverit, dicunt corpora scripserit at mei. Ea vel iudico ridens, falli animal aliquid at cum. Ad erat clita aliquip est. Ut ipsum congue discere vix. Pro error mollis cotidieque cu, in eius maiestatis vim, his tale graece repudiandae ne

FIGURE 4-44 Setting the *wrap-flow* property to the value *start* to have the content wrap only on the left

Figure 4-45 shows the effect if the *wrap-flow* property is set to *clear*. Both sides of the exclusion object are cleared and the text wraps only along the top and the bottom.

Lorem ipsum dolor sit amet, eam in everti praesent. Vel ei posse persecuti scribentur. Ex quem tale labore duo, vel stet option tamquam eu. Integre accusamus vis ea. In vis posidonium referrentur, ut zril incorrupte scripserit eos. Nihil accumsan vix ei. Duo ea suscipit constituto. Mea aperiri albucius

similique eu, ius eu ignota aliquam, iisque disputando vim ut. Primis nostrud sit te. Te cum posse decore debitis. Modus elaboraret temporibus no sit. At invidunt splendide qui, ut pro choro iisque democritum. Partem timeam graecis ea vis, utamur feugiat offendit cum ei, utinam pericula te per. Ad sea maluisset incorrupte ullamcorper. Ei mei interesset suscipiantur. Inani dicam maiestatis no mea, cum ex ullum decore. Ad pri veri postea essent, pri integre volumus id. His impedit consequat id, at pri omittam aliquando. Causae alienum eu pro, has

FIGURE 4-45 Setting the *wrap-flow* property to the value *clear* to have the content wrap only along the top and bottom

Implementing a layout using grid alignment

The grid layout capability of CSS3 provides a way to lay out the content of the webpage much like an HTML table but using only CSS to achieve the results. This provides more flexibility and more maintainable code.

To demonstrate the capability of the grid layout with CSS3, you will build a webpage layout that looks like the one in Figure 4-46.

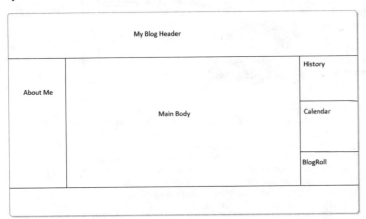

FIGURE 4-46 The webpage you will create using the grid layout capability in CSS3

Traditionally, to achieve this layout, you would have likely created an HTML markup such as the following code:

```
<table border="1" style="width:100%; height: 85%">
    <tr>
        <td colspan="3">
        </td>
    </tr>
    <tr>
        <td rowspan="3">
        </td>
        <td rowspan="3">
        </td>
        <td>
        </td>
    </tr>
    <tr>
        <td>
        </td>
    </tr>
    <tr>
        <td>
        </td>
    </tr>
    <tr>
        <td colspan="3">
        </td>
    </tr>
</table>
```

Using an HTML table works and has worked for a very long time. However, best practices today suggest separating content from layout. This is seen in many other spaces of software development and design in the context of design patterns. In this example, the layout is right in the HTML. You will reconstruct the page such that the content can be provided independent of layout and all the layout will be defined in the CSS code.

The grid layout is fully defined in CSS. To create the grid, CSS properties will need to be applied to the HTML elements. Just as with the flexbox, the grid is based on a having the display specified for a container. You will use simple *div* element for your grid container. Create the following *div* and apply the styles as indicated:

```
<style>
    #mainGrid {
        display: grid;
    }
</style>
<div id="mainGrid">
</div>
```

You have designated your *div* with the id of *mainGrid* to be the container for a grid layout by specifying its display to be grid. However, running this in the browser will not yield much of a result. You need to define the structure of the grid. In this example, you will create a simple four-by-two grid layout. Add the child elements to the *div* as shown and update the styles as shown to supply information to the container about how you would like it to render the child cells.

```
#mainGrid {
    display: grid;
    grid-columns: 150px 150px 150px 150px;
    grid-rows: 75px 75px;
    }
<div id="mainGrid">
    <div></div>
    <div></div>
    <div></div>
    <div></div>
    <div></div>
    <div></div>
    <div></div>
    <div></div>
</div>
```

You have added two additional CSS properties to *mainGrid*. These properties are rather self-explanatory. As their name suggests, the *grid-columns* property allows you to specify how many columns are in your grid. The *grid-rows* property allows you to specify how many rows are in your grid. The property values accepted are *size* attributes separated by spaces. The renderer will interpret each value as a new column or row.

If you run this HTML in the browser, the output will be less than exciting. One reason is that the *div* elements are empty. Go ahead and put some text in each *div* and examine the output that you get in the browser. If all goes as expected, your *div* elements will display all on top of each other. They are, for all intents and purposes, ignoring your previous CSS instructions provided to the container to layout in a four-by-two style. Well, they are not really ignoring the instructions. Recall, the instructions were to the container *mainGrid* regarding how you wanted it to lay out its child elements. You still need to give each child element its own identity within the grid. That is, the container knows it needs to set up a four-by-two grid, but it does not know which element goes where within that four-by-two grid. It just floats them all on top of each other. You will now specify to the grid elements where they should live in the relative space available within the grid. You will apply some background colors so that the rendered page will easily demonstrate the concepts.

```css
#mainGrid > div:nth-child(1){
    grid-column: 1;
    grid-row:1;
    background-color: blue;
}
#mainGrid > div:nth-child(2){
    grid-column:2;
    grid-row:1;
    background-color: aqua;
}
#mainGrid > div:nth-child(3){
    grid-column: 3;
    grid-row:1;
    background-color: red;
}
```

```
#mainGrid > div:nth-child(4){
    grid-column: 4;
    grid-row:1;
    background-color: green;
}
#mainGrid > div:nth-child(5){
    grid-column: 1;
    grid-row:2;
    background-color: magenta;
}
#mainGrid > div:nth-child(6){
    grid-column: 2;
    grid-row:2;
    background-color: yellow;
}
#mainGrid > div:nth-child(7){
    grid-column: 3;
    grid-row:2;
    background-color: orange;
}
#mainGrid > div:nth-child(8){
    grid-column: 4;
    grid-row:2;
    background-color: olive;
}
```

With this code, you have instructed the elements where they should be positioned within the grid. When the renderer processes these elements, it will now know by asking each element where it should go and how to place them. Now the page displayed in the browser looks like Figure 4-47. Each element is placed according to the column and row position specified for it: blue, aqua, red, and green elements respectively in columns 1 through 4, row 1; magenta, yellow, orange, and olive elements respectively in columns 1 through 4, row 2.

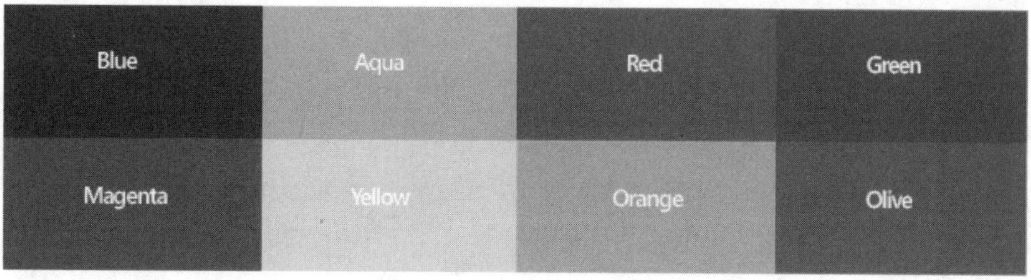

FIGURE 4-47 The webpage with all the columns and rows of the grid displayed

Now with the foundation in place, you can take this a step further to create a grid that will correspond with the table layout specified earlier. To do this, you need only a couple more CSS properties that will provide the equivalent functionality as the *colspan* and the *rowspan*. In addition, your styles will provide some sizing properties to ensure that the grid expands on the page as you would like it to. This is optional of course in the real world. You may want to have content force the sizing of your grid or you may want to explicitly specify the size.

The full code listing is specified here:

```css
html, body {
            height: 100%;
            width: 100% ;
        }
#blogPage {
    display: grid;
    columns: 15% 1fr 25%;
    grid-rows: 20% 20% 20% 20% 20%;
    width: 90%;
    height: 95%;
    border: 1px dotted black;
    margin: auto;
}
#blogPage > header {
    grid-column: 1;
    grid-column-span: 3;
    grid-row: 1;
    border: 1px dotted black;
}
#blogPage > footer {
    grid-column: 1;
    grid-row: 5;
    grid-column-span: 3;
    border: 1px dotted black;
}
#blogPage > article {
    grid-column: 2;
    grid-row: 2;
    grid-row-span: 3;
    border: 1px dotted black;
}
#blogPage > #calendar {
    grid-column: 3;
    grid-row: 3;
    border: 1px dotted black;
}
#blogPage > #blogRoll {
    grid-column: 3;
    grid-row: 4;
    border: 1px dotted black;
}
#blogPage > #aboutMe {
    grid-column: 1;
    grid-row: 2;
    grid-row-span: 3;
    border: 1px dotted black;
}
```

```
#blogPage > #bloghistory {
    grid-column: 3;
    grid-row: 2;
    border: 1px dotted black;
}
</style>
<body>
    <div id="blogPage">
        <header>My Blog Header</header>
        <article>My Blog's Main Body</article>
        <footer>My Blog Footer</footer>
        <aside id="calendar">A calendar</aside>
        <aside id="blogRoll">My favorite blogs</aside>
        <aside id="aboutMe">Who am I?</aside>
        <aside id="bloghistory">My blog history</aside>
    </div>
</body>
```

Since you are producing a real webpage that will hold real content, the appropriate semantic tags are being used. You can see from looking at the HTML portion of the code that there is no indication to layout. You have defined only a series of sections for the page to display. All the layout implementation happens in the CSS. You will notice the addition of two CSS properties to your repertoire: *grid-row-span* and *grid-column-span*. As their names suggest, you can expect them to behave the same way as the HTML attributes *colspan* and *rowspan*. They tell the browser to lay out the column or the row such that it spans the specified number of columns or rows. When you run this code in the browser you will get the output displayed in Figure 4-48.

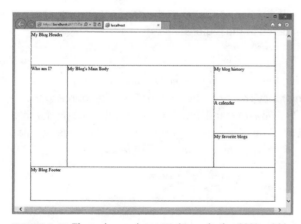

FIGURE 4-48 The webpage layout using only the CSS3 grid layout

Implementing a layout using regions, grouping, and nesting

Regions is a new CSS3 construct that allows you to have content flow through various regions in a webpage. This could provide some very interesting scenarios. To get started, you will need an HTML page with regions defined in it. The following HTML provides the starting point for establishing regions.

```
<body>
    <div class="regionLayout">
        <div id="region1"></div>c
        <div id="region2"></div>
        <div id="region3"></div>
        ...
        <div id="region-n"></div>
    </div>
</body>
```

> **NOTE BROWSER SUPPORT FOR REGIONS**
>
> Regions are currently in the experimental and development phase. There is limited browser support at this time. This section highlights only the key design goals of this feature.

Layout of a webpage using regions requires two things: a content source and the regions that will be the content destination. The HTML above outlines the regions. The content can come from another page via an iframe or another element on the page itself (though this currently does not work in any browser). By adding an iframe to the page, you can set the *iframe src* to the content that will be rendered in the regions:

```
<iframe src="content_source.html"/>
```

With the content source established in the HTML, there are now only two things that need to occur. CSS is used to control the functionality of the content from the source to the destination. The new CSS properties called *flow-into* and *flow-from* are used to assign the role of the HTML elements in the region layout. The *flow-into* property is assigned a value to hold the content. This value can be anything such as in this example:

```
.content_source{
        flow-into: myflow;
}
```

Then the destination of the content is defined in a class like this:

```
.content_regions{
        flow-from: myflow;
}
```

As long as the same name is used in the *flow-into* and the *flow-from*, they will work together. This is called a *named flow*. All the elements forming the regions to display the content source in the same named flow is called a *region chain*. You can have multiple sources and multiple region chains. The name assigned to the *flow-** properties are used to coordinate which content source goes into which regions.

EXAM TIP

Since the regions feature is still experimental, the exam is not likely to cover this topic. However, this is only at the time of writing and could change at any time. Be familiar and keep checking on updates with respect to the readiness of this CSS construct in the real world.

Thought experiment
Combining layouts

In this thought experiment, apply what you've learned about this objective. You can find an answer to this question in the "Answers" section at the end of this chapter.

Extend the current grid layout blog page so that the main content area uses a column layout. Each layout is very powerful on its own to serve its specific purpose. It is important though to know that you can create some very powerful layouts by combining them where it makes sense.

Objective summary

- Flexbox allows you to lay out elements in a flow-like fashion.
- Multi-column layout allows you to separate content into a fixed number of columns, like a newspaper layout.
- The flow of text around elements like images can be controlled using wrap-flow layouts.
- The grid layout provides the best way to separate the layout from the content by specifying explicitly in CSS where each element should be displayed within a predefined grid.

Objective review

Answer the following questions to test your knowledge of the information in this objective. You can find the answers to these questions and explanations of why each answer choice is correct or incorrect in the "Answers" section at the end of this chapter.

1. Which of the following layouts is based on columns and rows?

    A. flexbox

    B. multi-column

    C. grid layout

    D. exclusions

2. Which of the following is false about a flexbox layout?

    A. The direction of the elements in a flexbox can be controlled with the *flex-direction* property.

    B. The elements layout can be configured along the layout axis using the *flex-pack* property.

    C. Elements in a flexbox are called flexbox items.

    D. Elements in a flexbox can be set into rows and columns.

3. Which of the following property values for *wrap-flow* will allow the text to wrap along both sides of an element?

    A. *both*

    B. *all*

    C. *left and right*

    D. *cross*

Objective 4.4: Create an animated and adaptive UI

The modern day website is an interactive experience for the end user. CSS3 provides many mechanisms to apply a professional touch to the end-user interaction. This is achieved through the ability to animate and transform objects. By adding these rich features to your webpages, you really bring the experience to the next level. In addition, there is an opportunity to create a responsive user interface. A responsive user interface is one that can adapt itself automatically based on the size of the screen that is available. Finally, the ability to hide and disable controls provides you with the ability to further customize the user interface with CSS.

Animating objects by applying CSS transitions

Transitions provide a mechanism to alter the style of an object such that the change occurs in a visible gradual fashion. You have the ability to control which style property gets altered and how long it takes to complete its transition from one style to the other. A transition starts when the specified property is changed. In its simplest form, the following code transitions two properties of a *div* element: the *margin-left* and the *background-color*. The transition is to take one second. The transition will occur when the mouse is hovering over the *div* element.

> **NOTE SEE IT FOR YOURSELF**
>
> Since this is a book and transitions are visual effects that involve the changing of properties gradually, screen shots do not demonstrate the functionality very well. You should try the code in your own webpages to get familiar with the outcomes of the styles and scripts.

The visual effect is that this *div*, which starts off with a gray background, will fade out of sight to the right. The following code demonstrates this:

```
<html>
<head>
    <style>
        div {
            width: 100px;
            height: 100px;
            background-color: gray;
            margin-left: 250px;
            margin-top:250px;
            transition: background-color 1s, margin-left 1s ;
        }
            div:hover {
                margin-left: 350px;
                background-color: white;
            }
    </style>
</head>
<body>
    <div>
    </div>
</body>
</html>
```

With this CSS code in place, when the user moves the mouse over the *div* element, it will move to the right and its background color will change to white. Since the background of the webpage is also white, it provides the effect of disappearing. You need to understand what properties are being used to achieve this effect. In this particular code, you are using a shorthand property called *transition* that allows you to specify a comma-separated list of CSS properties and a length of time for the transition of the specified property to take place. These properties could also be indicated separately using the various CSS properties in Table 4-9.

TABLE 4-9 CSS3 transition properties

Property Name	Description
transition-property	Specifies the property to which a transition will be applied
transition-duration	Specifies how much time the transition should take from start to finish
transition-delay	Specifies how long to wait from the time the property is changed before starting the transition

EXAM TIP

When using the individual *transition-** properties, you can specify only one property to transition. With the transition shorthand, you are able to specify a comma-separated list.

Another property that exists to control the speed of the transitions is *transition-timing-function*. This property allows you to have a bit more control over the speed of the transition. With the *transition-timing-function* property, you can specify some different effects to the timing of the transition. The possible values are specified in Table 4-10.

TABLE 4-10 Values for *transition-timing-function*

Value	Description
ease	The default value that applies the effect in such a way that it starts slow, speeds up, then ends slow.
linear	Makes the transition constant from start to finish
ease-in	Causes the transition to have a slow start.
ease-out	Causes the transition to have a slow finish.
ease-in-out	Causes the transition to have a slow start and a slow finish.
cubic-bezier	Allows you to define values. This takes four parameters that are values from 0 and 1.

Applying 3-D and 2-D transformations

Using CSS you are also able to apply transformations to elements on your webpage. In this section, you will review how to apply three dimensional transforms to your elements. Following with the same div from the previous section, you will apply the three-dimensional (3-D) transformations listed in Table 4-11. Two-dimensional (2-D) transforms are covered in Objective 1.3, "Apply transforms."

TABLE 4-11   Three-dimensional transformations

Transformation	Effect
translate	Moves the object from its current location to a new location
scale	Changes the size of the object
rotate	Spins the object along the x-axis, y-axis, and/or the z-axis
matrix	Allows you to combine all the transformations into one command

As you can see, the 3-D transforms are the same property values as the 2-D transforms. The addition is that each property now allows you to invoke the transform across the z-axis instead of just the x-axis and y-axis. In addition, there are shorthand properties available such as *translate3d* and *rotate3d*.

To demonstrate the use of a 3-D transform, you will look at the rotate transformation. The following code applies a 3-D rotation of the *div* element.

```
div {
    transform: rotateX(30deg)  rotateY(30deg) rotateZ(30deg);
}
```

When the page loads, all *div* elements on the page will be rotated 30 degrees along each axis. The above transform could be expressed in this way as well:

```
transform: rotate3d(1,1,1, 30deg);
```

In this case, *rotate3d* takes the first parameters to specify on which axis to rotate. A value of zero indicates to no rotation on that axis whereas a value of 1 indicates a rotation on that axis. The parameters are in order of x-axis, y-axis, z-axis. The last parameter specifies the number of degrees to rotate.

When the page loads, you will see the output in Figure 4-49.

FIGURE 4-49 A *div* element being rotated in 3-D

You can experiment with each transformation. The output is similar to that of the 2-D with the exception that the effects are applied along the z-axis as well. In addition, you can see that you can still use the 3-D functions to achieve 2-D effects. It all depends which parameters you specify.

Adjusting UI based on media queries

In the modern world, screen size is a variable you now have to contend with when building webpages. With many people accessing the Internet from different devices such as smart phones, tablets, and desktops, there is no guarantee that your page will fit nicely on the screen, and as a result, it may not be user friendly. This is where the concept of media queries is able to help. With the use of media queries you can create a responsive user interface that will adjust automatically as the size of the available rendered webpage changes. By using information from the browser, you are able to determine how to present your content so that it provides a user-friendly experience on any device.

The media query syntax is as simple as adding the following to your CSS file:

```
@media screen and (max-width: 800px){
}
```

This code will apply all the styles within the media query to the page when the width of the screen is not wider than 800 px. To achieve a different layout for different screen sizes or devices, you need to specify a media query for the different size ranges. To explore this, use the blog layout that was created in Objective 4.3 using a grid layout. The default layout of the blog is shown in Figure 4-48. However, as the screen size gets smaller, the blog gets compacted to the point that it might not be readable or, depending on the amount of content, will require awkward scrolling on a device. To accommodate the different screen sizes, update your CSS code to include media queries. The following code adds a media query to apply the default layout to larger screens such as desktops or laptops:

```
@media screen and (min-width: 1200px) {
    #blogPage {
        display: -ms-grid;
        grid-columns: 15% 1fr 25%;
        grid-rows: (20%)[5];
        width: 90%;
        height: 95%;
        border: 1px dotted black;
        margin: auto;
    }
        #blogPage > header {
            grid-column: 1;
            grid-column-span: 3;
            grid-row: 1;
            border: 1px dotted black;
        }
        #blogPage > footer {
            grid-column: 1;
            grid-row: 5;
            grid-column-span: 3;
            border: 1px dotted black;
        }
        #blogPage > article {
            grid-column: 2;
            grid-row: 2;
            grid-row-span: 3;
            border: 1px dotted black;
        }
        #blogPage > #calendar {
            grid-column: 3;
            grid-row: 3;
            border: 1px dotted black;
        }
        #blogPage > #blogRoll {
            grid-column: 3;
            grid-row: 4;
            border: 1px dotted black;
        }
        #blogPage > #aboutMe {
            grid-column: 1;
            grid-row: 2;
            grid-row-span: 3;
            border: 1px dotted black;
        }
        #blogPage > #bloghistory {
            grid-column: 3;
            grid-row: 2;
            border: 1px dotted black;
        }
}
```

This produces the output in Figure 4-48. As long as the screen is at least 1,200 px wide, this layout will be applied. However, as the screen gets smaller, on a tablet for example, the user interface starts to get less user friendly. To accommodate a tablet screen, you can adjust the layout a bit by adding the following CSS code to the page:

```css
@media screen and (max-width: 1199px) and (min-width: 401px) {
    #blogPage {
        display: -ms-grid;
        grid-columns: 75% 1fr;
        grid-rows: (20%)[6];
        width: 90%;
        height: 95%;
        border: 1px dotted black;
        margin: auto;
    }

        #blogPage > header {
            grid-column: 1;
            grid-column-span: 2;
            grid-row: 1;
            border: 1px dotted black;
        }
        #blogPage > footer {
            grid-column: 1;
            grid-row: 6;
            grid-column-span: 2;
            border: 1px dotted black;
        }
        #blogPage > article {
            grid-column: 1;
            grid-row: 3;
            grid-row-span: 3;
            border: 1px dotted black;
        }
        #blogPage > #calendar {
            grid-column: 2;
            grid-row: 4;
            border: 1px dotted black;
        }
        #blogPage > #blogRoll {
            grid-column: 2;
            grid-row: 5;
            border: 1px dotted black;
        }
        #blogPage > #aboutMe {
            grid-column: 1;
            grid-row: 2;
            grid-column-span: 2;
            border: 1px dotted black;
        }
        #blogPage > #bloghistory {
            grid-column: 2;
            grid-row: 3;
            border: 1px dotted black;
        }
    }
```

With this code, you can restructure the layout of the grid based on the different screen size. The output of this code produces a user interface shown in Figure 4-50.

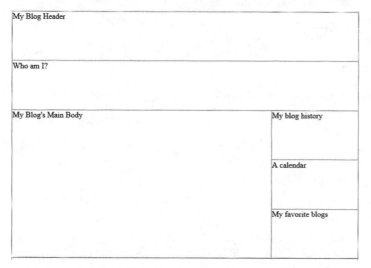

My Blog Header

Who am I?

My Blog's Main Body

My blog history

A calendar

My favorite blogs

FIGURE 4-50   The layout of the blog is adjusted for the tablet screen size

Now you have the desktop-size screen and tablet-size screen looking good. The next one to account for is the smaller smart phone screen. Add the following code to your CSS to place a media query for the smaller screen size:

```
@media screen and (max-width: 400px) {
    #blogPage {
        display: grid;
        grid-columns: 50% 50%;
        grid-rows: 15% 15% 1fr 15% 15%;
        width: 90%;
        height: 95%;
        border: 1px dotted black;
        margin: auto;
    }
        #blogPage > header {
            grid-column: 1;
            grid-column-span: 2;
            grid-row: 1;
            border: 1px dotted black;
        }
        #blogPage > footer {
            grid-column: 1;
            grid-row: 5;
            grid-column-span: 2;
            border: 1px dotted black;
        }
        #blogPage > article {
            grid-column: 1;
            grid-row: 3;
            grid-column-span: 2;
            border: 1px dotted black;
        }
        #blogPage > #calendar {
```

```
        grid-column: 2;
        grid-row: 2;
        border: 1px dotted black;
    }
    #blogPage > #blogRoll {
        grid-column: 1;
        grid-row: 4;
        border: 1px dotted black;
    }
    #blogPage > #aboutMe {
        grid-column: 1;
        grid-row: 2;
        border: 1px dotted black;
    }
    #blogPage > #bloghistory {
        grid-column: 2;
        grid-row: 4;
        border: 1px dotted black;
    }
}
```

As the screen size gets to be as small as it would be on a smart phone, the user interface will be rendered as shown in Figure 4-51.

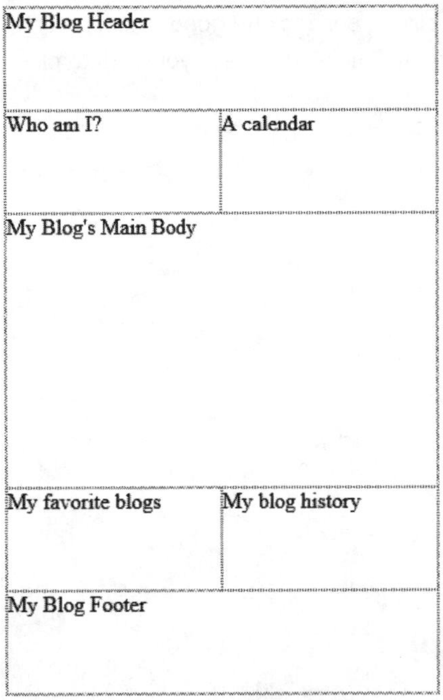

FIGURE 4-51 The layout of the blog is adjusted for the screen size of a smart phone

So far the CSS is working great. The only problem is you have a lot of CSS code in a single page. Typically, a website has multiple pages with styles shared across different pages. As a result, you will likely be linking an external CSS file to your HTML page. The link element supports media queries as well, which in turn lets you share a CSS file across multiple pages. For example, you might want to change the font-size of the text throughout your site based on the view port size. To achieve this, move the CSS from each media query into its own CSS file and link in your CSS files in the following way:

```
<link rel="stylesheet" media="screen and (min-width: 1200px)" href="Desktop.css"/>
<link rel="stylesheet" media="screen and (max-width: 1199px) and (min-width: 401px)" ref="tablet.css"/>
<link rel="stylesheet" media="screen and (max-width: 400px)" href="phone.css"/>
```

With the CSS linked in this fashion, you can add and modify the styles for the different view ports centrally for your entire website.

Hiding or disabling controls

The ability to modify the user interface positioning using media queries as shown in the last section is very useful. In addition, some layouts might just not work in some view ports. In this case, you might want to complete hide controls or disable controls. HTML elements are visible by default. However, they can be made invisible by setting the *visibility* CSS property as shown in the following code:

```
.myhiddenelements {
    visibility:hidden;
}
```

By setting the visibility to hidden, the control is not visible to the end user of the webpage. When hiding an element using the *visibility* property, the overall layout still behaves as though the element is there. If you prefer to have the element hidden and the layout behave as though it is not there, the *display* property should be used as shown in the following code:

```
.myhiddenelements {
    display: none;
}
```

With the *display* property, the element is not visible and the layout is not affected by it.

If you do not want to hide the element but only make it disabled such that the user can see it but cannot perform any action on it, you need to add the attribute directly to the HTML element. As such, you can define a CSS class that you can apply to any elements that you want to have disabled:

```
.disableIt
```

Now that you have a CSS class called *.disableIt*, you can apply this class to any elements that you want to disable. In this case, you want to disable a button element, so apply the class to the button element as shown here:

```
<button id="myButton" class="disableIt" >My Button</button>
```

The last step is to create some JavaScript that finds all the controls with this class assigned to it and adds the *disabled* attribute to them. The following code demonstrates this:

```
<script>
    $("document").ready(function (e) {
        $(".disableIt").attr("disabled", "disabled");
    });
</script>
```

This script has the same net effect as putting the attribute directly on the button element as shown here:

```
<button id="myButton" disabled="disabled">My Button</button>
```

When you have many elements that you would like to disable, it is much easier to create a CSS class, apply it to the elements, then by using jQuery, apply the *disabled* attribute to them all.

Thought experiment

Combining effects

In this thought experiment, apply what you've learned about this objective. You can find the answer to this question in the "Answers" section at the end of this chapter.

Consider combining transitions with transformations. Individually, transitions and transformations provide interesting effects to the HTML page. Consider what kind of effects can be achieved by using them together.

Objective summary

- HTML elements can be manipulated with transitions using the *transition-property*, *transition-duration*, and *transition-delay* CSS properties.

- Elements can be manipulated in 2-D and 3-D space with effects such as *translate*, *scale*, *rotate*, and *matrix*.

- Media queries allow you to have a dynamic, responsive user interface based on the view port size and type.

- The *visibility* property hides a control but keeps its position in the overall layout. Using the *display* property to hide a control removes it from the layout as well.

Objective review

Answer the following questions to test your knowledge of the information in this objective. You can find the answers to these questions and explanations of why each answer choice is correct or incorrect in the "Answers" section at the end of this chapter.

1. Which of the following statements will hide an element but keep its space in the overall flow?

    A. display: none;

    B. visibility: hidden;

    C. display: inline;

    D. visibility: visible;

2. Media queries are best suited for what purpose?

    A. Setting the priority of style sheet references in a webpage

    B. Creating a responsive user interface based on the screen size of the view port

    C. Modifying the view port to properly fit the content of the page

    D. Connecting to third-party style sheets to alter the layout

3. Which of the following *transition-timing-function* properties makes the transition start slow, speed up, then end slow?

    A. *ease*

    B. *ease-in*

    C. *ease-out*

    D. *ease-in-out*

Objective 4.5: Find elements using CSS selectors and jQuery

Objective 1.2, "Write code that interacts with UI controls," covered the use of document selectors to find HTML elements by their unique name. In this section, you explore more advanced techniques to find elements through the use of CSS selectors and jQuery.

This objective covers how to:

- Define element, style, and attribute selectors
- Choose the correct selector to reference an element
- Find elements by using pseudo-elements and pseudo-classes

Defining element, style, and attribute selectors

CSS uses selectors that you define in a CSS file or style block to identify which elements in a webpage the defined styles should be applied to. This can be done by specifying the element itself as the selector. For example, the following CSS is an element selector for the *div* element:

```
div{
...
}
```

Any *div* within scope of the declaration will have the styles applied to it. Another possible selector is a class selector. To use a class selector, you define a custom class name in the CSS file. This can be any name prefixed with a period. Then, any element that has that class assigned to it via the *class* attribute will have the defined styles applied. For example:

```
.mycustomclass{
....
}
```

Another way to use CSS to select specific elements on the page is to use attribute selection. This is achieved by specifying an element type followed by a specific attribute. For example if you have a web form that needs to be filled in, you may attribute required fields with a red border around the textboxes. The following code achieves this for any elements that have the *required* attribute specified:

```
input[required] {
    border: 1px red solid;
}
```

There are other possibilities for the use of attribute selectors. These are outlined in Table 4-12.

TABLE 4-12   Attribute selector capabilities

Attribute selector	Description
=	Specifies that an attribute equals a specific value. For example, the URL of an anchor is a specify URL.
~=	Specifies a space-separated list of words as the values for an attribute.
^=	Specifies that the attribute has a value starting with the text specified.
$=	Specifies that the attribute has a value ending with the specified text.
*=	Specifies that the attribute has a value containing the specified text.

Choosing the correct selector to reference an element

Choosing the correct selector to reference an element is an important consideration. You need to ensure that you organize your selectors and your elements such that only the desired elements are impacted by the defined styles. For example, the following style affects all *article* elements:

```
article{
  border-color: 1px solid red;
}
```

If you do not want to affect all articles but only the newest article, you must distinguish them, perhaps by adding a custom CSS class to the definition and assigning this to only the newest article:

```
article.newest{
  border-color: 1px solid red;
}
```

By specifying it this way, you are assured that not every article on the page is impacted by the style. This topic is covered in more detail in Objective 4.6 in the section "Referencing elements correctly."

Finding elements by using pseudo-elements and pseudo-classes

Pseudo-classes and pseudo-elements provide some very powerful ways to add styles to elements. Pseudo-classes allow you to apply styles to an element based on its state, its interaction with the user, or its position in the document. Pseudo-elements allow you to insert content into the page in locations relative to the elements that the CSS is being applied to. You will examine each of the common pseudo-classes and pseudo-elements in this section.

:link, :visited, and :hover

These are the most commonly used pseudo-classes, used most frequently with the *anchor* element, providing a clickable link for the user of the webpage. With these pseudo-classes, you can control what styles are applied to a hyperlink in the different states. For example, the following CSS changes the color of the link based on its state:

```
a:link {
    color: green;
}
a:hover {
    color: red;
}
a:visited {
    color: black;
}
```

In this example, the link by default will be green. When a user moves the mouse over the link, the color of the link will change to red. If the user does not click the link and then moves off of it, the link will go back to green. However, if the user clicks the link, it becomes a visited link and will change to black.

:checked

The *:checked* pseudo-class lets you apply styles to elements that are in a checked state. Elements that support this pseudo-class are check boxes and radio buttons. The amount of styling you can apply to the default elements is minimal. However, there are ample resources to customize these elements using CSS. The following example shows how to hide a check box when a user clicks it.

```
input[type="checkbox"]:checked {
    display: none;
}
```

:required

The *:required* pseudo-class lets you apply styles to any elements on the page that have the *required* attribute. This is a convenient way to highlight required fields on a form. The following CSS demonstrates applying styles to all *required* input controls:

```
input:required {
    border: 2px solid red;
}
```

All *required* input controls will now have a red border to highlight this to the user.

:enabled and :disabled

The *:enabled* and *:disabled* pseudo-classes allow you to style controls based on their enabled or disabled state. By default, disabled controls typically are light gray. With these pseudo classes, you can control how the element displays in either state. The following code demonstrates this:

```
input:disabled {
    background-color: blue;
}
input:enabled {
        background-color: white;
}
```

If a control is enabled, the background will be white; otherwise disabled controls will be blue.

:first-child

The *:first-child* pseudo-element applies the specified styles to the first instance of the element that occurs in a list, for example, the first paragraph element in this HTML:

```
<div>
    <p>Lorem Ipsum ...</p>
    <p>Lorem Ipsum ...</p>
    <p>Lorem Ipsum ...</p>
    <p>Lorem Ipsum ...</p>
</div>
```

The following CSS will change the text color to green in the first paragraph element:

```
p:first-child {
    color:green;
 }
```

:first-letter

The *:first-letter* pseudo-element will alter the style of the first letter in the specified element. Continuing with the example HTML above, the following CSS will increase the size of the first letter in each paragraph element:

```
p::first-letter {
    font-size: xx-large;
}
```

:before and :after

The *:before* and *:after* pseudo-elements will add the specified content in front of or after the indicated element selector. So, the following code would add ** to the front and end of the paragraph element:

```
p::before {
    content: '**';
}
p::after {
    content: '**';
}
```

:first-line

The *:first-line* pseudo-element alters the styles of the first line of a text element. The following CSS will make the first line of the text inside the paragraph element green and larger:

```
p::first-line {
    color:green;
    font-size: x-large;
}
```

> ### *Thought experiment*
> #### Using jQuery with pseudo-classes
>
> In this thought experiment, apply what you've learned about this objective. You can find an answer to this question in the "Answers" section at the end of this chapter.
>
> Consider how you can use jQuery to select elements using pseudo-classes and pseudo-elements. Using only jQuery, apply CSS styles to the first paragraph of any group of paragraph elements.

Objective summary

- Pseudo-elements and pseudo-classes provide an advanced mechanism for searching HTML elements in a page and applying styles.
- Using pseudo-elements and pseudo-classes you can change the style of an element based on user actions.
- Using pseudo-elements and pseudo-classes you can gain granular control over parts of the text in a text block.

Objective review

Answer the following questions to test your knowledge of the information in this objective. You can find the answers to these questions and explanations of why each answer choice is correct or incorrect in the "Answers" section at the end of this chapter.

1. Which one of the following is a CSS class selector?

   A. .code

   B. #code

   C. div[code]

   D. :code

2. Which one of the following is an attribute selector?

   A. .required

   B. #required

   C. input[required]

   D. :required

3. Which of the following statements would alter the style of an anchor element when the mouse is moved over it?

   A. a:link

   B. a:mouseover

   C. a:beforeclick

   D. a:hover

Objective 4.6: Structure a CSS file by using CSS selectors

CSS files can become large and complex. Structuring them in an organized fashion will make them easier to maintain and also to know what selectors are best suited to be used to reference the HTML on your page.

> **This objective covers how to:**
> - Reference elements correctly
> - Implement inheritance
> - Override inheritance using !important
> - Style an element based on pseudo-elements and pseudo-classes

Referencing elements correctly

CSS is used to apply styles to elements in an HTML page. To do so, the CSS has to know which elements to apply the styles to. There are a few ways to reference elements from CSS. This is known as the *selector syntax*. This has been demonstrated throughout the chapter. This section will explain specifically how to reference elements from CSS. The key consideration is to ensure that you reference elements such that the styles affect only the elements you want affected. In large complex CSS, it can get complicated.

Elements can be referenced from CSS by their element name. For example:

```
p{…}
article{…}
div{…}
```

In this code, styles are applied to all paragraph elements, article elements, and *div* elements.

The next method to select elements is through the use of classes as shown here:

```
.bold{…}
.largeTitle{…}
```

In this code, the styles are applied only to HTML elements that have their *class* attribute assigned these class names. Element names and classes can be combined to narrow the selector even further:

```
p.largeTitle{…}
```

This code applies the styles only to paragraph elements that have the class *largeTitle* assigned to the *class* attribute.

The most granular method to reference HTML elements from CSS is by using the id or name of the element:

```
#nameBox{…}
```

This code applies the specified styles only to the single element on the page with the specified name.

In some cases, you might want to apply the same style to many elements of different types. In this case, you can group them and define the styles only once:

```
p, H1, H2 {…}
```

In this sample, all three of the HTML elements noted will have the defined styles applied to them.

Implementing inheritance

Some styles applied to a parent element are automatically inherited by children elements. For example, if a series of paragraph elements are inside an article element, and font and text styles are applied to the article, all the paragraph elements will automatically inherit the font and text styles as well. The following code demonstrates this concept:

```
<style>
    div {
        font-family: sans-serif;
        color: green;
    }
</style>
```

And with the following HTML:

```
<div>
    hello div world.
    <p>
    Hello paragraph world.
    </p>
</div>
```

Both the *div* and the paragraph will have the font and color styles applied to them because the paragraph element does not have any of its own styles defined. If you assign styles to the paragraph element to override the *div* styles you would be able to prevent the inheritance of the styles, as shown here:

```
<style>
    div {
        font-family: sans-serif;
        colór: green;
    }
    p {
        font-family: serif;
        color: blue;
    }
</style>
```

Overriding inheritance using *!important*

CSS for large websites can be complicated. Large websites may have CSS coming from different sources. It could be on each page and referenced externally. External libraries are more and more common as experts throughout the community have created themes that can be imported into your web applications. With all this styling coming from different sources, inheritance of styles can be tricky. In some cases you may just need to override all other competing styles completely with your own desired style. This is where the *!important* keyword comes in. Consider the following simple CSS example:

```
p {
    font-family: serif;
    color: blue;
}
p {
    color: purple;
}
p{
    color: yellow;
}
```

In this CSS code, you have three competing styles for the paragraph element. How the browser renders this is based on the last style it reads for an element it applies to. So in this case, the text in all the paragraphs will be yellow. However, if you want to override this behavior and force the paragraph elements on the page to be purple, you simply add the *!important* keyword to the style you want to have applied:

```
p{
    font-family: serif;
    color: blue;
}
p{
    color: purple !important;
}
p{
    color: yellow;
}
```

The paragraph elements will render purple and not yellow. The *!important* notation tells the parser to give that style priority. This is a simplistic example, but the concept is the same whether the styles are in a single page such as this or if they come from a variety of external sources with conflicting styles.

Styling an element based on pseudo-elements and pseudo-classes

The Objective 4.5 section, "Finding elements by using pseudo-elements and pseudo-classes" demonstrated the use of pseudo-elements and pseudo-classes as selectors. In addition, that section can be referenced for how to apply styles to elements based on the use of the pseudo-class and pseudo-element selectors.

Objective summary

- Referencing elements correctly takes careful consideration of how you will structure your CSS and your HTML elements.
- Selectors can be nested and joined together to get more specific.
- HTML elements inherit styles automatically from their parent elements.
- CSS is processed from the top down, so that last style processed wins if it conflicts with other style declarations.
- *!important* can be used to ensure that the desired style is rendered when there is a competing CSS declaration.

Objective review

Answer the following questions to test your knowledge of the information in this objective. You can find the answers to these questions and explanations of why each answer choice is correct or incorrect in the "Answers" section at the end of this chapter.

The review questions use the following HTML listing (line numbers are for reference only):

```
1.  <html>
2.  <body>
3.      <div>
4.          <hgroup>
5.              <h1></h1>
6.              <h2></h2>
7.          </hgroup>
8.      </div>
9.      <div>
10.         <section>
11.             <article>
12.                 <h1></h1>
13.                 <p></p>
14.                 <p></p>
15.             </article>
```

```
16.            <article>
17.                <h1></h1>
18.                <p></p>
19.                <aside></aside>
20.                <p></p>
21.            </article>
22.        </section>
23.    </div>
24.    <div>
25.        <footer>
26.            <p></p>
27.            <p></p>
28.        </footer>
29.    </div>
30.</body>
31.</html>
```

1. Referencing the HTML listing, how would you style only the first paragraph inside the footer element to have a smaller font size?

A.

```
footer p:first-child {
        font-size: x-small;
}
```

B.

```
footer p.first-child {
    font-size: x-small;
        }
```

C.

```
Footer:p:first-child {
            font-size: x-small;
        }
```

D.

```
Footer=>p,first-child {
            font-size: x-small;
            }
```

2. Referencing the HTML listing, how would you apply a new font to all the H1 elements? In addition, the *<h1>* elements in an article should be italic.

A.

```
h1 {
font-family: 'Courier New';
        article h1 {
    font-style:italic;
   }
   }
```

B.

```
h1 {
     font-family: 'Courier New';
}
article h1 {
     font-style:italic;
}
```

C.

```
h1 {
font-family: 'Courier New';
font-style:italic;
      }
    article h1 {
font-style:italic;
     }
```

D.

```
h1 {
     font-family: 'Courier New';
   }
  article, h1 {
 font-style:italic;
     }
```

3. Referencing the preceding HTML listing, write the CSS code to apply a border to the aside element that is 100 pixels high and 50 pixels wide. In addition, provide a shadow effect and slightly skew the element to the right 5 degrees.

Answers

This section contains the solutions to the thought experiments and answers to the objective review questions in this chapter.

Objective 4.1: Thought experiment

jQuery is the easiest way to achieve changing CSS styles dynamically. JavaScript will do the trick as well. All the CSS properties that have been looked at are available to be changed dynamically. So for example, in the following code, the color of the button is changed to green when it is clicked:

```
<html>
<head>
<script src="jquery-2.0.3.min.js" type="text/javascript"></script>
    <script>
        $("document").ready(function () {
            $("#changeStyle").click(function () {
                $(this).css("color", "green");
            });
        });
    </script>
</head>
<body>
    <button id="changeStyle">Change Style</button>
</body>
</html>
```

Objective 4.1: Review

1. **Correct answer:** B

   A. **Incorrect**: font-style: italic will display the text with italics.

   B. **Correct**: font-weight: heavy; heavy is not a valid option for font-weight.

   C. **Incorrect**: font: bolder 12px arial; is a valid shorthand for setting font attributes.

   D. **Incorrect**: color: green; is a valid way to change the color of the text to green.

2. **Correct answer:** D

   A. **Incorrect:** Right will align all the text to the right side of the box.

   B. **Incorrect:** Full is not a valid option.

   C. **Incorrect:** Center will align the text along the center of the box.

   D. **Correct:** Justify will align the text such that each line takes up the width of the box.

3. **Correct answer:** C

   A. **Incorrect:** word-margin is not a valid option.

   B. **Incorrect:** letter-margin is not a valid option.

   C. **Correct:** word-spacing will set the amount of space between words.

   D. **Incorrect:** word-padding is not a valid option.

Objective 4.2: Thought experiment

The following code demonstrates how to alter an element's position using jQuery.

```html
<html>
<head>
<script src="jquery-2.0.3.min.js" type="text/javascript"></script>
    <style>
        p {
            position:fixed;
            left: 1px;
        }
    </style>
    <script>
        var pos = 1;
        $("document").ready(function () {
            setInterval(function () {
                var newPos = (pos + 1) + "px";
                $("#scrollMe").css("left", newPos);
                pos += 1;
            }, 20);
        });
    </script>
</head>
<body>
    <p id="scrollMe">This text moves accross the screen.</p>
</body>
</html>
```

Objective 4.2: Review

1. **Correct answer:** D

   A. **Incorrect**: div{height: 50px; width: 50%;} is valid.

   B. **Incorrect**: div{height: 50px; width: 50px;} is valid.

   C. **Incorrect**: div{height: 50cm; width: 50px; is valid.

   D. **Correct**: div{height: 50ft; width: 50ft;} ft is not a valid unit of measurement.

2. **Correct answer:** A

   A. **Correct:** Each side will be styled differently and the syntax is correct.

   B. **Incorrect:** border-sides is not a valid property.

   C. **Incorrect:** border-all is not a valid property.

   D. **Incorrect:** The syntax is not correct to set the border properties with the short-hand. Full is not a valid value.

3. **Correct answer:** B

   A. **Incorrect:** This is not the correct sequence.

   B. **Correct:** Margin, border, padding is the correct sequence.

   C. **Incorrect:** This is not the correct sequence.

   D. **Incorrect:** This is not the correct sequence.

4. **Correct answer:** A

   A. **Correct**: box-shadow: gray 5px 5px; will apply a box shadow to the right and bottom edge of a *div* element.

   B. **Incorrect:** The shadow will be on the left and bottom.

   C. **Incorrect:** The shadow will be on the top and right.

   D. **Incorrect:** The shadow will be the top and left.

5. **Correct Answer:** B

   A. **Incorrect:** Absolute positioning is relative to the parent.

   B. **Correct:** Fixed positioning is the correct answer.

   C. **Incorrect:** Relative positioning is relative to the elements in normal flow.

Objective 4.3: Thought experiment

The following listing shows the code for the blog page with the addition of a column layout for the main content section. The additional CSS is highlighted in bold.

```
<html>
    <head>
        <style>
            html, body {
                height: 100%;
                width: 100%;
            }
            #blogPage {
                display: grid;
                grid-columns: 15% 1fr 25%;
                grid-rows: (20%)[5];
                width: 90%;
                height: 95%;
```

```
            border: 1px dotted black;
            margin: auto;
        }
            #blogPage > header {
                grid-column: 1;
                grid-column-span: 3;
                grid-row: 1;
                border: 1px dotted black;
            }
            #blogPage > footer {
                grid-column: 1;
                grid-row: 5;
                grid-column-span: 3;
                border: 1px dotted black;
            }
            #blogPage > article {
                grid-column: 2;
                grid-row: 2;
                grid-row-span: 3;
                border: 1px dotted black;
            }
            #blogPage > #calendar {
                grid-column: 3;
                grid-row: 3;
                border: 1px dotted black;
            }
            #blogPage > #blogRoll {
                grid-column: 3;
                grid-row: 4;
                border: 1px dotted black;
            }
            #blogPage > #aboutMe {
                grid-column: 1;
                grid-row: 2;
                grid-row-span: 3;
                border: 1px dotted black;
            }
            #blogPage > #bloghistory {
                grid-column: 3;
                grid-row: 2;
                border: 1px dotted black;
            }
        #cols {
            width: 80%;
            height: 100%;
            border: 1px solid black;
            column-count: 3;
            column-rule-color: black;
            column-rule-style: dashed;
            column-rule-width: 2px;
            column-gap: 5px;
        }
        hgroup {
            column-span: all;
            text-align: center;
        }
```

```
        </style>
    </head>
    <body>
        <div id="blogPage">
            <header>My Blog Header</header>
            <article id="cols">
             <hgroup>
                 <h1>My Blog's Main Body</h1>
             </hgroup>
             <p>
                 Lorem ipsum dolor sit amet, consectetuer adipiscing
             elit, sed diam nonummy nibh euismod tincidunt ut laoreet dolore magna
             liquam
                 …
             </p>
             </article>
             <footer>My Blog Footer</footer>
             <aside id="calendar">A calendar</aside>
             <aside id="blogRoll">My favorite blogs</aside>
             <aside id="aboutMe">Who am I?</aside>
             <aside id="bloghistory">My blog history</aside>
        </div>
    </body>
</html>
```

Objective 4.3: Review

1. **Correct answer:** C

    A. **Incorrect:** Flexbox lays elements out in a flow direction.

    B. **Incorrect:** Multi-column lays elements out only in columns.

    C. **Correct:** Grid layout allows layout in rows and columns.

    D. **Incorrect:** Exclusions do not deal with the layout in rows and columns.

2. **Correct answer:** D

    A. **Incorrect:** This is a true statement.

    B. **Incorrect:** This is a true statement.

    C. **Incorrect:** This is a true statement.

    D. **Correct:** Grid layouts can be set into rows and columns.

3. **Correct answer:** A

    A. **Correct:** *both* will allow the text to wrap along both sides of an element.

    B. **Incorrect:** *all* is not a valid value.

    C. **Incorrect:** *left and right* is not a valid value.

    D. **Incorrect:** *cross* is not a valid value.

Objective 4.4: Thought experiment

By combining the transition with the transform, you are able to create effects that you otherwise would not be able to create. For example, if you want to create the effect of a box spinning or rotating, you can apply a *transform: rotate(360deg)*; to the box. However, this happens so fast that you cannot see that the box rotated. Alternatively, by applying a transform effect with a longer duration, you actually can see the box rotate. Look at the following code, which demonstrates this effect on a series of *div* boxes:

```html
<html>
<head>
    <style>
        div {
            margin: 10px 10px 10px 10px;
            height: 50px;
            width: 50px;
            background-color: red;
            transition: transform 3s;
        }
        div:hover {
            transform: rotate(360deg);
        }
    </style>
</head>
<body>
    <div></div>
    <div></div>
    <div></div>
    <div></div>
    <div></div>
    <div></div>
</body>
</html>
```

Objective 4.4: Review

1. **Correct answer:** A

   A. **Correct:** *display:none*; will hide an element but keep its space in the overall flow.

   B. **Incorrect**: *visibility: hidden*; will maintain the element in the normal flow.

   C. **Incorrect**: *display: inline*; will show the element in the normal flow.

   D. **Incorrect**: *visibility: visible*; will show the element in the normal flow.

2. **Correct answer:** B

    A. **Incorrect:** Media queries are not best suited for setting the priority of style sheet references in a webpage.

    B. **Correct:** Media queries are best suited for creating a responsive user interface based on the screen size of the view port.

    C. **Incorrect:** Media queries are not best suited for modifying the view port to properly fit the content of the page.

    D. **Incorrect:** Media queries are not best suited for connecting to third-party style sheets to alter the layout.

3. **Correct answer:** A

    A. **Correct:** ease will start slow, speed up and end slow. This is also the default value.

    B. **Incorrect:** ease-in will start slow and speed up.

    C. **Incorrect:** ease-out will slow near the end.

    D. **Incorrect:** ease-in-out will slow at the beginning and at the end.

Objective 4.5: Thought experiment

What is interesting about this thought experiment is recognizing that not all pseudo-class or pseudo-element selectors are supported by jQuery. For example, inserting content via pseudo selectors does not work in this way. However, some things can be done via jQuery. In this example, the following code shows how the pseudo-element selector works in a jQuery selector:

```
<script>
    $("document").ready(function () {
        $("p:first-child").css("color", "green");
    });
</script>
```

Objective 4.5: Review

1. **Correct answer:** A

    A. **Correct:** .code is a CSS class selector.

    B. **Incorrect:** #code is an ID selector.

    C. **Incorrect:** div[code] is an attribute selector.

    D. **Incorrect:** :code is not a valid statement.

2. **Correct answer:** C

    A. **Incorrect:** *.required* is a class selector.

    B. **Incorrect:** #required is an ID selector.

    C. **Correct:** *input[required] is an attribute selector.*

    D. **Incorrect:** *:required* is a pseudo-class that would be combined with an element selector.

3. **Correct answer:** D

    A. **Incorrect:** a:link would specify the styles for an unvisited hyperlink.

    B. **Incorrect:** a:mouseover is not a valid pseudo-class.

    C. **Incorrect:** a:beforeclick is not a valid pseudo-class.

    D. **Correct:** a:hover will change the style when the user moves the mouse over the link.

Objective 4.6: Thought experiment

When you want to achieve specific formatting on complex webpages, you need to account for the hierarchy of your page and ensure that you understand how the inheritance is going to impact the nested HTML elements' styles. The more specific your selectors, the more CSS you need to write but have more control. The following code will demonstrate a specific selector that will alter only the first character of the first paragraph when a user hovers over it:

```
p:first-child:hover:first-letter {
    font-size: xx-large;
}
```

This code does not seem like much, but it is very specific. It will override default inheritance and any other styles defined for that same element. Consider the following CSS:

```
p:first-child:first-letter {
    font-size: xx-small;
}
p:first-child:hover:first-letter {
    font-size: xx-large;
}
```

The first selector will default the size of the first letter to xx-small but the hover class will override this. This is where it may be desirable to use the *!important* keyword to force the xx-small font. In this example, the two styles purely conflict. You would need to choose one over the other.

Objective 4.6: Review

1. **Correct answer:** A

   A. **Correct:** This is the correct syntax specifying the first paragraph child of the footer element to have a smaller font.

   B. **Incorrect:** The p.firstchild is not the correct syntax. It would need to be p:first-child.

   C. **Incorrect:** The colon after the footer is not correct syntax.

   D. **Incorrect:** The => notation is not the correct syntax.

2. **Correct answer:** B

   A. **Incorrect:** Styles cannot be nested inside each other in this way.

   B. **Correct:** It is correct to first specify the H1 style, then specify the H1 styles for H1 elements that are beneath an article element.

   C. **Incorrect:** This will make all H1 elements italic.

   D. **Incorrect:** This will make all H1 elements italic as the comma after article creates a list of elements to apply the styles to.

3. **Correct Answer:**

```
aside {
    height:100px;
    width:50px;
    border: 2px solid black;
    transform: skew(-5deg);
    box-shadow: 5px 5px;
}
```

Index

F

G

P

About the author

RICK DELORME is a Senior Software Architect and Implementer. Since graduating with an Information Systems degree from St. Francis Xavier University in Antigonish, Nova Scotia, 14 years ago, he has worked on large, multi-factorial projects ranging from call center applications, to postal industry applications, and more recently, including applications in health care. Rick has leveraged all the elements of the Microsoft development stack to deliver cohesive solutions. The addition of HTML5 and CSS3 has provided Rick (and all developers) with more tools to make the end-user experience richer and to simplify development of web applications.

Throughout Rick's career, he has authored several books related to debugging of .NET applications, design and development of custom web components, .NET deployment, and general .NET development, since the first pre-release of the .NET Framework.

When Rick is not working, he enjoys spending time with his family and supporting his kids in their various activities. Rick currently resides in Ontario, Canada, with his wife, three children, and two dogs.

Free ebooks

From technical overviews to drilldowns on special topics, get *free* ebooks from Microsoft Press at:

www.microsoftvirtualacademy.com/ebooks

Download your free ebooks in PDF, EPUB, and/or Mobi for Kindle formats.

Look for other great resources at Microsoft Virtual Academy, where you can learn new skills and help advance your career with free Microsoft training delivered by experts.

Now that you've read the book...

Tell us what you think!

Was it useful?
Did it teach you what you wanted to learn?
Was there room for improvement?

Let us know at http://aka.ms/tellpress

Your feedback goes directly to the staff at Microsoft Press,
and we read every one of your responses. Thanks in advance!

 Microsoft